The
Oberammergau
Passion Play

A Lance against Civilization

Saul S. Friedman

Southern Illinois University Press
Carbondale and Edwardsville

Copyright © 1984 by the Board of Trustees,
   Southern Illinois University
All rights reserved
Printed in the United States of America
Designed by T. J. Campbell
Production supervised by Kathleen Giencke

87 86 85 84   4 3 2 1

Library of Congress Cataloging in Publication Data

Friedman, Saul S., 1937–
   The Oberammergau Passion play.

   Bibliography: p.
   Includes index.
   1. Oberammergau Passion play. 2. Holocaust,
Jewish (1939–45). 3. Anti-Semitism—Germany.
I. Title.
PN3238.F74 1984   792.1'6   83–17099
ISBN 0–8093–1153–4

For Earl and Liesel Friedman—teachers

Contents

Illustrations

Foreword

In a celebrated passage Friedrich Nietzsche makes a madman cry that God is dead—and, as he looks at his listeners, proceed that he has come too soon, that this enormous event has not yet entered the human consciousness. One is reminded of this passage as one reads the text of the Oberammergau Passion play, 1934 Nazi version and the expurgated and reformed 1980 version, together with Saul Friedman's critical study of the whole subject in all its ramifications. We say "1934 Nazi version" because, contrary to all the apologetics offered after 1945 to the effect that nazism never really penetrated Oberammergau, the spirit of nazism is unmistakably present in the picture of money-greedy, plotting, bloodthirsty Jews, coupled neatly with the claim that now, *anno* 1934, Christians are redeemed from them and their machinations. And we are reminded of Nietzsche's passage because the 1980 cleaned-up version, while eliminating overtly offensive expressions and ideas, shows no signs of a fundamental *metanoia*—a term quite inadequately translated by "repentance"—even after Auschwitz, for two millennia of Christian "teaching of contempt" (Jules Isaac) for Judaism and the Jewish people.

Were Nietzsche alive today he would have no stronger evidence for his claim that God is dead than the Nazi

Holocaust—the coldly methodically planned murder of six million Jews in the heart of what was once Christian Europe. And, foe of anti-Semitism, critic of Christianity, and discriminating diagnostician of the sickness of European culture that he was, he might have found the most profound, if not the sole, course of Jew-hatred in that very teaching of contempt that has accompanied Christian history from its beginnings. The Catholic theologian Rosemary Ruether states that Jew-hatred has been the "left hand" of Christianity, and that all depends now on whether future Christianity will be able to teach that "Christ saves" without adding, explicitly or implicitly, that "the Jews be damned." The 1934 version of the Oberammergau play damns the Jews explicitly. In the 1980 version this damnation is still implicitly present. After having searched it critically but by no means unsympathetically, Friedman lists no less than eight anti-Jewish stereotypes, among them avaricious Jewish money-dealers bent on revenge against Jesus, spiteful rabbis and Pharisees, a Jewish mob shrieking twenty-five times for the death of Jesus—all this and more contrasted with the image of a noble Pilate. There is in this version of the play no *metanoia*—no repentance that stems from a fundamental change of heart.

In his discussions with German Catholic clerics, Friedman was told that it "takes time" for such reconsiderations of Jewish-Christian relations as those of Vatican II to be reflected in popular Christian consciousness of which, of course, the Oberammergau play is a prominent expression. But it is just apologetics such as these that bring Nietzsche's madman to mind—and make one wonder whether he *is* mad, less because of what happened than because people are unable and unwilling to notice it. Just how long will it take for the ordinary Christian or German to take notice? And, in the meantime, are new seeds of the old hatred being sown, for some future explosion—and for a new catastrophe for Christianity, no less than for Judaism and the Jewish people? Just when will the required *metanoia* come, and what are its elements?

Perhaps the most powerful answer to this question has come from a German Catholic theologian. Johann Baptist Metz (who as he says "hails from a typical Catholic milieu") reports that even after the war, "the Jews" remained a "vague cliché," and that one's views of them were derived at best from Oberammergau. Metz demands that Christians, and especially German Christians, must stop "finding themselves innocent in their own self-judgment," must on the contrary judge everything, their Christianity included, by the standard of Auschwitz, so much so that any theology that could be the same before and after, is deficient for that reason alone. Rather than be content with vague expressions of goodwill, or "offering dialogue to victims," Christians must, at long last *listen* to Jews. Addressing himself specifically to German Christians, Metz concludes as follows:

> This moral recollection of the persecution of the Jews touches lastly the relation of the people of this country to the state of Israel. In this respect we have no choice, and I insist on this point over and against my leftist friends. After the Jews were carried in our most recent history to the brink of total annihilation, we should be the last people in the world to accuse Jews of an excessive desire for security. We should be the very first to believe Jews when they claim that they defend their state, not because of "Zionist imperialism" but rather as a "house against death," as the very last place of refuge of a people persecuted for centuries.

Whether any sort of Oberammergau Passion play can survive the *metanoia* demanded by Metz is more than doubtful. If so, it will be possible only if Metz's concluding admonition is heeded: "We Christians will never get back behind Auschwitz. And we will get beyond it, not alone and by ourselves, but only in togetherness with the victims."

Emil Fackenheim

New Testament Roots of Christian Anti-Semitism

Judson Shaver

Obviously the history of anti-Semitism raises a number of painful questions. Questions about the nature of God—and of man. It also raises some questions about Christianity. For those of us who are Christian, these questions are particularly acute. As Dr. Clark Williamson has written:

> Standing as we do on this side of the *Shoah*, that holocaust of our time in which six million Jews were sacrificed in the heart of Western, ostensibly Christian civilization and handed up for slaughter by at-least-nominal Christians, we have to ask ourselves some hard questions. Can we still make the convenient distinction between Christianity as in itself perfect—and therefore on principle non-indictable in such matters—and sinful "Christians" who in want of true faith have conducted themselves shamelessly? Or following almost two thousand years of a virtually unrelenting teaching and practice of contempt, does not such a slippery distinction become extremely dubious? Must we not demand to know, in fear and trembling, whether

there are factors near the very heart of the Christian tradition which have led Christians to an anti-Judaic posture which we must now condemn and overthrow?[1]

The intensity and the pervasiveness of anti-Semitism in prewar Christian Europe and the fact of the Holocaust force these questions upon us. But how could a Christian possibly be anti-Semitic? Christianity teaches that the God of Israel is the only God. That in Jesus, a Jew, God acted to reconcile all persons to himself and to each other. How then could a Christian possibly be anti-Semitic? How indeed! The answer to that question is disturbing. In light of statements made by some of Christianity's earliest and most influential theologians one *might* conclude that a Christian can be anti-Semitic because Christianity is essentially anti-Semitic. Listen to Origen, an important third-century theologian:

> We may thus assert in utter confidence that the Jews will not return to their earlier situation, for they have committed the most abominable of crimes, in forming this conspiracy against the savior of the human race. . . . Hence the city where Jesus suffered was *necessarily* destroyed, the Jewish nation was driven from its country, and another people was called by God to the blessed election.[2]

Listen to the fourth-century Bishop Gregory of Nyssa describing Jews:

> Murderers of the Lord, assassins of the prophets, rebels and detesters of God, they outrage the law, resist grace, repudiate the faith of their fathers. Companions of the devil, race of vipers, informers, calumniators, darkeners of the mind, pharisaic leaven, Sanhedrin of demons, accursed, detested, lapidators, enemies of all that is beautiful.[3]

Or Saint John Chrysostom (also fourth century):

Brothel and theater, the synagogue is also a cave of pirates and the lair of wild beasts. . . . Living for their belly, mouth forever gaping, the Jews behave no better than hogs and goats in their lewd grossness and the excesses of their gluttony.[4]

Where in the world would Christians, educated Christians, theologians, bishops, and saints get ideas like that? From the New Testament. According to the Acts of the Apostles, the Jews murdered Jesus. Listen to Stephen, the first Christian martyr, speaking to his Jewish killers: "You stiff-necked people, uncircumcised in heart and ears, you always resist the Holy Spirit. As your fathers did, so do you. Which of the prophets did not your fathers persecute? And they killed those who announced beforehand the coming of the Righteous One, whom you have now betrayed and murdered" (Acts 7:51–52).

According to Matthew, Pilate found Jesus innocent, but the Jews demanded his death and shouted, "His blood be on us and on our children" (Matt. 27:25). Thus, as Dr. John Chamberlain put it, "uttering the self-incrimination of all Jews in all times on the charge of deicide."[5] Further, Matthew, Mark, and Luke all include the parable of the Tenants (Mark 12:1–9 and parallels) in which the gospel writers present Jesus as claiming that God had rejected the Jews in favor of the Gentiles, and Paul describes Jews as children of the slave woman, not the children of promise, as branches broken off in order to graft on Gentiles.[6] Passages could be multiplied, but this is enough to answer the question asked by Williamson. Are there "factors near the very heart of Christian tradition that have led Christians to an anti-Judaic posture?"[7] Yes, we cannot avoid it, there are.

But that raises the question: Why? Why do the Gospels contain—besides the good news—such clear contradictions of it? I think the answer can be found in an examination of the circumstances of the first century.

First-century Judaism had deep inner divisions. There were the Sadducees who cooperated with the Roman rule of

Palestine and the Zealots who resisted it violently. There were also the Pharisees whose more liberal views were detested by the Sadducees, and in the desert there were the Essenes who regarded everyone else as apostate. Another group within first-century Judaism came to be known as the Christians. That Christianity originated as a Jewish sect is true, even if we sometimes forget that Jesus was a Jew, that his earliest followers were Jews, and that his bible was the Hebrew Bible. All those groups existed side by side in disharmony and sometimes open antagonism until ca. 70 C.E. when the Romans sacked Jerusalem and burned the Temple. Only the Pharisees and the Christians survived the destruction. By then, many Gentiles were Christians. They had been taught by Paul and others that they need not follow Jewish dietary laws or be circumcised. This of course to the Pharisees, and some Christians, including apparently even Peter, was apostasy. The battle lines were drawn.

Christianity and Pharisaic Judaism *both* claimed the God of Abraham as their authority, used the same sacred book, claimed to be the sole interpreter of God's will, and competed with each other for members.

The battle itself was regrettable; the language used to describe the enemy, some of which I have quoted, may be understandable in its historical context, but is no less deplorable. What is worse, however, as Rabbi Sandmel has pointed out, is that the Christian side of this bitter debate came to be included in Christian Scripture.[8]

Williamson's final question bears repeating: "Must we not demand to know, in fear and trembling, whether there are factors near the very heart of the Christian tradition which have led Christians to an anti-Judaic posture which we must now condemn and overthrow?"[9] Yes, there are, and yes, we must condemn and overthrow them.

Can that be done without condemning the New Testament or Christianity itself? Again, I believe the answer is yes. Like every movement, group and individual Christianity must own up to its sins. The historically conditioned New Testament that Jews murdered Jesus is, on the historical evidence, false. And the claim that God rejected the Jews is simply bad theology. These ancient claims must be understood and dismissed as the words of men. Jews *and* Christians await the fulfillment of the divine word, the promise of the God of Abraham to reconcile all of humanity, indeed the whole of creation, to himself.

Preface

Perhaps the best way to start a book about Oberammergau is with an explanation. As a professor of Jewish
history, I had traveled through several European countries
before arriving in Germany in June 1980. Frankly, I had
avoided this land which was the source of so much anguish
for my people. When a younger brother, a doctor, was
stationed with U.S. forces in Swabia twelve years ago, I recall writing him, "How can you walk the streets knowing
what happened? Don't the stones feel hot beneath your
feet?" No amount of monetary compensation, I felt, could
repair the horrors of the Holocaust. Of necessity, though, I
was drawn to Frankfurt, Munich, Vienna, and Nuremberg.
The following lines were written June 15, 1980, my first day
in Germany:

> DACHAU. What can I say about Dachau that hasn't al-
> ready been written by poets? It is a sad place. No, it is
> not completely made over, as others have suggested.
> The huge *Appelplatz* is covered with gravel—just as it
> was between 1933 and 1945. The gate leading through
> the former main entry (now blocked to the public) still
> jeers "Arbeit Macht Frei." Only two of the more than
> 50 barracks stand in the quadrangle that house the

prisoners—and these, to be sure, have been carefully reconstructed. The people who entered the barracks and gazed at the wooden *pritschen* were all appropriately respectful. How pathetic, though, to note that the planks are covered with "Kilroys" from Finland, Portugal, Canada, Italy, the USA, Greece, Ecuador, Iran, and even Israel. It brings to mind George Will's column on the Anne Frank house and how a D. Gonzalez of Leadville, Colo., carved his name into the window sill where Anne once dreamed of freedom.

It is a slow, trudging walk along the path of the barrack foundations. Others may not feel it, with the beautiful blue skies and poplar trees, but I tried to listen for the sounds of what really went on here. The barracks sprawled over an area at least 300 yards by 200 yards. I know because I paced it off. A quick stop at the Christian pavilions—and then to the impressive memorial to the thousands of Jewish dead. 12,000 alone were rounded up and sent here on *Kristallnacht.* I was fortunate. I was alone at the monument. I said Kaddish.

Two crematoria were located at the opposite side of the memorials. The photographs I took tell enough of these barbarities.

I found the museum devastating, at least as powerful as the Yad va-Shem in Jerusalem. Here is a map of all the Nazi concentration camps. Here you can see up close the insane wooden shoes that must have cut into the wearer's feet, the insubstantial pajama uniforms which could not possibly have offered protection against the Bavarian winter, the color chart denoting what kinds of badges had to be worn by asocial Jews, rabbis, lawbreaking Jews, homosexual Jews (pink on the Magen David), etc. And then there is the film—30 minutes of dramatic testimony. The Germans mince no words about their guilt. Their genocide is fully documented—and the Jews are highlighted as their principal victims.

What struck me was the attitude of the people in the

camp. There were only a few dozen at Dachau when I arrived early on Sunday. By the time I left (three hours later) the number had grown to many hundreds, many young people—from the States—with Duke and Princeton sweaters—families—student groups from Germany. One group of Americans standing at the bus stop, discussing what they had seen, had just been to Oberammergau the previous day. Their spokesman, a man in his fifties from Illinois, told me he had intended to come out to the camp on his own. When six others in his tour heard that, they opted to accompany him. I don't know if they made any connection, saw any irony, but the fact that they went was significant.

The leader of that particular group remarked how quiet the theater was when the film was rolling. People had seen pictures like this before—but not in such a setting. It wasn't totally quiet—a bambino was sounding off—but the only word for the 200 people who sat through the Dachau film was reverential. This was what impressed me—repeatedly. At the torture blocks and disinfection chambers, a German mother stopped her 10- or 11-year-old boy from going into the oversized "ice boxes." When he protested, she said, "No, you don't go into such a terrible place." And later, at the pictorial exhibit, before the large photos of Jewish children who starved in the Warsaw Ghetto, another German woman, accompanied by her husband, broke into tears. Those tears mean more than all the millions of reparations.

For me, Dachau was a place of sadness, "the sadness that comes when someone you know has died—and you were too late to help." That same feeling of impotence was expressed by Pater Gregor Rümmelein of Ettal monastery when he told me how he wished he could have reformed the Oberammergau Passion play years earlier. Instinctively, Pater Rümmelein acknowledged the link between the anti-Semitic staging of the Passion and the ovens at Dachau.

My research into Oberammergau dates back six years and

stems from an invitation to offer a historical address on the significance of the Passion. In preparing the talk, I learned that few books had been written about the play itself, and those which had been published were either synopses, paeans of praise, or memoirs of uncritical spectators who had achieved "a religious experience" at Oberammergau. Although editors, Jewish community workers, clerics, and a handful of other professionals purportedly "knew" of the anti-Jewish nature of the Passion, their struggle against this vestige of medieval bigotry was, for the most part, being waged in advertisements, pamphlets, and newspaper condemnations which appeared and were ignored every ten years.

Having scrutinized various editions of the Passion text dating back to 1890, it was my feeling that the play was not only injurious to Christian-Jewish understanding but also unfaithful to Christian holy writings. Somewhat vaingloriously, I undertook this project with the idea of at least sensitizing spectators to the potential harm of the Passion, if not achieving some changes in the text itself. I was encouraged in the process by Simon Wiesenthal who told me in November 1979: "I believe it was in 1947 when I was on a train in Bavaria with some U.S. officers. We went through Oberammergau and they were talking about putting on the play again. All of the people in the town had been Nazis except one, and he had played Judas. Much work must be done on this play, to show the world how anti-Semitic it is."

Fortunately, much work has been done in recent years. Through the persistent efforts of the secretariat for Catholic-Jewish Relations of the National (American) Conference of Catholic Bishops, Dr. Leonard Swidler, professor of Catholic thought at Temple University, Theodore Freedman, director of programs of the Anti-Defamation League, and Rabbi Marc Tanenbaum of the American Jewish Committee, major changes have been wrought in the Passion. Much work remains to be done before the Passion is performed again in 1984, the 350th anniversary of Oberammergau's vow of piety. As I write this, a conference of German bishops is laboring over revisions.

It is my hope that this book will complement, rather than usurp, the labors of the above groups by addressing the following issues: What is the historical evolution of Passion plays? Why is the Oberammergau Passion unique among medieval mystery plays? How did the Passion originate in Oberammergau, and how has it managed to survive? Can the traditional text be reconciled with the Gospels? Does the play generate harmful, stereotypic images of Jews? Can the text be reconciled with what we know of ancient Jewish laws and institutions? Can the text be reconciled with what we know of Roman imperial administration and the person of Pontius Pilate? Is the text faithful to church theology as outlined by Vatican II? What is the psychological impact of such performances upon relatively unsophisticated viewers? What is the impact upon spectators in a post-Holocaust world? Is the underlying motivation for the Passion religious piety or has financial gain subverted the intentions of the Oberammergauers? Is the Passion immune from contemporary political pressure, or can it be manipulated for propaganda? How and why was it possible to revive the Passion after World War II? Where did the money necessary to fund the revival come from? Could an alternate version of the Passion, known as the Rosner version, a baroque edition, employed in the eighteenth century, be offered? Could an entirely new version of the Passion, based on the Book of Luke, be attempted? What future changes are possible in the existing text? Is the Passion truly a "hymn of reconciliation" or is it, as Nietzsche said of Wagner's *Meistersinger,* a "lance against civilization"?

To answer some of these questions, I traveled to Oberammergau to attend a performance of the Passion. In the course of my visit in Germany, I interviewed Msgr. Curt M. Genewein of the archbishop's office in Munich; Dr. Hans Lamm, *Rosh Kehillah* of the Jewish community in Bavaria; Bürgermeister Ernst Zwink of Oberammergau; rival play directors Hans Schwaighofer and Hans Maier; Pater Rümmelein; Gregor Breitsamter, one of two men who portrayed Christ; and numerous other townsfolk. I have also discussed the Passion with the ADL's Ted Freedman, Rabbi Tanenbaum, Phil Baum and Howard Stanislavsky of the American Jewish Congress, Pater Stephan Schaller of Ettal, former U.S. High Commissioner for Germany John J. McCloy, Professor Swidler, and several psychiatrists who supplied me with insight into the reactions that such religious dramas may evoke in viewers.

Throughout the compilation of this book, I have anticipated some criticisms. Analysis of various scripts has compelled the use, at times, of the historical present. Hopefully, before lapsing into this normally unacceptable tense, I have warned the reader. While some may also prefer a different form of organization (with earlier discussion of economic factors involved in perpetuating the passion), I have opted for a combined chronological-conceptual approach. As for my credentials in playing historian-psychologist-theologian ("who is this man from Youngstown?"), I refer to four years as a social worker in the inner city Hough District of Cleveland, eighteen years teaching ancient Near East and Jewish history at various universities in Ohio, and five books published on Jewish subjects.

From the outset, I wish to make it clear that I believe the Oberammergau Passion survives because of (a) religious zealotry derived at first from fear of plague in the seventeenth century; (b) a deep-seated racial arrogance and anti-Semitism not uncommon in Bavarian peasants or art; and (c) a developed sense of lucre, profit. I may be chastised for making an oblique attack upon the Gospels, but when I began this project I hoped to show that the Passion was far removed from traditional Christian theology. I have merely attacked those portions of the play which are unhistorical or unfair. That may present problems for the Christian uncomfortable with the knowledge of Jewish persecution for the past nineteen hundred years, yet unwilling to allow any link between his theology and that persecution, but I will retract none of my findings.

Finally, this project could not have been attempted without the assistance of Dr. George Chalou of the National Archives Records Center in Suitland, Maryland; Hildegarde Schnuttgen of Youngstown State University's Maag Library and Earl and Liesel Friedman of the Park School in Buffalo, all of whom assisted with translations of colloquial German; Holocaust survivors George Jacobs and Dr. James Elder of Youngstown, both of whom were temporarily housed as displaced persons in Oberammergau after the war; a cadre of Youngstown State University graduate students—Frank Butvin, Stephen Ard, Andrea Fesz, Steve Darvanan, Gary Noday, James Russo, Nafiseh Shihabi, and Mary Anne Seman—who belie the notion that the best young minds can only be found at prestige institutions; and those individuals who gave inspiration and substance to this project—my wife, Nancy, and our children, Jonathan, Molly, and Jason.

The Oberammergau Passion Play

1

The Way to Oberammergau

As they swept across Central Europe, Attila's hordes exclaimed: "To Bayern! To Bayern! There dwells the Lord God himself!" While partisans of Olympus or Mecca may dispute the residence of divinities, it is difficult to imagine a more idyllic land than Bavaria. In the sixty-five miles from Munich to Oberammergau, rolling hills covered with beech, pine, and fir give way to white-capped peaks, ideal for winter sports. Near the Austrian border, the jagged mountains rise as high as ten thousand feet. Below, as if placed there by some master designer, quaint little villages with bulbed church steeples and chalet-style homes punctuate the lush, green valleys.

Centuries before the Huns reached Bavaria, Romans blazed the first roads through the Wettersteingebirge. No Appian Ways, merely trails, wound from Verona over the Brenner Pass to Zirl (Teriolis) and Mittenwald (Scarbia), Partenkirchen (Parthanum), Weilheim and Augsburg (Augusta Vindelicorum). Another branch eventually linked with Munich through the Isartorgasse. Along this road, at the base of a four-thousand-foot mountain overlooking the present town of Oberammergau, the legions constructed a fortified halt called *ad coveliacas*. Both names of the mountain (now called Kofel) and Oberammergau (which was Latinized to Ambre) are of Celtic origin, and mounds marking prehistoric tombs on the road testify to the ancient strategic importance of this site. For the Graswang Valley commands passes leading to the rest of Bavaria in the north, Tyrol in the south, and Swabia to the west.[1]

During the Middle Ages, merchants passed through Oberammergau because it sat astride a main commercial road from Italy into Germany. In the past century, however, perhaps as many as five hundred thousand persons in a given summer would come here for a different reason—to witness a re-creation of the Passion of Jesus Christ, which the villagers had been presenting every ten years, with few exceptions, since 1634. They came, wrote village historian Hermine Diemer, as pilgrims: "People they are who still believe, and who, by looking at their representation, want to live through the sufferings of our Lord. People who have lost their faith in the world and who want to find it again in the play of the simple-minded folk, sanctified as it is by the centuries."[2]

What Diemer wrote fifty years ago was confirmed in 1960 by a survey conducted by Frau Pastorin Timm of Hamburg who found that Protestant visitors to Oberammergau came away impressed with a deep sense of piety which the play had awakened.[3] Another survey, conducted for the Catholic church by Annemarie Weiss of Heidelberg offered the same conclusions, that "those who had a ticket to Oberammergau in their pocket were convinced of the good of the play" and that it was a "positive religious experience for a great part of the visitors."[4] For Dr. Josef Ziegler, professor of theology at the University of Mainz, people come to Oberammergau "not only to see a theater, but rather to find answers to questions which perplex them, questions of isolation, questions of frustration. They seek answers and they find them by identifying themselves with the events of the Passion."[5]

Religious pilgrimage was only one of several motives which impelled thirty-three persons to make the journey to Oberammergau with me in June 1980. Since the Oberammergauers long ago had ordained that playgoers must spend the night preceding a performance in the village, a packaged tour was, the German National Tourist Office advised, the only way to guard against currency fluctuations, scalpers, and "other surprises." In short, I joined a tour to avoid "the nightmare" and "mad scramble for tickets and accommodations."[6] But I was also curious to learn why the others had come.

All of the people in my group were English-speaking, as were the majority (an estimated 300,000) of the visitors to Oberammergau in 1980.[7] With the exception of one black woman from California, those I encountered were middle-class, middle-aged-to-aged whites. Like the two ancient ladies who collapsed in the lobby of the Platzl Hotel in Munich before the start of the tour, most had scrimped to make this one pilgrimage before they died. Several persons were from Australia, including two spinster schoolteachers, sisters who had traveled over much of the world and were making a specific detour to Oberammergau to see "the Lord's Passion." Another Australian Catholic, a widow named Moskovitz, had been married to a Jewish Holocaust survivor from Rumania. She had been to Israel several times, but now was going to Oberammergau "because I'm a Christian." An old beer drinker from Melbourne, a white-haired gentleman named Davis also gained inspiration from religion—the teachings of Garner Ted Armstrong—and went on at length about belief in the resurrection of Christ, the destruction of the Antichrist, and the 144,000 blessed among men who would be protected by the mark of God.

For the Americans, revivalism was only one of several factors leading them to Bavaria. The Zielinskis of Iowa had just visited their native Poland and, matter-of-factly, decided to add Oberammergau to their itinerary on the way back home. The Marquadts, devout Catholics from Long Island, had whisked through ten German cities in twenty-one days. Mr. Beagle, a government trade expert, was returning from a professional trip to Egypt and was on his way to Rome with his family. His wife planned to do a report on the Oberammergau experience for the Sacramento city schools. Their son, an instructor at a junior college in Olympia, Washington, summarized the feelings of many visitors to Oberammergau in 1980 when he said, "I think my parents were curious. They just wanted to see it. Besides, who knows what'll happen by 1990?"[8]

We traveled to Oberammergau by air-conditioned bus. Before the electric railroad was extended from Munich to Murnau, and finally Oberammergau in 1900, the trip could take as long as eighteen hours by foot or cart. The path near town was especially crude. Till 1929, there was no bridge over the dreaded mountain of Echelsbach. The Ettal road was described as "bad going up, worse coming down." The steep cliffs offered no room to turn around. Often, buggies would tip and fall, horses might stampede, and the valley would be filled with the shrieks of women passengers and the curses of drivers. By the end of the nineteenth century, the wayside was punctuated with little crosses, *Marterl*, designating the sites of fatal accidents.[9]

Today's tourists doze as they motor along the sleek autobahn from Munich to Oberammergau in little more than one hour. There is almost a surrealistic air to the journey as the countryside whizzes by to the sound of Beethoven's *Pastoral* coming over a stereo loudspeaker. It is an impressive landscape, one rich in romance, history, and legend.[10] Mühltal, near Munich, is reputed to be the birthplace of Charlemagne. At Berg, on the Starnberger See, Ludwig II, the mad king of Bavaria responsible for a "positive orgy of castle-building," drowned on Whitsunday, 1886.[11] The Wessobrunn monastery contains what may be one of the oldest documents in German literature, dating from 800 A.D. Polling was the home of Jorg Banghofer, architect of the cathedral and old town hall in Munich. Tegernsee was the source of "Ruodlieb," the first novel written on German soil. Near Murnau is a hut said to be the dwelling place of the Volsungs, made famous by Wagner's *Nibelung* tetralogy. Murnau, sixteen miles from Oberammergau, derives its name from a legendary dragon that supposedly lived in a nearby valley. The *Bärenloch* (bear's den or cave) close by Oberammergau is the source of another host of fables. And the Kofel, that outcropping of granite which looms over the village of Oberammergau, where May Day pageants were celebrated in medieval times and marriage betrothals announced more recently, allegedly still conceals a witch that kidnaps children out after dark.[12]

Then there is Ettal, the charming Benedictine abbey three kilometers north of Oberammergau. One tale has it that Ettal owes its origins to an embittered old nobleman named Ethiko who retired here with twelve armor bearers at the end of the ninth century. The name Ettal may well be derived from Ethiko-Tal or Ethiko's Valley. More likely, the monastery was founded by Ludwig IV of Bavaria at the beginning of the fourteenth century. Overjoyed at God's sparing his land the ravages of war, Ludwig promised to establish a Benedictine retreat upon his return from Rome in 1314. The emperor brought with him a heavy, alabaster figure of the Madonna, supposedly given to him by an angel but actually fashioned by the Italian sculptor Pisano.[13] As Ludwig's horse climbed the steep hill near the Kienberg Gully, it collapsed under the weight of the statue. Though the steed was prodded to its feet three times, it repeatedly fell. The monarch, accepting this as a sign from heaven, decided to build his sanctuary for incapacitated knights on the spot.[14]

The monastery's foundation stone was laid in 1330, and the original, dodecagon building consecrated in 1370. Four centuries later, the abbey, church, and library were destroyed in a fire sparked by lightning. Ettal's prior risked his life, however, to rescue the Madonna's statue, which has been venerated to the present. The monastery itself was rebuilt under the direction of Josef Schmutzer of Wesobrunn, the architect responsible for the ostentatious parish church of Saint Peter and Saint Paul in Oberammergau. Schmutzer's main structure at Ettal is topped by the largest cupola (65.4 meters in diameter) in Bavaria and bears a painting of the history of the Benedictine order. The splendor of this cloister has been described by one German journal as "fröhlich baroque."[15]

During the Napoleonic period, Ettal was secularized. In 1803, part of the convent was pulled down and a brewery installed in its place. Without shame, the distillers inscribed their product, "God Bless the Beer of Ettal." Though the

Benedictine brothers were permitted to return in 1900, they continued to issue liqueurs and reap profits from the sale of fine wines under the Ettal label.[16]

Throughout its history, the monastery has enjoyed a unique relationship with the people of Oberammergau. Many villagers have been educated at the monastery school. Even today, it is not unusual to see a fleet of BMWs, Audi 5000s, and Mercedes pull up before the gates of Ettal in the bleak, gray dawn and deposit children wearing blue jeans and Indian headbands. Some students have returned to serve as pastors in the village. Ettal has also supplied Oberammergau with the redactors of all its Passion plays, from the celebrated Ferdinand Rosner, Ottmar Weis, and Alois Daisenberger in the eighteenth and nineteenth centuries to contemporaries Stephan Schaller and Pater Gregor Rümmelein.

The symbiosis between village and monastery stems from the Oberammergauers' strong commitment toward their religion. Rupert, bishop of Worms, introduced Christianity to the region in 696 A.D. It was not until Saint Boniface, the apostle to the Germans, came to Kapelle on Lake Staffelsee forty years later, however, that Christianity took root among the mixture of indigenous Celts and Bajuwari Germans. From the moment a missionary priest named Thasso established the first parish in 750,[17] through the change of dynasties from Guelph to Hohenstaufen to Wittelsbach, the south Bavarians were unwavering in their faith. Such loyalty was not without its compensations.

When Ludwig IV needed manpower to complete his holy project at Ettal, his vassals in Oberammergau complied. About the same time, they also furnished the labor necessary for the construction of Ulrich von Rothenbuch's convent at Berchtesgaden. In return, the villagers were accorded an extraordinary privilege for the fourteenth century—emancipation from serfdom. More important, in 1332, Ludwig gave "the burghers and peasants of the Ammer Gau the right to lodge all traders and to store all merchandise passing through their village."[18] Where previously only a few had profited as guides leading traders along the Augsburg Road, now the people organized into guilds of *Röttmanner* (teamsters). Their monopoly was reconfirmed in 1420 when the Dukes Wilhelm and Albrecht declared, "Nobody except those of the Ammer Gau shall have the right to help with horse the merchant passing by."[19]

The carriage trade could not provide the village with adequate income during the winter when medieval roads were impassable. In the fifteenth and sixteenth centuries, some Oberammergauers turned to prospecting for gold and silver—with little success. Others devised a different source of bad weather revenue—wood carving. Either because of the abundance of timber or idle time during winter snows, this section of Germany, together with northern Italy, has acquired a reputation for excellence in the manufacture of everything from puppets to icons. As one writer put it, the tradition of wood carving was "born and bred in the very blood of these Bavarians."[20]

In a region cursed with sparse arable land, nearly every family trained its young men as *Holzschnitzer* (woodcarvers). Publicity photographs for the 1930 Passion play show Alois Lang (Christ), Johannes Lang (John), Andreas Lang (Simon of Bethany), Joseph Mayr (Rabbi Archelaus), Hugo Rutz (Caiaphas), Peter Rendl (Peter), Guido Mayr (Judas), Anton Lang (Prologue), Joseph Albrecht (Malchus), and Melchior Breitsamter (Pilate) all working in their shops on religious scenes.[21] Similar shots of humble wood-carvers were offered of George Land (the director), Hans Schwaighofer (Judas), Hans Maier (Peter), and Melchior Breitsamter (again Pilate) when the village tried to drum up international enthusiasm for the play in 1950.[22] The same was true of 1980 flyers which emphasized carvers stooped over a near lifesized Christ figure.[23]

Four hundred years ago, the villagers crossed Central Europe with their wares strapped to their backs in quest of markets. The wood carvings were never crude barn figures but finely chiselled representations of the Last Supper, the Madonna, a kneeling apostle, crucifixes. In 1682, the prince elector upgraded what had begun as a pastime to a "free profession." By the end of the nineteenth century, a full-fledged carving school had been established in town under the direction of experts imported from Munich, Nuremberg, and Fürth. Agencies for Oberammergau pieces could be found as widespread as Saint Petersburg, Quebec, Cadiz, Venice, Manila, and New York.[24]

Oberammergau's artistic fame carried a price with it. Already in the midst of the Reformation, the village's economic boom began to attract derelicts and vagabonds. According to Vernon Heaton, early in the sixteenth century, the warden of Murnau helped purge Oberammergau of "undesirables."[25] The latter were chained and dumped over the border into Austria. Although the villagers have acquired a reputation as "the friendliest, most cheerful, most at peace with the world,"[26] this purge was not a singular, nor even the most important, case of Oberammergau inhospitality.

The year 1632 brought another unwelcome visitation to southern Bavaria. In the midst of the devastation wrought by invading armies of the Swedish king Gustavus Adolphus, the village of Oberammergau suffered an outbreak of plague. While most authorities assume it was bubonic, Heaton goes further, suggesting it may have come from "the dark continent," with traders who moved from Egypt or Libya on to Venice.[27] Another commentator, Winold Reiss, without any supporting evidence, identified the "Schwartze Tod" as smallpox.[28] Still another, J. J. Walsh, maintains the plague may have been influenza, which began its ravages in the late fall of 1632 and ceased when better weather developed toward the end of Lent in 1633.[29] Walsh's interpretation is appealing, as the climate about Oberammergau is not invigorating. Residents have a saying that it rains 365 days a year. Though this upland district (three thousand feet above sea level) may be striking when skies are clear, chilly, rain-bearing clouds may come blowing off the mountains in a matter of minutes. I experienced precisely this kind of perpetual mist in the village one frosty morning in June 1980. Even in this age of antibiotics, such a locale would be ripe for Russian, Asian, Hong Kong, or Spanish Flu. The only drawback with this interpretation is that all contemporary accounts of the plague mention that the sickness was first manifested in the form of sores, a symptom not normally associated with any of the flu pandemics.[30]

Whether bubonic plague, smallpox, or even typhus, whatever ravaged Bavaria in the seventeenth century was the result of a breakdown of society, coupled with the absence of practically any uniform system of sanitation. Bavaria, which had escaped relatively unscathed from the wars of the Reformation, was a principal battleground in the Thirty Years' War. Though some tales of destruction, like roving packs of wolves feasting off the remnants of once thriving farms or cannibalism in cities, may have been fabricated to win a tax reduction or other favor,[31] perhaps one-third of the population in Germany and Bohemia lay dead as a consequence of attacks by pillaging soldiers and disease. As with all wars, much farmland was ruined, giving rise to food shortages and starvation. Armies parried from Prague to Lutter to Breitenfeld to Alsace and the Pyrenees, and tens of thousands of people were left homeless refugees. Rotting corpses and animals littered the fields, roads, and water systems, exacerbating the atmosphere of despair.

As the villagers in Oberammergau tell it, "fear was widespread over Bavaria" in the spring of 1632. Swedish troops had crossed the Lech River on April 15 and entered Munich unopposed on May 17. Some days later, advance units of the invaders swept into Ettal, sacking the church and killing the monastery's porter and organist who tried to protect some of the sacred objects. Only the linkup of Wallenstein's troops with those of the Palatinate League forced a withdrawal of the Swedes. In their wake, however, they left the countryside a shambles and many persons suffering from a contagion which was labeled plague. Scattered *Landsknechte* (mercenaries) bearing marks of the sickness on their bodies spread the scourge through the Loisach and Ammer valleys, from Ohlstadt to Partenkirchen.[32]

Somehow, Oberammergau was spared till midsummer. The village elders established a council to supervise a regime of stringent hygiene, quarantine, and prayer. Homes were scrubbed from floor to rooftop, along with bed linen and clothing. The Alpine streams which supplied water for mandatory baths were checked regularly for their purity. Watchmen armed with clubs were posted beside "pest fires" at all mountain passes, to keep strangers from entering the Upper Ammer Valley. Only those residents of Oberammergau who worked outside the purification perimeter were readmitted. When the plague descended upon the neighboring village of Eschenlohe, three miles off, killing two of every three persons in ten days, the Oberammergau council banned all outside visits. Unfortunately, one Kaspar Schisler worked in Eschenlohe and was there the day the council banned reentry. As the Oberammergau village chronicle of 1733 recounts:

> By diligently guarding the village we succeeded in warding off any contagion until church-ale. Then a man by the name of Schisler, who had been employed throughout the summer by one Mair of Eschenlohe, brought the pestilence into the village. He had come to celebrate churchale with his family. The evening before he had crossed the mountain of Eschenlohe, and since his house was the first one of the whole village up near the Laine, he was suffered to enter. He went back to Eschenlohe by the way he had come, but already on Monday following church-ale he died. From this day on until October 28th, 84 persons died.[33]

Schisler's saga is a compelling one. Barred from his village, he may have roamed for days, even weeks, alone and frightened. Then, one day before he died, possibly feverish, he struck out over the steep hills for his home. He arrived on *Kirchweih* (the anniversary of the consecration of the village church) celebrated in the fall. Several days after his departure, his wife and children died, then those who had contact with him. Though the villagers redoubled their efforts at quarantine, it was too late. Plague victims were immediately buried in a deep pit beyond the town limits. Houses of the stricken were nailed up, till the relatives inside also perished. While the Oberammergau Memorial Book of the Year of the Plague lists eighty-four dead, Vernon Heaton maintains "the toll of dead must have exceeded that shown in the written record." Heaton estimates that perhaps as many as half of all the villagers died that winter, as "great gaps" appear in the registry of deaths, and no children's names are listed at all.[34]

The plague lasted till Simoeon and Judae's Day, early in the summer of 1633. Then, at the urging of their parish priest, all of the survivors, including the sick, assembled at the church for a special mass. They vowed that they and their descendants would enact a Passion play every ten years "for ever" if God would lift the affliction. The first performance was held in the churchyard in the spring of 1634. "Since that vow was made," reported the village chronicle, "not one person died of the plague, although some of us already had the marks of pestilence on their bodies."[35]

Perhaps it happened in exactly this fashion. The idea of bartering with God was not new. In 1497, the people of Chalons-sur-Saône had offered a play *Saint Sebastian* to ward off pestilence.[36] At about the same time the Oberammergauers made their vow, the villagers in Kohlgrub promised to restore their church of Saint Rochus every hundredth year if the plague ended. Not even the idea of a Passion was exactly novel. Nearly every village in this part of Bavaria had staged a Passion, based on a script from either Frankfurt in 1501 or Heidelberg in 1513. Murnau performed such a cycle in the sixteenth century. Even the little-known town of Dachau, fifteen miles northwest of Munich, celebrated a Passion in 1791. The development of Oberammergau's Passion will be traced in the next chapter. Whether it stems from the activities of Kaspar Schisler or not, Hermine Diemer's assessment that the Oberammergauer measures time by "passions," "divides his life by passions,"[37] just as the ancient Greeks lived from one Olympiad to another, still holds true.

To this day, the five thousand villagers of Oberammergau regard their vow as a *Gepflegt,* a sacred trust. Practically all who have visited the town have been impressed with its charm, the sincerity of its people. "A wild mountainflower," gushed John Stoddard in 1897. "The world is wide, but it contains no sight like that of Oberammergau."[38] Others found the village "unforgettable,"[39] "a bit of heaven on earth."[40] Its inhabitants were praised for their remarkable dignity,"[41] "easy and unstudied grace,"[42] or their "simple, childlike belief . . . imbued with an inherent mission."[43] A bewitched Reinhold Niebuhr wrote, "Oberammergau is a democracy and there seems to be neither rich nor poor in this village, where everything points to thrifty competence."[44] William Allen Butler was moved to rhapsodize:

> Fair Oberammergau! to thy pure shrine
> How many thoughts to-day revert with mine!
> From over distant seas, from every zone,
> What memories claim thee as their own![45]

I, too, was impressed with the physical appearance of the village. There is only one word to describe it—*gemütlich.* As one enters from the north, he is immediately confronted with houses covered with fresco paintings of children's fairy tales—*Hänsel and Gretel, Little Red Riding Hood.* Further on, in the town center more than two dozen buildings, including some inns, are plastered with biblical scenes—the flight into Egypt, the expulsion of Hagar, the healing of Tobias, the conferring of the keys on Saint Peter. With few exceptions, these outdoor treasures, including the one resplendent piece known as the Pilatushaus, were executed by Oberammergau's so-called *Luftmaler,* Franz Zwink, between 1769 and 1788.

The streets are no longer dirt paths as they were in Stoddard's day. If anything, the amount of blacktop in Oberammergau would make an American county commissioner bristle with envy. The gingerbread homes, replete with side porches and flower boxes, are further removed from the roadway now. There are no rocks on the roofs to keep unnailed shingles in place.[46] Accommodations are superior to a time when people "paid Waldorf-Astoria prices to sleep in rooms reminiscent of the manger; for the acrid smell of manure pervades them."[47] Some things never change—the omnipresent crucifixes above each bed, the thick eiderdown quilts, inadequate toilet facilities, and the Kofel, brooding sadly over the village.

But something else has changed. The people no longer greet every stranger with a traditional "Grüss Gott!"[48] Montrose Moses once wrote, "The people of Oberammergau are aloof,"[49] and when you see them in their cafes, ignoring the visitors who self-consciously sport ill-fitting Alpine hats and *Lederhosen,* you understand why. After three hundred years, perhaps they, too, have grown weary of the cloying approach to the outside world. Despite the open reception we received from the Bürgermeister, actors, waitresses, and others in the village, the feeling remained nonetheless that all of this was a well-rehearsed facade. The correspondent for the *Frankfurter Allgemeine Zeitung* had warned that the people of Oberammergau could be "tenacious and thick-headed."[50] Another German reporter warned of an *Eigensinn* (obstinate) or *Dorftrotz* (provincial) mentality in the village.[51] That unbecoming side emerged when our tour group arrived, tired and hungry at the Post Hotel one afternoon. In a scene reminiscent of a "Saturday Night Live" skit, we were told there would be no substitutions for "pork chops, pork chops, pork chops." When several of the Australian ladies requested glasses of water (which were free) instead of apple juice or some other commercial beverage, the waiter muttered under his breath in German, "Wasser, wasser. If you want water, go jump in the river." So we were welcomed into Oberammergau.[52]

2

The Origins of the Passion

To fully appreciate the significance of the Oberammergau Passion, it is essential that one understand the historical bases and evolution of such religious dramas. Two points must be noted at the outset: (1) Oberammergau's *Passionsspiel* is not the first attempt in history to reconcile elements of religious ritual and secular drama; and (2) Oberammergau's play is not even unique within the Christian community. The Bavarian phenomenon is a product of millennia of human experiment, fear, and artistic striving.

In his book *Thespis: Ritual, Myth, and Drama in the Ancient Near East,* Theodor Gaster states it is a worldwide custom "from time immemorial" to usher in the new year or bring to the end the old year with some kind of public ceremonies.[1] Gaster was not speaking of the frenzied spirit of alcohol and mayhem which accompanies the celebration of the new year in America (though one could make a case for the institutionalization of football and Guy Lombardo which has occurred here). Rather, he was speaking of solemn religious ceremonies which he labeled either rituals of *kenosis* or *plerosis.* The former were acts of "emptying," associated with abstention from work or sex, fasting, self-mortification, what Gaster termed "periods of suspended animation." Plerotic rites, on the other hand, served the purpose of "filling," through mating, sexual activity, magic, or purgation. Whether "emptying" or "filling," both sets of rituals attempted to renew the vitality of a people, ensure its continuity, and achieve what the ancient Greeks called *soteria*, salvation through a closer contact or union with God.[2]

The number of plerotic or kenotic parallels which Christianity shares with other religions is striking. One good example is the Lenten custom which Gaster indicates has been universally observed since ancient times. The Babylonians ushered in the new year with the recitation of the *Enuma Elish* poem and a sixteen-day period of religious introspection. Similar rites were found among the Greeks, Romans, Mayans, Incas, the Cherokee and Choctaw Indians of North America, and the Chinese. In Southeast Asia today, the Tet festival supposedly commands a suspension of sex, work, and war. The autumnal ingathering (Sukkot) among Jews is preceded by Yom Kippur, their most sacred day. Among Muslims, this fast, originally known as *Ashura*, was extended to an entire month, the holy period of Ramadan.

A more extreme form of Lent or kenosis is self-flagellation. Among Christians it may take the form of confession and penance. With Jews, it is evident during the Yom Kippur service, as they pound their chests and recite a litany of sins committed or acts omitted during the year. Shiite Muslims openly flog themselves with chains on the tenth of Muharram, the date commemorating the martyrdom of Hussein, grandson of Muhammad, in 680. More important, for several hundred years, the Shiites have performed their own passion on this holiday. In one emotional exchange between Hussein and the vision of the prophet before Hussein is beheaded, Muhammad declares, "Dear child, thou hast at length suffered martyrdom by the cruel hand of my people. This was the reward I expected from them." To which Hussein responds in Christ-like fashion, "I would offer my soul not once or twice but a thousand times for the salvation of my people."[3]

The tenth of Muharram is celebrated in the fall. Generally, however, a people's high holidays occur at the time of the winter solstice (the shortest day of the year), the vernal equinox (when the day and night are of equal length), or midsummer (when the day is at its longest). Almost invariably, there is a communal meal offered in honor of the gods. Thus, the ancient Persian deity known as Mithra, the God of a thousand eyes, ten thousand ears, a god of agriculture, contracts, and war, was honored for his special association with the sun. The birthday (*dies natalis invicti solis*) of this popular deity which at one time challenged Christianity for supremacy in the Roman Empire was, coincidentally, celebrated on December 25. The cult's rites were conducted in underground vestibules, not totally dissimilar from chambers in the Roman catacombs. There, in the privacy of these mithraeums, the god's epiphany, a bull, would be slaughtered and initiates baptized in its blood. Afterward, all would partake of a communal feast of wine and beef.[4]

Whatever date is assigned to specially honor a people's god, whether rites be kenotic or plerotic, it is certain they will be propitiatory in nature. Just as the people of Oberammergau sought to placate their God by swearing to do something they thought "He" would appreciate, so people have always tried to curry favor with their patron deity. That was precisely the point of the *akhitu* ceremony in ancient Babylon, wherein the priests sought to stave off destructive flooding of the Mesopotamian lowlands by praising the deeds of Marduk. It was essentially the same purpose in what was probably the most ancient Passion drama, the Sed ceremony in ancient Egypt. Evidence from mace-heads of the fourth millennium B.C. shows a pharaoh nicknamed "Scorpion," wearing the white crown of Upper Egypt, engaged in blessing the waters of the Nile. The king wore a tail (symbolic of a clan which held the wolf as its totem) and a goatee (representative of another clan which identified with Osiris) and held agricultural implements in his hands. As he walked about, in specific directions, he was followed by priests who offered chants to the gods. This fertility ritual, common to this day among some Nilotic tribes of Africa, was conducted at the beginning of the summer when the waters of the Nile began to rise and was intended to guarantee that the inundation would be sufficient for farming in the coming year.[5]

There are a host of other examples in history where the line between religious ritual and drama is finely drawn: repetitious Sumerian hymns, the Bacchic orgies in Greece, pagan May Day fetes in Western Europe, the lighting of bonfires in England to ward off evil spirits at Halloween, the resurrection of Tammuz in the Middle East, the baptism by fire in the Isis cult, Indian rain dances, Ukrainian ancestor worship at Christmas. It is not surprising, therefore, that Christians too have succumbed to the universal theophanic impulse to stage religious pageants. The play at Oberammergau is precisely one such attempt to accomplish *soteria*, to bring people nearer to God. As Dr. Josef Ziegler put it, "God embodied his redemption in Jesus Christ, graphically as historical fact, and that gives us not only the possibility, but rather the mission to carry on this visible principle embodying redemption."[6]

While the continuity of Oberammergau's performances may be remarkable, the actual staging of a Passion drama is not, even for Germany. Not just small towns like Murnau, Weilheim, and Dachau but larger cities like Innsbruck, Vienna, Frankfurt, and Berlin attempted such plays. Nor was the impulse confined to Germany. During the late Middle Ages, practically every hamlet from Italy to England felt constrained to offer its version of a biblical tale at Easter, Pentecost or Whitsunday, Trinity Sunday (the festival following Pentecost) or Corpus Christi Day (the Roman Catholic festival in honor of the Eucharist, celebrated the Thursday after Trinity Sunday).

The scholar Sandro Sticca attributes this widespread Christian zeal to what he terms "the Christocentric mysticism and piety" of the eleventh and twelfth centuries.[7] Certainly, a good case can be made that this was an age of religious fanaticism. The superstitious Christian world was in a state of expectancy. A magical thousand years had passed since the Crucifixion and church dogma preached an impending second coming. Now that the Holy Sepulchre was in the hands of the Turkish Antichrist, many simpleminded folk believed the End of Days was at hand. Hundreds of thousands of the faithful volunteered to march in Crusades to hasten the age of salvation. More stayed at home to do God's bidding by killing Jews whom they accused of ritual murder, host desecration, and eventually well-poisoning.

There was also a major spiritual transformation in Christianity at this time. Where the life of Jesus had been regarded as a triumph and Jesus himself portrayed as *Pantocrator*, ruler of the universe, church teachings now began to emphasize the human nature of Christ. The historian Karl Young maintains that previous representations of the Crucifixion had been deliberately avoided because "the Mass itself was felt to be sufficiently effective."[8] After the eleventh century, however, it was increasingly common in art and drama to dwell on the suffering of Jesus, to show him on the cross, bloodied, head down.[9]

Sticca attributes the change to Saint Anselm (1033–1109), Saint Bernard (1091–1153) and the Cistercians.[10] But there is little doubt that the change struck a responsive chord among the common people who craved something more than a Latin rite which few could understand. The standard Passion play, then, sprang from several disparate roots: (*a*) the classical Graeco-Roman tradition of tragedy; (*b*) church-related art; (*c*) secular medieval entertainment; and (*d*) services tied to the mass during Holy Week or Christmas.

The link between classical drama and the traditional Passion is indisputable.[11] It is apparent in the technical aspects of staging in Oberammergau where a huge stage, 150 feet wide, stands open, unprotected by any roof, just as an ancient Attic amphitheater. Nine yards from the orchestra pit is a curtained proscenium opening. A series of archways permit entry and exit of a chorus, directed by a Prologue who speaks in much the same manner as a Roman drama reciter leading a group of mimes from the pulpit. The chorus is as controlled and unemotional, their faces as stern as any mask from the theater of Aeschylus, Sophocles, or Terence.

The figures, too, within the Passion, were overdrawn caricatures of good or evil. When the Saxon nun Hrotswitha authored the first popular religious dramas in the tenth century, her villains—Dulcitius, the evil governor who persecuted Christians in the time of Diocletian, and Sisinnius, the wizard who tortured young girls—the violence and melancholy of her work owed much to Agamemnon or Medea. Later mystery plays prominently featured veiled angels and Marys, along with bemasked devils and the seven deadly sins, the latter cavorting onstage, sneering asides to the audience, encouraging men to stray from the path of righteousness.[12] The same principle of good versus evil was manifest in old Hollywood westerns where the heroes wore white and villains black. Such characters may have disappeared from the Oberammergau stage today, but the simplistic identification of good people and bad still operates. Evil priests wear no masks, but they do wear horned headdresses and lavish robes. Conspiratorial traders are marked by striped tunics. When these nemeses speak, they shout. Meanwhile, Jesus and his coterie of disciples wear unpretentious, single-hued garments and, with the exception of Peter, speak in subdued tones. The contrast, as in ancient Greece, is unmistakable.

The second element contributing to the development of a formal Passion was medieval church art. The Crusader epoch saw the development of illuminated manuscripts— hymnals and missals with elaborate biblical scenes. One such example was the *Biblia Pauperum* (Poor Man's Bible) which was constructed in such a fashion that Old Testament prophecy was affixed to the Gospels in adjoining columns. A third column, containing a primitive woodcut or some colored illustration, explained the written passages to the illiterate. Even before the development of the printing press, however, the same catechistic purpose was served by inscriptions on portals, statues in city squares, frescoes and stained-glass windows of churches, all showing scenes from the Old and New Testaments.[13] It is no coincidence that the Oberammergau play originally included twenty-four *tableaux vivants*, living pictures or "freezes" from the Old Tes-

tament, "carved expressions of histrionic art" Joseph Maria
Lutz called them, whose purpose it was to offer some
prophetic message to the audience. Some of these—the adoration of the brazen serpent, Moses' receipt of the decalogue, Hebrew spies carrying clusters of grapes, Abner
slain by Joab—were exact duplicates of medieval scenes in
the Poor Man's Bible.

Reliance upon religious illustrations, in print, art, or
onstage, paved the way to greater expression by lay entertainers and troubadors in the Middle Ages.[14] These included
mummers, whose biblical pantomimes often bordered on
the lewd. Indeed, the term *ludus*, meaning amusement, was
the generic term applied to liturgical works of the twelfth-
century playwright Nicolai Hilarius, as well as to plays and
games dealing with Father Christmas and Saint George.[15]
Religious mummery had been introduced at trade fairs as
early as the eighth century. It was soon complemented by
profane puppetry, ballads, and poems. Indigent minnesing-
ers and jongleurs, composers of the *Carmina Burana* (collections of popular, bawdy songs) and the *comoedia elegiaca*
(rhyming couplets developed in France in the twelfth century), attached themselves to monasteries and began reciting
chansons de geste (songs of heroism) in order to attract pilgrims to a particular site.[16] This *Ordo Vagorum* (order of
wandering scholars) also chanted long biblical odes or created vernacular plays in which they juxtaposed Hercules,
Adam, and Nicodemus.[17]

Ultimately Thespis, diversion and art came together in the
church. Though some historians trace the roots of the Passion to innocent Resurrection plays like the *Concordia Re-
gularis*, from England at the end of the tenth century, or the
Planctus Mariae, lamentations of the Marys sung on Good
Friday, and only dating from fourteenth-century Italy, the
germinal truly was the mass itself during Holy Week. As
early as the fourth century, clergy and congregation at
Jerusalem had observed the *Adoratio Crucis, Depositio
Crucis*, and *Elevatio Crucis*, the lifting, adoring, and kissing
of the cross.[18] The rituals were performed in some stan-

dardized form by the tenth century, for a *Peregrinatio* (travelogue), transcribed at Monte Cassino, the Benedictine abbey sixty miles south of Rome, treats at length Holy Week observances in different parts of Italy.[19]

Sometime during the medieval period, *melisma* (humming of wordless melodies) was introduced to church choirs. Then *tropes* (short texts or interpolations featuring specific choral members) were added to the Easter service. Already by the ninth century, priests were permitting the troping of the Introitus, Kyrie Eleison, and Gloria hymns. It was only a matter of time before the clergy, probably at the urging of minstrels and other entertainers, permitted the acting out of little scenes at the side of the altar.[20]

The scene which seems to have the greatest claim to serving as a rudimentary Passion play is the *Visitatio sepulchri* (the visit of the Marys to the tomb of the crucified Jesus).[21] Some four hundred versions are known to have existed by the year 1000, most of them beginning with the query *Quem quaeritis?* While the congregation was reciting the third lesson of the Easter liturgy, four priests would costume themselves, three in long, flowing gowns as the Marys, the other as an angel in white. The "angel" would enter the hall and go to the altar (tomb) where he would sit quietly, holding a palm branch in hand. When the third response was completed, the "Marys" would enter, carrying illuminated censers. They would proceed slowly to the altar, as if looking for something, while the one at the "tomb" sang softly, "Quem quaeritis in sepulchro, Christicolae?" ("Whom seek ye in the sepulchre, o Christians?") The Marys would answer: "Ieusum Nazarenum crucifixum, o Caelicolae." ("Jesus of Nazareth, the Crucified, of dwellers in heaven.") Again the angel: "Non est hic, surrexit sicut praedixerat. Ite, nuntiate quia surrexit de sepulchro." ("He is not here; he hath arisen as was prophesied. Go ye and proclaim that he hath arisen from the tomb.") The Marys finding only the linens from Christ's body, put down the censers and turned to the congregation, proclaiming, "The Lord is truly risen, as he hath said: behold, he shall go before you into Galilee, where you shall see him. Hallelujah! Hallelujah!" The officiants then resumed the regular service with a Te Deum Laudamus.[22]

The *Quem quaeritis* is, in abbreviated form, almost identical with the apotheosis of Christ in the current Oberammergau Passion. There also the Marys, having found the entrance open and nothing but wrappings inside, are told by an angel in white and spangles, "Fear not, you seek Jesus of Nazareth who was crucified. He is not here. He has arisen from the dead! He will go on before you to Galilee. You will see Him there, as He told you." The women proclaim, "Hallelujah, He has arisen!" and are then joined by the entire chorus in a chant of hallelujahs, while the triumphant Christ appears onstage flanked by Moses, Adam and Eve, the apostles, and winged angels bearing the cross and chalice, another carrying a flag.[23]

The finale at Oberammergau is, in a sense, the culmination of a process which began with fertility rites in the ancient Near East and wound through medieval *Visitatio*. Once the barrier to presenting the liturgy in a dramatic fashion had been broken by the Christian church, there was no turning back. Choral bits and dialogues were added for Christmas, Epiphany, and Ascension Day, with prologues and sequels telling of the creation of man and his final judgment. At Easter, scenes showing shepherds in the field, the Nativity, Rachel and her children, and Herod's massacre of the innocents were staged in the nave or exterior of a church. The only restrictions were that such vignettes be recited in Latin and that they be true to the Gospels.[24]

As with other forms of art, the focus of religious dramas underwent a transformation during the Crusader period. Once more, the emphasis was upon the martyred Christ. Monte Cassino provides the earliest example of a complete *Passionsspiel*, dating from 1150. The twelve acts are extremely short, consisting of only 320 lines. The performance, beginning with Judas's bargain with Caiaphas and ending with the lament of the Virgin while her son is on the cross, could not have taken more than one-half hour.[25] Most of these early plays were short, 58 lines in the case of the so-called Northern Passion, 250 at York,[26] as if the performers were somewhat tentative about overstepping the bounds of propriety. In fact, one preacher warned, "Men shulden not pleyn the passion of Crist, upon peyne myche grettere than was the venjaunce of the childre that scornyden Helisee. For siker pleyinge of the passion of Crist is but verre scornyng of Crist."[27]

The church, however, permitted secular performances because, as Saint Ethelwod and Saint Thomas Aquinas suggested, they might be catechistic and edifying. Professor Sticca adds: "The function of the medieval drama is quite clear. It constitutes a powerful dramatic statement of the Christian faith at its richest and most complex. The aim of medieval drama is that which motivated the medieval church as a whole—to express in visible, dramatic terms, the facts and values of the accepted body of scripture and theological belief."[28]

Emboldened by church dogma which emphasized the suffering of Christ, playwrights concentrated on the dramatic Crucifixion, to the exclusion of more benign scenes. The Wakefield Passion consisted of only 450 lines, almost all of them given over to the Crucifixion. As it opened, Pilate, surrounded by sycophants, harlots, and "dastards," bade peace to everyone. Jesus was then brought in, accompanied by four torturers who mocked "this fals chuffer." The torturers spoke and laughed among themselves, as they prepared him for his execution. "Knyt thou a knott . . . tyll it com to the bone," said one. "Dryfe a nayll ther thrugh outt," said a second. "Hold down his knees," said the third. "Draw out hys lymmes," said the fourth, as they invited the audience to participate in the brutal murder. There followed a short exchange between Jesus and Mary, then for 70 more lines the torturers taunted Jesus demanding a miracle and regaled the audience with what they had done.[29] The emphasis on pain and agony was even worse in a German play from Alsfeder where 700 lines, more than the complete Monte Cassino Passion of 1150, dealt with torture.[30]

Before the fifteenth century, many such pageants were being offered throughout Europe. While these plays dealt principally with the Crucifixion, the Passion of Jesus was not an exclusive subject. Scenes from the earlier life of Christ were introduced. Old Testament tales which tended to confirm the mission of Christ were also dramatized, until a complete cycle, from the Creation to Judgment Day, was achieved. At York in the fourteenth century, some forty-eight plays were staged, with specific guilds being assigned responsibility for a mini-drama. Thus, the tanners offered the creation and the fall of Lucifer, the glovers did Cain and Abel, the bookbinders did the sacrifice of Isaac, and the shipwrights appropriately did the building of the ark.[31]

So many individual plays could not be performed in a single day. As much as a week might be given over to the religious cycle in Siena, Padua, or Friuli in Italy; York, Chester, Coventry, or Towneley in England. The burghers did not complain. Protestations to the contrary notwithstanding, the plays represented an economic boon to such communities. Religious shrines have always attracted pilgrims eager to part with their monies for a blessed trinket. It was so in Rheims, where 16,000 attended a Crucifixion play in 1490, at Auton where 80,000 persons packed a theater during the season of 1516, and at Valenciennes where the townsfolk earned almost 5,000 livres from admissions to their play in 1547.[32] Like their predecessors elsewhere, the villagers of Oberammergau have felt the tension between piety and profit. And like their counterparts in Britain, who made participation in the sacred drama a monopoly of the citizens, the Oberammergauers have clung to the tradition that no outsider may perform in their pageant.

In Germany itself, the first prototypical Passions or *Visitatio sepulchri* may have been performed in Bavaria as far back as the ninth century. Four hundred years later, the first German-language Passions were developed at Klosterneuburg, Benediktbeuern, Rothenbuch, and the Benedictine abbey at Saint Gall. The latter especially offered a precedent for Oberammergau's Prologue (the chief angel who serves as a kind of interlocutor through the performance), for at Saint Gall, a priest, representing Augustine, was chosen to speak the Prologue and offer comment during the action. The Reformation gave rise to no fewer than five hundred plays in the Lower Rhine, as nearly every respectable town in this part of Germany had its own Passion.[33]

It is possible that the village of Oberammergau may have been introduced to its first Passion play three hundred years before the staging of its celebrated plague-ending pageant in 1634. Oscar Cargill claims the Benedictine order generally was the most tolerant of innovations in church music and liturgy, and certainly the Passion translations rendered into the vernacular at the Benedictine abbeys noted above bears this out.[34] It is, moreover, no coincidence that the Ettal monastery, a Benedictine outpost, was established in the fourteenth century. Ettal was under the supervision of the convent at Rothenbuch. It does not strain credulity to suggest, as others have done, that monks from Rothenbuch brought this religious innovation to the village about the same time.[35]

What does strain credulity is the rapidity with which the unsophisticated Oberammergauers were able to implement their vow, in less than one year. Wrote one critic, "It is not probable that simple villagers would make a vow to perform a play totally unknown to them, and even in its rudest form demanding such capacity and preparatory study."[36] Said another: "He who knows what pains must be taken for years and what preparations are necessary in order to perform a play involving several hundreds of actors will admit that the idea could not have come to the minds of the Oberammergauers all of a sudden, in one night so to speak, especially as it would have been an impossibility with country folk lacking in experience."[37]

Research conducted by Dr. August Hartmann into the oldest extant text, that of 1662, established that the work was really a composite of four distinct manuscripts. Some of the text may have been taken from a Passion offered in the jubilee year of 1600 by the Augustine abbey at Polling. The principal portion stems from a fifteenth-century playbook deposited with the chapter of Saints Ulric and Afra at Augsburg. Several thousand lines were literally copied from a sixteenth-century text written by Sebastian Wild, Meistersinger of Augsburg who was also a pupil of Nuremberg's Hans Sachs. Dr. Hartmann also found slips of paper, containing passages from a Passion written by Johann Aelbl, curate of Weilheim, glued to the 1662 copy.[38]

Oberammergau's village historian Hermine Diemer conceded that the saga of the Passion vow was "convenient" and "circumstantial" and added that the villagers must have been using a copy of the Augsburg play for decades before the onset of the plague. Wrote Diemer, "If the Ammergauers had not had a passion play before 1634, it is not to be supposed that they would have adopted a text that had been written nearly two centuries ago, then a text that needs must have been obsolete in both language and conception."[39] The invasion of the Swedes and onset of the plague may actually have led not to the beginning but to a temporary suspension of a tradition. Again Ms. Diemer: "It is very probable, that in Oberammergau, as in other villages, passions were performed a great deal earlier than that, presumably already in the 15th century."[40] Even the former parish priest of Oberammergau, Dr. Franz Bogenrieder, reluctantly agrees, stating there may have been regular performances in the village two hundred years before the Thirty Years' War.[41]

The oft-cited tale of panicked villagers swearing a vow to stave off bubonic plague may appeal to romantics and gullible tourists, but it has little validity. The Passion at Oberammergau is a product of ten thousand years of human aspiration and experiment. It is a cousin, however distant, of the pagan rites of Sed and the tenth of Muharram. It owes much in style to ancient myth and theater. It evolved through the course of centuries in Europe, with its own unique Christian elements taking form. And it was refined in modern times by a series of gifted editors, who, as chance would have it, lived in the isolated Bavarian village.

3

The Daisenberger Passion

At no time was the Oberammergau Passion text considered immutable. Notations on copies preserved in the parish archives dating from the seventeenth and eighteenth centuries bear comments like "has again been revised and rewritten."[1] Shortly after the 1740 performance, the task of revision was assigned to Ferdinand Rosner, keeper of equipment at the Ettal monastery. Rosner's mammoth work (nine thousand lines, more than twice the length of the 1662 text)[2] introduced what is regarded as a Jesuit influence to the play, that is, two parallel actions proceeding side by side. The series of tableaux, Old Testament freezes which presaged events in Jesus' life, were inserted between acts. For the first time, there was orchestral accompaniment, reminiscent of Italian opera. Rosner employed traditional, allegorical characters like Despair, Sin, Avarice, and Envy. But their stilted lines, recited in iambic tetrameter, the meter employed by Goethe in *Faust,* caused much unhappiness among the cast, which found such lines difficult to speak, and the audience, which could not suffer the length or symbolism of the play.[3]

In 1780, another Ettal priest, Magnus Knipfelberger, was asked to simplify Rosner's text, for a reason other than local discontent. Between 1770 and 1810, several Bavarian monarchs, including Maximilian Joseph, Charles Theodore, and Maximilian II, attempted to ban religious folk plays which they feared bordered on the sacrilegious. The villagers of Oberammergau wished to avoid such criticism. In their decennial applications to the archbishop of Munich seeking a *missio canonica*, they emphasized the purity of their intentions and reminded the authorities of the privileged status they had been accorded for assisting in the construction of Ettal. Because of either the remoteness of the village or the sympathy of the church hierarchy, the Passions were performed in 1634, 1644, 1654, 1664, 1674, 1680 (when for no apparent reason other than convenience of calculation the presentations were shifted to years ending with zero), and every decade thereafter until the Napoleonic period.[4]

Combat between French and Austrian troops in the Ammer Valley in July 1800 forced a suspension of performances for the first time. The villagers did offer four belated presentations in 1801. Wartime conditions interfered once more in 1810. Still worse, secular officials, who had winked benignantly at Oberammergau's Passion before, now declared the village's privileged status at an end. The Bavarian Imperial Court, led by Count Montgelas, a minister hostile to every petition of the Ammergauers, prevailed upon the prince elector to warn the villagers in September 1810 that they would be fined thirty *Reichsthalers* (a symbolic amount linking the villagers to Judas) unless they complied with the ban.

Undaunted, a delegation from Oberammergau went to the capital to appeal. The group was headed by Georg Lang, whose grandfather had immigrated to the Ammer Valley in 1723, and whose descendants would play leading roles in subsequent Passions. Though the villagers were at first rebuked and ridiculed by members of the imperial court, their project was saved by Georg Sambura, a clerical councillor who used his influence with the *Kurfürst* to secure an exemption. In an action worthy of Herod Antipas, Maximilian adjudged the Oberammergau Passion "a harmless affair" to be considered "more or less a rural festivity" and permitted its resumption in 1811.[5]

There would be only three more interruptions of what Alois Lang, Christus in the 1930 and 1934 pageants, called "the feast of reconciliation."[6] All of these, too, were related to war. In 1870, twenty performances were scheduled, but only sixteen given because of the outbreak of the Franco-Prussian War.[7] Josef Lang, who played Jesus that year, and a number of other actors were called to safe duty in Munich. The men were not even required to cut their long hair or beards, grown for their roles in the passion. The villagers were not so fortunate in World War I, however. Sixty-seven men of Oberammergau died on the battlefields, and the resentment generated against Germany caused a postponement of the pageant until 1922. There were no performances in 1940 because of the Second World War.

The text employed in recent times no longer was that of Pater Rosner. A drastic revision was accomplished by another Ettal monk, Othmar Weis (1769–1843), after the Benedictine abbey was secularized in 1803. Weis and several colleagues were permitted to remain in a wing of the converted brewery, as Hermine Diemer puts it, "to lament over the ruins of their Jerusalem."[8] In the silence of his cell, the young priest from Schongau devised an entirely new concept for the Passion. Gone were Rosner's demons and the medieval concept that man was not totally responsible for his actions. Gone too the allegorical figures and the flowery singsong. Tableaux, chorus, and Prologue were retained. But now the central themes of the play were the villainy of men, the sacrifice and triumph of Christ the Messiah.[9]

Another change which figured prominently in the 1815 production was the addition of major musical pieces. Where previously the play had included Gregorian chants, arias, and a few orchestral interludes, symphonic music now became an essential part of the Passion. The innovation is attributed to Rochus Dedler (1779–1822), son of an Oberammergau innkeeper who trained as a teacher in Ettal and Munich, then returned to his native village to write the accompaniment for Weis's text. The story is told that all of this original music was consumed by fire in 1817, and Dedler had to compose it over again from memory. It would have been a remarkable achievement even for a man who had written numerous Te Deums, litanies, and musical comedies. What finally emerged was a score which owes much to Beethoven and Mozart. Heavy brass passages which seemed to herald the age of Wagner were edited out by Professor Eugen Pabst in 1950.[10]

While Dedler's music has remained relatively intact for 175 years, the same cannot be said for Weis's text. In 1850, the third major revision of the Oberammergau Passion was undertaken by Joseph Alois Daisenberger (1799–1883). Born in the neighboring village of Oberau, Daisenberger had studied under Othmar Weis and viewed his former teacher with a respect approaching piety. Ordained at Uffing in 1821, Daisenberger accepted the position of curate at Oberammergau in 1839. Before his death, he earned the title of "beloved Geistlicher Rath" (beloved spiritual counselor) from his parishioners. In 1850, and again in 1860, Daisenberger, who served as stage manager for the Passion, applied himself to shortening some passages and eliminating obsolete expressions.[11] His declared purpose, precisely as Aquinas and Ethelwod had advised, was "the edification of the Christian world."[12] Moreover, he wrote, "May it be that the sight of the Redeemer's great love for mankind may draw tears from the eyes of the sinners, and these tears aided by God's good spirit may be the way by which the Good Shepherd seeks and finds His lost sheep."[13]

The Passion text used in Oberammergau till 1980 essentially was Daisenberger's edition. It consisted of eighteen acts (compressed to sixteen in recent years), sixty scenes, and twenty-four tableaux vivants. Between acts, the chorus of forty-nine men and women dressed in drab gray robes and wearing headbands of gold tramps out to set the stage, while their leader, the Prologue, in the fashion of Augustine offers an explanation of the accompanying biblical scene. A single performance normally lasted eight hours, the first section beginning at 8 A.M. and lasting till noon when an hour intermission permitted lunch, then resuming from one till five in the afternoon. Religious zealots might start their day joining members of the cast for a six o'clock mass in the village church.

The events of Holy Week, as dramatized by Daisenberger, may be summarized in the following manner:

Prelude. The Prologue and chorus greet the audience. Two tableaux are presented. In the first, Adam and Eve, wearing sheepskins, are banished from the Garden of Eden by a winged angel who holds a sword in the form of a flame. Behind the angel stands a burst of gilded rays symbolizing the tree of forbidden fruit. The second living picture traditionally showed a number of girls and smaller children surrounding a cross at center stage. The adoration has been retained but transformed to represent the time in 1633 when villagers swore their vow before a huge crucifix bearing a twelve-foot-high Jesus.

Act 1. Jesus and the Money Changers. Jesus enters Jerusalem atop a donkey, to the shouts and exultations of the people on Palm Sunday. He drives the money changers and traders from the Temple, then returns to Bethany. The traders plot for revenge.

Act 2. Conspiracy of the High Council. In the past, this act began with a tableau showing the sons of the patriarch Jacob conspiring to kill Joseph in the Plain of Dothan. Though the freeze has been deleted from the 1980 presentation, the act itself consists of discussions between the traders and Sanhedrin who agree that Jesus must be arrested to preserve Mosaic law.

Act 3. Parting at Bethany. Two tableaux presage the action. In the first, the young Tobias departs from his parents, while the angel Raphael, played by another boy, waits, crook in hand, stage left. In the second, the loving bridesmaid from the Song of Solomon laments the loss of her groom. In the play, Christ is anointed by Mary Magdalene, then takes leave of his mother and friends. Judas is angered by the waste of the spikenard of oil.

Act 4. The Last Journey to Jerusalem. A controversial tableau (now deleted) showed Queen Vashti dishonored at the court of King Ahashuerus. The old queen (Judaism, explains the Prologue) has been displaced by Esther (Christianity). Jesus sends two disciples to secure a Paschal lamb. He enters Jerusalem for the last time and weeps over the fate of the city. Judas contemplates betraying his master and is tempted by Dathan and other merchants.

Act 5. The Last Supper. The Passover Seder or Last Supper is celebrated in a scene evocative of Da Vinci's painting. Jesus washes the feet of his disciples and institutes the mass with wine and thick, brown, leavened bread. Two tableaux show Moses with rays or horns protruding from his head, bringing manna and grapes to the people in the wilderness.

Act 6. The Betrayer. In a tableau, Joseph, a boy nude to the waist, is sold by his brothers to the Midianites for twenty pieces of silver. In accompanying action, Judas appears before the Sanhedrin and promises to deliver Jesus for thirty pieces of silver. After his departure, the Pharisees plan at great length the death of Jesus.

Act 7. Jesus at the Mount of Olives. Two more Old Testament scenes introduce the soliloquy of Jesus in the Garden of Gethsemane. The first, a nonsequitur, which we are told explains that man must earn his food by the sweat of his brow, shows Adam, in sheepskin and assisted by a brood of similarly attired children, drawing a plow across a field. The second freeze more appropriately offers a helmeted Joab, surrounded by soldiers, stabbing an unsuspecting Amasa in the ribs. In the actual Passion, Christ agonizes over his fate while his apostles doze. Judas enters with an armed band and betrays Jesus with a kiss.

Intermission.

Act 8. Jesus before Annas. The Old Testament parallel has Micah, slapped on the cheek by Zedekiah, priest of Baal, for daring to predict that King Ahab would die in battle. In like manner, Jesus is taken before a waiting, eager Annas and is struck on the face for his insolence. Soldiers also deride Christ as he is led through the streets by a rope.

Act 9. Condemned by the High Council. Two more tableaux emphasize the humiliation of Christ. In one, the aged Naboth is condemned by false witnesses and is stoned to death by the sons of Jezebel. In the other, Job, sitting atop a dunghill, is railed at by his friends, servants, even his wife and children. Meanwhile, Jesus is questioned by Caiaphas about his messiahship and is condemned. A tortured Judas tries to get the Sanhedrin to repeal its verdict. When his efforts prove unsuccessful, he tosses the money back at them and storms off.

Act 10. Despair of Judas. Judas and all who identify with him are linked with Cain in the opening tableau. The battered body of Abel appears at center stage. To the right is Cain, clad in a leopard skin and holding a club in one hand. His other hand is at his brow, attempting to conceal the brand of God. In what for the play is a remarkably short act, Judas offers a speech of remorse, then hangs himself.

Act 11. Christ before Pilate. Originally, there was a freeze which heralded Christ's first appearance before Pilate. The tableau of Daniel in the great pillared hall of Darius has been deleted from twentieth-century productions. Pilate's interrogation, coupled with news of his wife's dream, convinces the governor that Jesus should be prosecuted by Herod Antipas for lese majesty.

Act 12. Christ before Herod. The scene stands without the original living picture which showed a blinded Samson mocked by the Philistines. Herod treats Christ with scorn, demanding a miracle, then sends him back to Pilate, cloaked in a red mantle of royalty. Responding to the urgings of the Sanhedrin, Pilate reluctantly agrees to have Jesus scourged. Roman guards beat Jesus and press a crown of thorns into his scalp.

Act 13. Christ Sentenced to Death on the Cross. Two horrible pictures showing the presentation of Joseph's bloodied coat to Jacob and Abraham about to stab Isaac on Mt. Moriah have been rejected from contemporary versions of the Passion. Retained, however, are tableaux which show Joseph riding a sedan chair as vizir of Egypt and another which supposedly represents the scapegoat offering of Yom Kippur. Following the tableaux, the stage is aswarm with action, as priests and Pharisees bring mobs from every direction.

Pilate gives Jesus another hearing, then offers the people a choice between Jesus and Barabbas. They demand and receive a final judgment on Christ.

Act 14. The Way to the Cross. The final segment of the Passion is introduced by a more sublime image of the *Akedah,* or binding of Isaac. In this tableau, the boy, like Jesus, carries wood on his back as he and Abraham climb Mt. Moriah. Another freeze, showing Moses and a brazen serpent intertwined about the cross, has been deleted. When the chorus withdraws from the stage, Christ bears his cross to Golgotha. As he passes through the streets, he encounters his mother, Veronica, and Simon of Cyrene. The women of Jerusalem weep for him.

Act 15. Jesus on Calvary. For the first time, the chorus appears in black, traditional mourning garb. There is no tableau. Christ is raised upon the cross. He is mocked by members of the Sanhedrin and the soldiers, and utters his last words. The legs of the criminals are broken. A soldier pierces the side of Christ with a lance and blood gushes forth. Jesus' followers slowly and reverently take down the body and lay it before his mother in a replica of the Pieta. The Sanhedrin insists that guards be posted before the tomb which is to hold Christ's body.

Act 16. Resurrection and Apotheosis. For once, action precedes tableau. Roman guards see a light at the tomb. Mary Magdalene and the other women encounter an angel and recite the same lines as *Quem Quaeritis.* The final tableau shows Jesus, resplendent in white, with his apostles, angels, the Virgin Mary, and Moses. The Passion ends with the chorus proclaiming:

> Praise to you, conqueror of death,
> Who once died on Golgotha.
> Praise to you, Saviour of all sinners,
> Who conquered on Golgotha.
> Praise to you who on the altar
> Gave your life for us.
> You have purchased our salvation,
> We die, to live in you.

Halleluja, praise, renown, adoration, power and
   glory
be thine for ever and ever.[14]

Daisenberger's play called for upward of five hundred
participants, ranging in importance from Christ, the Marys,
and apostles to the high priests, Pilate, guards, traders,
members of the mob, and children who doubled as cherubs
and those who welcomed Jesus to Jerusalem on Palm Sunday. Selection of principals was done in a secret meeting of
the Bürgermeister and town council (sixteen men, including
the Catholic priest and Evangelical minister of Oberammergau) together with six other men, usually those with exper-
tise in staging the Passion, who were named by the council.
Traditionally, each member of the committee would drop a
white or black ball into an urn as candidates came up for
decision. To guarantee sufficient rehearsal time, decisions
were usually made in the spring of the year preceding production. In other words, cast selection for 1980 was made in
the spring of 1979.[15]
   Certain restrictions were imposed in the casting process.
In keeping with the provincial nature of European Passions,
only persons born in Oberammergau or resident in the village for twenty years could participate. To qualify for a modest part, one must have led a "blameless life." In a town
which historically has known no jail, poaching on the land of
nobility was sufficient to have someone disqualified. No
wigs or false beards could be used. To conform to the image
of what Jesus and his followers supposedly looked like, the
village men had to grow beards. No married woman or female over the age of thirty-five could play the role of the
Virgin Mary.[16]
   Important roles went to the town's leading wood-carvers,
reflecting, perhaps, a spiritual link between the Passion and
the manufacture of votive objects. As John Jackson noted in
1880, "the best players in the village, almost without exception, were woodcarvers."[17] Not coincidentally, in a society
where merit alone was supposed to serve as the basis of
selection, families with ancient ties in the community ac-

quired almost a proprietary claim to specific roles. The Zwinks, who claim to have arrived in Oberammergau as far back as 1446, supplied the Christus for productions in 1800, 1811, 1815, 1820, and 1980. In the same period, members of the Lang family filled the role on five occasions. Langs also directed most of the Passions in the twentieth century. Traditionally, the Virgin Mary has been played either by girls from the Mayr or Rutz clans, both of which trace their roots in Oberammergau back four hundred years. In the nineteenth century, Judas was played nine times by Johann Lechner or his son Gregor. Even Reinhold Niebuhr, who praised the democratic atmosphere of the village, wondered about Oberammergau's strange "aristocracy of artistic achievement."[18]

The actor-historian Eduard Devrient brought Oberammergau's Passion to notoriety in 1850 after being mesmerized by Tobias Flunger's performance as Jesus. In an article for the *Illustrierte Zeitung* of Leipzig, Devrient called the passion the last remnant of medieval religious plays. Wrote Devrient: "Rising before us, perfect in its old German atmosphere, as fresh and alive as if it had been conceived yesterday; its innocence, its untroubled childlike joy seems to call us: be of good cheer, the ancient store of folk-art in Germany is inexhaustible; only believe in it, and it will enrich you beyond measure."[19]

Within a decade, Devrient's panegyrics were matched by other notables. In October 1860, Dean Stanley lavished praise upon this "mysterious" and "sacred" drama for *MacMillan's Magazine*. Shortly after, the Baroness Tautphoeus devoted a chapter to this region in her romantic novel *Quits*.[20] Most significant, perhaps, was the endorsement of Hans Christian Andersen. The gentle Dane had gone to Oberammergau with some skepticism in 1860. Like others, he came away charmed by the "unimagined" beauty of the countryside, by the "majesty," "dramatic power," and "truthfulness" of the Passion. Wrote Andersen, "The entire play was like a going to church where the priest is not heard, but is seen as a living worker." Oberammergau he said was not comedy-playing but "a holy harmony, a real assumption of the Christ-man." As he watched the silent crowds leaving by foot or in wagons, Andersen likened Oberammergau to a holy festival, with each person "raised in spirit, filled with that soul of love that gave itself for unborn generations."[21] With such notices, it was only a matter of time before everyone from European nobility to Henry Ford and John D. Rockefeller was making pilgrimage to the once-obscure Bavarian village.

Since Devrient and Andersen penned their articles, the critical response to Oberammergau's Passion has ranged from praise to damnation. Some contend it is no liturgical act but rather "good, homespun folk art."[22] John Elliott, writing in the *New York Herald-Tribune* in 1930, compared the original collaboration of Weis and Dedler with that of Gilbert and Sullivan.[23] Elliott's contemporary, Hannen Swafer of the *London Daily Express* found the crowd scenes "worthy of Reinhardt," the Crucifixion "beautiful."[24] Others have noted "the naive simplicity of the scenes" and "the public earnestness of the actors."[25] Reinhold Niebuhr found it purged of the "sublime and ridiculous" which made medieval plays so offensive. "The play is the ripe fruit of a rich tradition toward the perfection of which many generations have collaborated," wrote Niebuhr. "It is the tragedy of the 'Soul of Love' accepting the fate which his uncompromising devotion to high truth makes inevitable."[26]

Niebuhr did, however, criticize the sameness in motive of every scene, the overlong choral interludes, and farfetched allegories upon which some Old Testament tableaux rested. He also suggested that the musical score might be strengthened by integrating some of Bach's *Saint Matthew Passion*. These were precisely the aesthetic failings which prompted other critics to label the Passion "a mixture of Lourdes and summer stock,"[27] "edifying *Rührstück* for old women,"[28] "kitsch," and "one of the biggest pieces of falderal ever palmed off on the innocent masses."[29] Said W. A. Darlington in 1930: "If you were to go to Ober-Ammergau simply with the idea of witnessing a work of deliberate art, you would, I think, be disappointed. Judged by a rigid standard of criticism, the music is nothing out of the ordinary and many of the costumes—particularly those of the chorus—reflect the least attractive religious painting. The singing is good—for a village; the technique of the acting is good—for a village. But if you refuse to make allowances and expect a finished professional production, your thousand-mile pilgrimage will have been wasted."[30]

Darlington's colleague, J. B. Priestley, echoed his sentiments. Considered as a production of wood-carvers, potters, workmen in a remote Bavarian village, the play, Priestley conceded, was "an astounding achievement." "If you came across it, by accident, you would never stop talking about it." Unfortunately, he continued, it had ceased to be an affair of a few, unsophisticated peasants attempting to fulfill a religious vow. It was by 1930 one of the great tourist attractions in the world, and as such "it is not good enough." Priestley attacked the music, which required the hand of a Bruno Walter, and the acting, which *required* a good director like Reinhardt. He likened the lengthy performance to "the dreariest periods" in school when students suffered the "agony and fury of tedium."[31] For this, Priestley blamed not the actual scenes in the play but the prologues and singing. As he explained:

> Before each scene, there entered, in a slow, solemn procession, the speaker of the prologue (the famous Anton Lang) and a choir of forty-eight men and women who were supposed to be guardian spirits. Considered as a village choir, these singers were unusually good, but they were certainly not good enough to be given such scope, for before we had done we must have had four hours of them, and four hours of mediocre singers going rather tamely through a great deal of mediocre music are too much for any man. Moreover, these guardian spirits went through the same slow ritual of entrance and exit before each scene, and, as you can imagine, there are a great many scenes. The first, second, or third time they did it, I was quite pleased to see them, but after that their entrance either irritated or depressed me, and long before I had seen the last of

them, I think that if the man sitting next to me (he spent all his time either yawning or dropping sandwiches) had turned a machine-gun on them, I should not have put out a restraining hand. Oh, how I came to hate those guardian spirits.[32]

An even more scathing indictment of Oberammergau was issued in 1922 by the celebrated critic Deems Taylor. Had Taylor, instead of Devrient, been the first outsider to write about Oberammergau, the town would have remained in permanent obscurity. At his most generous, Taylor judged the Passion "a bore" because of "the careful, traditional acting, the conventional scenery, the bad music, and above all, the deadly interludes." Some of these problems he felt could be attributed to the lack of imagination of "this Bavarian peasantry" which failed to comprehend the beautiful and spiritual possibilities of a Passion. The principal villain in the production, to Taylor, was Pater Daisenberger whose script offered "a frank and naive scoundrelism such as exists only in the movies." Taylor accused Daisenberger of "spoiling" the wise and dispassionate story of the gospel by conceiving the Pharisees as "simple villains." Additionally, Taylor took exception to (a) the entry into Jerusalem, which was "spoiled by the dreadful Moody and Sankoy hymn with which the rejoicing populace welcomes the Saviour"; (b) the Last Supper, which "drags on interminably by reason of a silent foot-washing ceremony that devotes a good minute and a half to every one of the twelve apostles"; (c) the Crucifixion, which was "fifteen minutes too long" and "lacks dignity and concentration"; (d) the tableaux, which "look exactly like the lithographed cards of Bible stories that one used to get at Sunday School, except that the cards were better lighted"; and (e) the actors who lacked "magnetism" and seemed "overwhelmed by the theological significance of their roles." In short, "The production is too elaborate to be excused for its crudities and too unimaginative to be impressive."[33]

Such rebukes cannot be written off to foreign insensitivity. German critics fifty years ago exceeded Priestley, Darlington, or Taylor in their condemnations. The Catholic journals *Kreuz Zeitung* (Berlin) and *Leipziger Neueste Nachrichten* scored the Oberammergau Passion as "a disedifying travesty," "an unconscious parody." The critic for *Germania* found fault with the staging, particularly of the Crucifixion, which was cleverly, if unconvincingly portrayed. He disliked the singsong recitation of the "wretched doggerel lyric." The script either lacked power as pathos or was too sickly sweet. That such "irreverences" were permitted at all, said Germany's largest Catholic journal, could be attributed to their appeal to "theatrically childish Americans."[34]

The passage of time has not muted such criticism. In 1950, the Evangelical publicist Hugo Schnell said, "The play is for our time too long, not tight in individual scenes, too uneven in speech."[35] In 1960, an unnamed critic for *Time* found the scenario "often less lively than the begat-begat-begat chapters of Genesis."[36] That same year, Tom Driver, now Paul Tillich Professor of Religion at the Union Theological Seminary, offered a blistering critique on the order of Deems Taylor. For Driver, then drama critic of Niebuhr's *Christian Century*, it was essential that the Passion be tested by the normal criteria for works of theater art. Did it have vitality? Was it faithful to some respectable idea of reality? Were the artists in control of their medium? Did it exhibit good taste? His conclusion: "On any or all of these counts the Passion Play at Oberammergau falls down miserably."[37]

According to Driver, the play was "lugubrious, plodding." The seven-hour script was devoid of humor or irony. The acting was amateurish: Christ, for example, was "wooden"; the participants in crowd scenes, "from the worst Hollywood tradition." Dedler's music was described as "inferior Mozart," the chorus "unbelievably stilted." The tableaux, which were "linked by dubious typology" to incidents in the Passion, were "atrocious beyond my power to describe."[38]

Length has always been a built-in defect of Daisenberger's work. When Theodore Freedman of the Anti-Defamation League returned from Oberammergau in May 1980, his first comments related to pacing and to the same

choir that Priestley cursed fifty years earlier. Recent editing
cut the performance time to five hours, but still Freedman
complained: "To me, it moved slowly. It did not have the
drama Americans are accustomed to. The choral group
comes on stage. There is an individual who is the narrator
and one or more voices singing. They step back and form a
semicircle. The curtain opens and there is a tableau. Then
the chorus moves back to where they were. Finally, they
march off the stage. If you do that many times, it becomes
longer. There were many more freezes and scenes kept intact than were really warranted."[39]

I personally was not troubled by the length of perfor-
mance. Perhaps it is that traditional Sabbath services or Yom
Kippur rites have fortified my *zitzfleysh* (staying power).
Certainly the five hours I spent watching this melange of
summer theater and Gloria was no more difficult on my person than sitting through every episode of a 1940 movie
serial at an art theater one evening in Cleveland in 1965.
The chorus and living tableaux were quite another thing.
Tom Driver likened the former to "resigned workhorses."
"Never once in seven-and-a-half hours did any one of the 49
smile; they obviously enjoyed it as little as I did."[40] My
own comments, jotted down in a notebook, read: "I'd hate
to meet male or female in a dark alley. They are a gloomy,
stocky, sour, dour, *zaftig*, dumpy, frumpy, glowering
group."

That the chorus is so serious is understandable, considering the nature of the Passion. There is no excuse for some of
the living pictures. Already in 1970, Dr. Hans Mallau of
Mexico noted many fallacies which should have led to the
dropping of more than just those freezes dealing with the
brazen serpent, Daniel and Darius, the bloodied cloak of
Joseph, and the rejection of Vashti. Mallau declared, "The
living pictures contribute little to the illumination of the
passion events and frequently are misleading." The connection between Tobit's leave-taking and the parting of
Jesus and Mary at Bethany was "confusing," since the mother's fear in the Book of Tobit proved to be unfounded. The
scene of the lamenting bride, "a somewhat shallow du-

plicate" of the previous tableau, was, to Mallau, sacrilegious, considering the "sensual, lustful" nature of the Song of Songs. The tableau where manna is provided in the wilderness implied that salvation was guaranteed, regardless of one's behavior. Cain's story should not be superimposed over that of Judas, for God punished the former, while Judas took his own life. The picture showing the sacrifice of the scapegoats as a parallel for the choice between Jesus and Barabbas was "absurd nonsense" for a number of reasons, not the least of which was that on the Day of Atonement neither ram was set free. Mallau found the elevation of Joseph "fully hazy," the scene with Naboth "a cheap pretext," that of Job "not particularly suited to the commentary," the sacrifice of Isaac "superfluous." As for Joab's assassination of Amasa, "Outside the kiss, the betrayal of Judas and the murder of Amasa have not much in common." According to Mallau, Joab used the kiss to get near his hated rival, so he could make short shrift of him. Judas used the kiss to identify Jesus, who was then given a formal hearing. Concluded Mallau, "Probably even a Neanderthal could conclude both kisses hardly have a common form."[41]

While the artistic merits of the *Lebende Bilder* may be debated,[42] some of the other faults of the play are incontestable. The casting frequently has proven incongruous. In 1980, the number of performances required the use of two persons for most of the leads. At times, eighteen-year-old blond Martha Wiedemann played Mary to forty-seven-year-old brunette Gregor Breitsamter's Jesus. Breitsamter's alter ego was twenty-year-old Rudi Zwink, the mayor's son, who looked every bit the dental student he was. Zwink seemed uncomfortable directing his *Jünger* (apostles). His uninspiring performance, more suited to a production about the "laid-back" generation of the 1960s, seemed unlikely to prompt white-haired Hermann Haser as Peter to proclaim, "Lord and Master, wherever you stay, there I stay too. Where you go, I will go too."[43] Perhaps because of Zwink's lack of dramatic flair, the rest of the principal characters, including Anton Preisinger as Pilate, Peter Stückl as Caiaphas, and Melchior Breitsamter as Annas, compensated by overacting.

If the principals were weak, little better could be expected from the rest of the cast. When temple guards dispatched to arrest Jesus first encounter the Nazarene, they suddenly and awkwardly sprawl out on the stage. Their Roman counterparts are no more graceful. Assigned to guard the tomb of Christ at the end of the play, they too fall down in a wink. The guards' performances, like the special effects— flashes and drum rolls which purportedly represent lightning and earthquakes, the offstage thuds which accompany the clubbing of the legs of the criminals crucified alongside Jesus—can only be termed overdone.

Other aspects of the Passion are just ludicrous. Whenever the action or a tableau requires a scene representing the palace of a Jewish king or the Sanhedrin, a gigantic menorah is trundled onstage for immediate identification. Over the throne of the high priests or monarch is set a table of laws, easily recognized as the decalogue of Moses. The Ten Commandments are inscribed, however, not in Hebrew, but in Roman numerals, from I to X. The aversion to Hebrew is readily understandable. On those few occasions when a Hebrew word is attempted (as when Jesus expires on the cross or when Mary Magdalene comes before the opened tomb), the pronunciation comes out a garbled "El-oyay! El-oyay!" or "Rabooni!"

The *Schweinebraten* and *Semmelknödel* of Oberammergau are reputed to be among the best in Bavaria. But skill in the kitchen does not necessarily translate to skill on the stage. The Passion-play acting is, at best, mediocre. In like manner, while the people of Oberammergau may be noted for their merriment and fondness for folk songs, they do not constitute the germ of another Mormon Tabernacle Choir. Dedler's music is better than some have warranted. The Oberammergau chorus is not. Alois Daisenberger may have been one of those rare souls, pure of heart and rich in intellect as Hermine Diemer suggests, but he was no master of dialogue or setting. His script generates little tension, for it is almost as if Jesus lingers about, waiting for someone, any-one, to do him in.

Despite its shortcomings, Oberammergau still has its de-fenders who maintain the Passion must be evaluated in terms of "contemporary aesthetics." Citing a "blatantly ra-cist song" from upstate New York, one correspondent has written, "The issues aren't as clear-cut as we might prefer." Another compares the Oberammergau phenomenon to a re-vival of Stephen Foster melodies or a minstrel show. A third concludes that Oberammergau was "no worse than the usual anti-Semitism of the Middle Ages."[44]

It is, frankly, astonishing to encounter scholars who ratio-nalize the use of stereotypes and race hatred under the guise of "aesthetics," a term which "pertains to a sense of the beautiful" or "emotion or sensation as opposed to pure in-tellectuality."[45] The folk song mentioned above ("Take the Night Train to Selma") was written by Dorrance Weir, an obscure figure from Oaksville, New York.[46] Limited in notoriety, it can in no way be compared with a serious reli-gious spectacle which attracts 500,000 persons in a summer. Although Henry Glassie of Indiana University suggests Weir seeks only to evoke laughter and brotherhood, it is difficult to be sympathetic to a ditty which redounds with references to "Wops," "Niggers," "Dagos," and "Guineas."[47] As for Stephen Foster, none of his lyrics urge lynchings. No decent person stages blackfaced minstrel shows today. There are no "aesthetic" re-creations of the *autos-da-fe* or Goebbels's anti-Jewish films.

Even conceding the point that cultural and historical tastes may change,[48] the Oberammergau Passion fails practi-cally every test of the true aesthetic experience. According to Mikel Dufrenne, an aesthetic object is one which "pro-vides answers to every question," "discourages every idea of erasure or correction, and in which nothing rings false."[49] Oberammergau's Passion has repeatedly been criticized by Christians as well as Jews. It has been revised periodi-cally. It still contains serious theological and historical flaws. To every question asked of the aesthetic experience by Swarthmore's Monroe Beardsley—does it relieve tensions and quiet destructive impulses; does it resolve conflicts in the self and create inner harmony; does it refine perception and discrimination; does it develop imagination and the ability of putting oneself in the place of others; is it conducive to mental health; does it foster mutual sympathy and understanding; does it offer an ideal for human life[50]—we must answer no.

The Daisenberger Passion falls into that catalogue of bad taste which, Gillo Dorfles claims, leaves "permanent aesthetic scars."[51] Affected, trite, redundant, and repetitious; replete with nonsensical metaphors, exaggerations, and distortions; hypersentimental and laced with "precious poses," Oberammergau's Passion is not something that must be probed for hidden meaning. It is devoid of tenderness, irony, tragedy, grace, delicacy, wit, or humor.[52] Crude and obvious, the Passion stands marked as aesthetic vulgarity—kitsch. Aesthetically, as art, then, the Oberammergau Passion play fails. As propaganda it is quite another thing.

4

Guidelines Rejected:
A New Covenant

All Passion plays owe their inspiration to one or more of the Gospels, the selection of which determines the tone of a particular pageant. In Oberammergau, the books of Matthew and John served as the basis for Daisenberger's text. Vernon Heaton maintains that only three lines in the 1970 Passion could not be attributed to the Bible.[1] Other scholars concur that the play "is an authentic interpretation of the Holy Writ."[2] Pater Gregor Rümmelein of Ettal, who edited the 1980 presentation, feels the play currently "is sound and faithful to the Gospels." Former Bürgermeister Ernst Zwink put it more succinctly, telling me, "This is the Evangelium."[3]

In fact, neither the Gospels nor the Oberammergau Passion constitutes "jejune historical tracts."[4] According to Professor S. G. F. Brandon of the University of Manchester, early Christian documents are "suspect as *ex parte* accounts."[5] In like manner, much of what was written or takes place onstage at Oberammergau has been fabricated to suit the needs of the people. In 1970, Sister Louis Gabriel from the Jesuit faculty at Frankfurt conceded that the Gospels, written forty to sixty years after the death of Jesus, could not be interpreted literally. She faulted the villagers in Oberammergau for falling into this historical trap. Still worse, she warned that the Passion, as performed, was in conformity with neither the truth nor spirit of Christianity. A member of a special ecumenical group assembled for the purpose of scrutinizing the Passion, Sister Louis condemned the villagers for a number of inventions "for which there isn't a shred of evidence in the Gospels."[6] Specifically, she denounced the effort to paint the Good News as a conflict between the church and synagogue, between "goodies and baddies," with priests represented as "irresponsible men guided by blind hate and jealousy" and "blood-thirsty Pharisees" frequently clamoring after the death of Jesus. The German nun worried that thousands of uncritical or naïve persons who went to Oberammergau would get "a distorted and often false version of what the Gospel intended."[7] Such was precisely the concern of the ecumenical council, consisting of Protestant, Catholic, and Jewish clergy from the Arbeitsgemeinschaft Ökumenischer Kreise in Deutschland and the Deutschen Koordinierungsrat der Gesellschaften für Christlich-Jüdische Zusammenarbeit, which, noting the play's "historical and theological distortion," "retention of medieval cliches," and "false appositions," called for a major revision.[8]

The same sentiments were expressed in a series of position papers prepared by the Secretariat for Catholic-Jewish Relations of the National Conference of Catholic Bishops in America between 1968 and 1970. As summarized for the Anti-Defamation League by Dr. Leonard Swidler, professor of Catholic thought and interreligious dialogue at Temple University, in 1980, these guidelines urged that the Passion at Oberammergau:

1. Avoid creating the impression that most Jews of Jesus' day willed his death.

2. Avoid depicting Pilate "whom history and the Gospels have shown to have been a ruthless tyrant, a coward and a perverter of justice" as an innocent and kindly bystander.

3. Not speak of the "Old" Testament or covenant.

4. Not give exclusively to enemies of Jesus recognizably Hebrew Bible names.

5. Not give the impression that most of Jesus' opponents were Pharisees, nor should there be any "rabbis" among his opponents.

6. Not conceal the fact that Jesus is a Jew (that is, Jesus and his followers should look and act like the Jews they were, and his opponents should not be cast as ugly stereotypes of Jews).

7. Not depict Jesus as opposed to the Mosaic law (Torah).

8. "In summary: Passion plays should not portray the events leading to the death of Jesus as a struggle among Jews. It should make Gentile Christians grateful that they have been led to the one true God and to God's teaching through the Jew, Jesus."[9]

Lamentably, few of these suggestions have been implemented, to date, at Oberammergau. The 1980 production gave no hint of the aspirations of the Jewish people in that ancient period. Jews had been seething under the rule of rapacious Roman governors and puppet kings for almost a century. Many, victimized by taxes like the *stipendium* (quartering tax), *portoria* (customs duty), or *decuma* (a form of personal or property tax), had abandoned their lands. For others, economic survival was challenged by Greeks, Samaritans, and Romanizing Jews. The very fabric of Judaism was being compromised, much as it had been in the age of Antiochus Epiphanes. The Maccabees had miraculously rescued Jews and Judaism in 165 B.C. Their triumph, translated into a national holiday, Hanukkah, combined with the tradition of providential deliverance, fixated the Jewish people throughout the period of Roman domination. Jesus of Nazareth was one of a host of messianic pretenders, including Judah the Galilean, Simon Bar Giora, Simon Bar Kochba, the less violent Teacher of Righteousness, Theudas, and an unnamed Egyptian Jew, who appeared in Judaea between 63 B.C. and 135 A.D. "The play should have conveyed something of the helplessness of the people under these conditions," wrote Judith Banki, "the climate of desperation mixed with fervent hope, the political hazards amid which the Jewish authorities had to maneuver."[10] There frankly is no effort to place Jesus within such a historical framework.

Nor for that matter, is there any effort to show Jesus as a Jew. Rarely is he referred to as Jesus, never as Yeshua or rabbi. For several years, Professors Swidler and Gerard Sloyan have urged the community of Oberammergau to address Jesus as a Jew. "By underscoring the Jewishness of the 'founder' of Christianity and all the first 'Christians,' " they declared, "a giant step toward the elimination of Christian anti-Semitism will have been taken."[11] For their part, the villagers protest that *everyone* knows that Christ (as they consistently refer to him) was a Jew, that if Americans don't understand this, it is an American problem.[12]

Preliminary findings of a five-year study conducted by the Anti-Defamation League in 1966 did reveal that large numbers of Americans, indeed a majority of Southern Baptists, considered Moses, David, and Solomon Christians! Given the option of labeling Peter, Paul, and the other apostles Christians or Jews, two-thirds of the Protestants polled, three-fifths of the Catholics, referred to the New Testament figures as Christians.[13] That such opinions are not confined to America was noted by Annemarie Weiss when she visited Oberammergau in 1970 and found residents who were adamant in affirming, "No, Jesus was no Jew."[14]

Such statements are, of course, vestiges of a recent time when many Germans subscribed to the view of Richard Wagner, Houston Stewart Chamberlain, Adolf Hitler, and other Teutomaniacs that Jesus was actually the offspring of a German soldier in the Roman ranks.[15] While that spurious tale of genealogy has been laid to rest by rational people, every effort is made to distinguish Jesus and his apostles from the rest of the Jews onstage at Oberammergau. The followers of Christ, including the disciples, the Marys, Simon of Bethany, Nicodemus, and Joseph of Arimathaea, traditionally have worn simple, single-hued garments. They appear well groomed, fair in complexion, even Nordic. Their speech is clear, almost lyrical; their movements are generally graceful. By way of contrast, Jesus' enemies per-

sonify evil. They include Barabbas, a thoroughly dirty ruf-
fian, whose selection by the mob underscores its perfidy;
Judas, who slinks across stage in a re-creation of Lionel
Bart's Fagin; the ubiquitous temple merchants, easily de-
noted by their multicolored *keffiyahs* and cloaks; and the
priests, resplendent in bejeweled mantles and horned
headdresses.

The priests' costumes are especially striking. The tunics,
ephods, and pectorals with their precious stones conform
fairly well to descriptions in Exodus 28:13–30. The Oberammergau production, however, erroneously suggests that
the priests go about, day and night, draped in formal raiment.
Flavius Josephus, on the other hand, mentions that the stole
and other vestments of office were normally kept in a stone
chamber of the Antonia, under triple seal, in the custody of
the procurator (Ant. 15:403 and 18:90). Such garments were
taken out only during formal rites such as the high holy days
or accession to office of a new Roman subgovernor.[16]

A more serious problem exists with the priests' head-
pieces. Till the present century, these consisted of bound
turbans, in the midst of which were inserted feathers or
cones. Such designs conformed with biblical instructions for
a *mitznefet* (mitre), the Hebrew root for which means "to
wind around." Appended to the *mitznefet* was a tiny piece
of gold, possibly in the form of a flower (as in ancient
Sumeria), called a *tzitz hazahav*. A symbol of life and salvation, the gilded flower was inscribed "consecrated to Yah-
weh." The entire headpiece was known as the *nezer
hakodesh* (holy crown).[17] Today, the only persons onstage
who wear bands of gold, symbols of honor, about their
foreheads are the Roman magistrates. Since 1900, the high
priests have worn headgear that billow out in the form of
horns. There is more of Wagner than Leviticus in these
crowns. No one knows how the concept originated, though
Oberammergauers freely offer that it is a "tradition." They
find no stigma in the concept, for Michelangelo's famed
statue of Moses, on display in Rome's Saint Peter's in Chains
Cathedral, shows the patriarch with horns. Moses is also
seen in two tableaux of the Passion play with the horns, a

product of a mistranslation of the Hebrew word *qaran* (rays).

Jews are quite sensitive about such images. High priests cavorting about the stage in horned headdress brings back memories of a time when the wearing of the *pileum cornutum* (horned hat) by the Jewish pariah was mandatory, because Christian masses believed Jews to be creatures of the devil. The medieval period was a time when people spoke of the *Judenblick* (evil eye), *Judenpech* (the fuel of hellfire, which was, in reality, bitumen), the *Jüdel* (a demon which inhabited Gentile ovens), and the *Judensau* (an evil hybrid pig-female that represented Judaism). In churches from Magdeburg to Saint Mark's, the Jew was portrayed as a gnarled, decrepit being with sharply pointed features and the goatee of Satan's familiar. Though "weak-kneed" and "woebegone," this insidious creature perpetually lacerated the body of Christ by his *Judenspiess* (Jewish spear) of usury.[18] Wrote Rosemary Ruether, "The image of the Jew deteriorated in the minds of Christians to that of a deformed monster, with horns, tail, cloven hoofs and sulphuric odor to betray his fundamentally diabolic character." It was, she added, "the basic image of the Jew up to its use by Nazism."[19] Noting how such caricatures led to periodic massacre, spokesmen for the Anti-Defamation League and American Jewish Committee have repeatedly requested that Oberammergau cease its use of horned headdresses, which are suggestive of the medieval devil canard. To date, their efforts have proved unsuccessful.[20]

The conspiratorial, wheedling image of the Jew continues to flourish onstage at Oberammergau. Until recently, the play included a figure referred to simply as "Rabbi" (now defined as Rabbi Archelaus). A particularly sinister person who champions the lynching of Jesus,[21] the rabbi in his black gown and hat doubtless represented a contemporary stereotype of all European rabbis for the people of Oberammergau. A number of other priests on the Sanhedrin are given Old Testament names like Ezekiel, Zadok, Joshua, Samuel, and Nathan, as if to underscore the division between Jew and Christian.[22] They try to outgesture and outshout one another, when they are not leering or sneering their plots at the audience. The priests manipulate the mob, press Roman authorities for the execution of what obviously is an innocent, and mock Jesus at the cross.

The worst malefactor is the aged high priest Annas, who is portrayed sharing authority with his son-in-law Joseph Caiaphas. According to Paul Winter, the determination of these priests as the principal villains in the Gospels was purely arbitrary, for "no tradition of any sort existed that preserved the name of the Jewish high priest in Jesus' time. The Third and First Evangelists, independent of each other, found it necessary to supply that name from outside information, and the information on which, respectively, they based their statements, differed."[23] Retrospectively, the gospel writers also offered the impossible tale of two high priests concurrently sharing power. Relying upon such misinformation, Daisenberger's original text contained a lengthy scene showing Annas wringing his hands as he awaited news of Jesus' arrest. No fewer than thirty-four lines were given to express Annas's anxiety and contempt. "I can find no rest tonight until I hear that this disturber of the peace is in our hands," said the doyen of high priests. "Oh, how I wish the enemy of the Synagogue were in fetters." Then, continuing to skulk about the stage, Annas offered, "Oh, I cannot think of anything save: Death to this criminal! This corrupter of Israel!"[24] None of this appears in the Gospels. Yet even today, in an abbreviated scene, Annas's delight knows no bound when runners inform him that Jesus has been apprehended. It is all invention. It is a performance worthy of nineteenth-century melodrama, and would be laughable if it were not so pathetic.

The estrangement between Christ and the Jews is reinforced in an unhistorical manner throughout the Passion. The crucial Passover, *Passatag* in German, is referred to as *Osterfast* in the Oberammergau text. It may be a little thing, for such a term may make it easier for Christians to identify events within Holy Week, but the references to *Osterfast*, itself originally a pagan rite of spring, is inaccurate. Jesus

came to Jerusalem to celebrate one of three pilgrimage festivals within Judaism, yet there is nothing in the Last Supper
scene to suggest that it is a *seder*. Though the participants
were supposedly all observant Jews, none wear skullcaps or
head coverings. They recite no standard blessings over the
wine and bread, no verses from Exodus which form the basis
of the Passover *Haggadah*. Even the thick, rich twist of
bread which Jesus shares with his apostles during the service is wrong. Passover bread must be flat, because it derives
from the unleavened *matzos* which the tribes of Israel carried out of Egypt. Dr. Hans Lamm, *Rosh Kehillah* (head) of
the Munich Jewish community, minimized such shortcomings when I spoke with him, asking, "Do you mean they
should have a *matzah* instead of bread? So then the
Catholics or cantonians can say what a funny bread they have
in Jerusalem. Oberammergau cannot be an introduction to
Jewish customs or Jewish History."[25] Perhaps not, but the
"canton" might be more faithful to its own Christian sacraments. As the German theologian Bo Reicke has pointed out,
the bread must be "ungesauerten" because it constitutes the
basis of the wafer of the Eucharist.[26]

Other Christian theologians, like James Parkes, Paul Tillich, Niebuhr, Gregory Baum of the University of Toronto,
and Douglas Hare, dean of the Pittsburgh Theological
Seminary, have insisted that for any telling of the Passion to
have validity, it must not only show Jesus and his followers
as Jews but must demonstrate a continuity, rather than a
break, between Judaism and Christianity.[27] Professor Swidler of Temple detects that continuity in the Beatitudes of
Matthew, where Jesus proclaims:

> Do not think that I have come to destroy the Law or
> the Prophets. I have come not to destroy, but to fulfill.
> For amen I say to you, till heaven and earth pass away
> not one jot or one tittle shall be lost from the Law till all
> things have been accomplished.
>
> Therefore whoever does away with one of these least
> commandments, and so teaches men, shall be called

least in the kingdom of heaven; but whoever carries them out and teaches them, he shall be called great in the kingdom of heaven. [Matt. 5:17–19]

For others, like Rosemary Ruether, Alan Davies, and Douglas Hare, a better, more historical, less anti-Judaic source of that Judaeo-Christian continuity is the Book of Luke.[28] According to the late Samuel Sandmel of Hebrew Union College, Christians in the Book of Luke are portrayed as "undeviatingly faithful" to Judaism. Sandmel offers several examples: Zechariah and Elizabeth, parents of John the Baptist, "who walked in all the commandments and ordinances of the Lord blameless"; Joseph and Mary, who took Jesus to be circumcised at the end of eight days, "in accordance with the law," who offered up sacrifice "according to what is said in the law of the Lord," and who returned to Galilee after having performed everything "according to the law." Jesus' appearance in the Temple, where he astounded the rabbis, also occurred when the family went to Jerusalem "according to the custom of the feast."[29]

As for Jesus himself, eighty years ago Rabbi Joseph Krauskopf of Philadelphia declared, "There was nothing that Jesus ever preached or taught that had not the heartiest endorsement of the Rabbis of Israel."[30] The historian Heinrich Graetz, who was otherwise not notably kind to Jesus in his monumental *History of the Jews,* agreed in principle, writing:

Jesus made no attack upon Judaism itself, he had no idea of becoming a reformer of Jewish doctrine or the propounder of a new law; he sought merely to redeem the sinner, to call him to a good and holy life, to teach him that he is a child of God, and to prepare him for the approaching Messianic time. He insisted upon the unity of God, and was far from attempting to change in the slightest degree the Jewish conception of the Deity. To the question once put to him by an expounder of the Law, "What is the essence of Judaism?" he replied, " 'Hear, O Israel, our God is one,' and 'Thou shalt love thy neighbor as thyself.' These are the chief commandments" (Mark xii 28). His disciples, who had remained true to Judaism, promulgated the declaration of their Master—"I am not come to destroy, but to fulfil; till heaven and earth pass, one jot or one tittle shall in nowise pass from the Law till all be fulfilled (Matthew v. 17). He must have kept the Sabbath holy, for those of his followers who were attached to Judaism strictly observed the Sabbath, which they would not have done had their master disregarded it. It was only the Shammaitic strictness in the observance of the Sabbath, which forbade even the healing of the sick on that day, that Jesus protested against, declaring that it was lawful to do good on the Sabbath. Jesus made no objection to the existing custom of sacrifice, he merely demanded—and in this the Pharisees agreed with him— that reconciliation with one's fellow-man should precede any act of religious atonement. Even fasting found no opponent in him, so far as it was practised without ostentation or hypocrisy. He wore on his garments the fringes ordered by the Law, and he belonged so thoroughly to Judaism that he shared the narrow views held by the Judaeans at that period, and thoroughly despised the heathen world. He was animated by that feeling when he said, "Give not that which is holy unto the dogs, neither cast ye your pearls before swine, lest they trample them under their feet and turn again and rend you."[31]

One need not consult only Jews for a sense of Jesus fitting into the historical and theological community of Judaism. The Christian scholar Paul Winter concluded that the ethics of Jesus were identical with those of *Pirke Avot*, the Pharisaic tradition. "In the whole of the New Testament," wrote Winter, "we are unable to find a single, historically reliable instance of religious differences between Jesus and members of the Pharisaic guild, let alone evidence of a mortal conflict." He added: "Jesus was a Jew. He lived among Jews, he learned from Jews, he taught Jews. The successes he enjoyed and the adversities he suffered throughout his life were shared with other Jews. Those of whom he approved and those of whom he disapproved were likewise Jews. It is only natural, therefore, that the persons with whom, on occasion, he disagreed were also Jews."[32]

In the past quarter century, the Catholic church also has stressed the spiritual links between Judaism and Christianity. In its fourth and final version of its "Declaration on the Relation of the Church to Non-Christian Religions," issued in October 1965, the Second Vatican Council declared:

> The Church, therefore, cannot forget that she received the revelation of the Old Testament through the people with whom God in his ineffable mercy concluded the Ancient Covenant. Nor can she forget that she feeds upon the root of that cultivated olive tree into which the wild shoots of the Gentiles have been grafted (cf. Rom. 11:17–24). Indeed, the Church believes that by His cross Christ Our Peace reconciled Jews and Gentiles, making both one in Himself (cf. Eph. 2:14–16).
>
> The Church keeps ever in mind the words of the Apostle about his kinsmen: "theirs is the sonship and the glory and the covenants and the legislation and the worship and the promises; theirs are the fathers and from them is the Christ according to the flesh" (Rom. 9:4–5), the Son of the Virgin Mary. She also recalls that the Apostles, the Church's mainstay and pillars, as well as most of the early disciples who proclaimed Christ's Gospel to the world, sprang from the Jewish people.[33]

That declaration was followed by similar statements issued by the American Bishops' Committee for Ecumenical and Interreligious Affairs (June 1970) and the French Bishops' Committee for Relations with Jews (April 1973). Though the original Vatican document alluded to "people of the New Covenant" and "the new people of God,"[34] *Nostra Aetate 4* implied the existence of several, interrelated covenants. Along these lines, a special Vatican study paper in

1969 noted that Jesus "represented himself as continuing and fulfilling the anterior Revelation, the basic teachings of which he offered anew, using the same teaching method as the rabbis of his time." The points on which he took issue with the Judaism of the first century were "fewer than those in which he found himself in agreement with it." Whenever he opposed the established religion, it was "always from within the Jewish people, just as did the prophets before him."[35]

Such a position is decidedly at odds with the traditional text employed at Oberammergau. The breach between Christianity and Judaism, the operation of only one *Heilsgeschichte*, was apparent to all who viewed the living picture of the Persian Queen Vashti. Before it was excised from the 1980 text, this scene was introduced by the Prologue who reproached "poor Jerusalem" for her blindness and deafness. Just as Queen Vashti was rejected by Ahashuerus, "Thus too will the synagogue be thrust away. From her will the Kingdom of God be taken and entrusted to another people who shall bring forth the fruits of righteousness." Then, in the form of redundant overkill so typical of the Daisenberger text, the chorus joyfully proclaimed that "the time of grace" for the synagogue has passed away, much as Ahashuerus cast out the proud Vashti. God, they sang, rejected the proud nation of sinners and declared, "Better people I will choose."[36]

The model for this tableau may have been ancient Roman coins which showed a woman weeping as *Judaea devicta.* More likely, the scene derives from portraits of Old Testament characters in medieval biblical illuminations. Invariably, these craven, unattractive figures would be styled after contemporary Jews and would be contrasted with the dignified, almost ethereal characters of the New Testament. Such images, wrote Joseph Reider, were used "as pegs on which to suspend the poisonous darts of spiteful wit and malicious satire."[37] One of the most popular motifs juxtaposed two females, one gloriously attired, the second downcast, in mourning garb and blinded with a veil. The former, crowned by Jesus who held a chalice and cross, represented the church; the latter, like Vashti, the synagogue.[38] What Professor Swidler terms this "crass rejectionist theology"[39] was preached by Saint John Chrysostom, Hrabanus Maurus, Augustine, Ambrose, Aurelius Clemens, Prudentius, and Venatius Fortunatus.[40] It was successfully translated to the portals of windows of town halls, the cathedral at Bourges, and, despite objections from at least one Protestant minister one hundred years ago, the stage at Oberammergau.

While the Vashti tableau is now gone, the Oberammergau Passion continues to emphasize the rupture between Judaism and Christianity. Act 4, which deals with the Last Supper, begins with a tenor solo where God declares, "Ich stifte euch ein neues Mahl" (I establish for you a new feast). As the accompanying twin tableaux unfold, showing the Children of Israel receiving manna and grapes in the wilderness, the entire chorus proclaims a *Neuer Bund* (new covenant) no fewer than *four* times: "Das Wunder in der Wüste Sin, weist auf das Mahl des *Neuen Bundes* hin" (the miracle in the Sinai desert points to the feast of the new covenant): "Des *Neuen Bundes* heilig Brot, bewahrt die Seele von dem Tod bei würdigem Genusse" (when worthily enjoyed, the holy bread of the new covenant preserves the soul from death); "des *Neuen Bundes* heil'ger Wein, wird selbst das Blut des Sohnes sein" (the holy wine of the new covenant will be His Son's own blood); and "Im *Neuen Bunde* reichet er sein Fleisch and Blut im Saale" (in the new covenant he gives his flesh and blood in the upper room).[41] Christ informs his disciples of the "beginning of a *new covenant*." He tells them to drink from "the cup of the *new covenant*." To which, Peter loudly responds, "This holy feast of the *new covenant* shall always be celebrated by us in this way." During the presentation of the scapegoat tableau, which presages the condemnation of Christ, a contralto sings, "This is the sacrifice of the *old covenant*." Later, she joins a bass in chanting, "In the *new covenant* the Lord no longer requires the blood of goats." The concept of a new covenant is implicit also throughout the scene of Christ's apotheosis.[42]

Pater Rümmelein of Ettal, who was responsible for emending the Vashti freeze, is reluctant to delete references to a new covenant. "We Christians insist we live in the *Neuer Bund* according to the Gospels," he told me. "We cannot abandon this idea."[43] Rosemary Ruether has a different opinion. "As long as the Christian Church regards itself as the successor of Israel, as the new people of God substituted in the place of the old," writes Ruether, "and as long as the Church proclaims Jesus as the one mediator without whom there is no salvation, no theological space is left for other religions, and, in particular, no theological validity is left for Jewish religion."[44] Adds Gregory Baum, any monopolistic claim to divine truth by a dominant church group generates "grave injustices that eventually accumulate to become major crimes" like the Holocaust.[45]

For more than three hundred years, the villagers of Oberammergau have celebrated the Passion of a figure called Jesus or Christus, not Yeshua as he would have been known in ancient Judaea. Few have been troubled by the failure to portray Jesus or any of his followers within a Jewish context or to demonstrate a continuity between Christianity and Judaism. For renowned psychologist Stanley Milgram, however, this is the "most galling" aspect of the Passion—the opposition between Jesus and the Jews "without recognizing that Jesus was a Jew, a contribution of the Jewish people." Addressing the conflict between theology and stark, historical reality, Milgram asks, "Is a religion entitled to its own mythic?" then answers, "In principle yes, but not when such myths are injurious to other groups."[46] Msgr. Curt M. Genewein of the archbishop's office in Munich maintains that it takes time for theological reforms in the church to filter down to the masses.[47] But even allowing for culture lag and provincialism, the failure to show the spiritual connection between Jesus and his people in the Oberammergau Passion is inexcusable.

5

History Ignored:
The Sanhedrin and Pilate

The traditional Daisenberger script contains more serious flaws which cannot be written off to artistic inexperience or provincialism. As Rabbi Krauskopf stated eighty years ago, the Oberammergau Passion is "unhistoric in fact, false in interpretation, and cruel in inference."[1] The problem may stem not so much from invention as from a rigorous adherence to the outline of Holy Week provided in the Gospels. These New Testament imperfections troubled Henry Bamford Parkes who wrote: "The whole story of his [Jesus'] triumphal entry into Jerusalem, his last week of preaching and his arrest, trial and execution is unintelligible in its surviving form; it is filled with contradictions and impossibilities, and at the same time includes a number of details that sound like authentic memories but cannot be easily reconciled with the accepted versions of Jesus' mission."[2]

The very opening of the Oberammergau Passion presents a problem. Jesus rides a small burro onto the stage, as hundreds of the faithful, including small children wave palm fronds in his path. The scene supposedly fulfills the biblical prophecy (Isa. 62:11 and Zech. 9:9) that stipulates the manner by which the Messiah would enter Jerusalem. Isaiah, however, says nothing about the mode of transportation, and Zechariah, which was not part of the ancient Hebrew canon operative at the time Jesus lived, specifies that there be both an ass and a colt, suggesting perhaps that the Jewish savior should enter Jerusalem via a palanquin or sedan chair. There is, moreover, disagreement among the Gospels themselves. In Matthew (21:2–5), Jesus asks for two animals. In Mark (11:2) he requires a colt, in Luke (19:30) the colt of an ass, and in John (12:14) a young ass.

Such discrepancies may seem trivial, but problems raised in the scene which immediately follows are not. Professor Parkes was perplexed by the sudden reversal of support among the masses in Jerusalem. Five days after they hosannaed Jesus, they shrieked for his execution. The only overt act which might have alienated the masses (leaving aside, for one moment, the instigation of the priests) was Jesus' behavior toward the money changers (Matt. 21:12–15, Mark 15:17, Luke 45:47, and John 2:14–16). The story is told, with some varying details, that Jesus overturned the tables of money changers and those who sold doves for sacrifice, casting out all who were selling and buying in the Temple. Asks Israeli Supreme Court Justice Haim Cohn, who has written one of the most comprehensive studies of the trial of Jesus from the standpoint of Jewish *Halakhah* (law): Why wasn't Jesus arrested immediately? Why was he permitted to worship at the Temple? Why did the Sanhedrin suffer his criticisms for another five days?[3]

Apart from the Gospels, there is no historical evidence that such an incident took place. Wrote Heinrich Graetz, "An act that must have given rise to intense excitement would not have been omitted from other chronicles of that period."[4] Josephus, for example, discusses at some length, the tumult which accompanied Roman efforts to place imperial standards at the gates of Jerusalem and to expropriate funds from the Temple for use in constructing an aqueduct.[5] The only recorded instance of an altercation between merchants and a religious celebrity involved Simeon ben Gamaliel, president of the Sanhedrin, before the destruction of Jerusalem in 70 A.D. The priest's anger was sparked by the merchants' doubling the price of their pigeons.[6] Hugh Schonfield, author of the controversial *Passover Plot*, maintains the gospel story of Jesus and the money changers raises numerous questions over credibility.[7] Professor Brandon would agree, noting that "it takes little reflection . . . on the manifest improbabilities of such an account to realise that the actual event must have been very different."[8]

According to Brandon, only a naif would suppose that Jesus was protesting the conduct of the Jerusalem vendors. For one thing, money changers were essential to the operations of the Temple complex, particularly during religious festivals. Pilgrims came to Jerusalem from Mesopotamia, Egypt, Greece, and Rome. Much as Muslims making the Haj to Mecca or any foreigner traveling in Europe, these visitors needed to convert their money into local currency. The only convenient spot was the Temple compound, a rectangular esplanade covering more than thirty-five acres in the heart of Jerusalem. A small portion of this area was reserved for the hundred-foot-high sanctuary constructed by Herod. In what was otherwise a hilly town of congested alleys, the Temple, with its open courts, fountains and colonnades, served the same purpose as the ancient agora of Athens. People came here to talk, trade, and pray.

If money dealers were a necessity, so too were those who traded in small birds. For better or worse, ancient Judaism was a sacrificial cult, much like every other Semitic religion, and, for that matter, Christianity, which continues to revere the blood and body of Christ in its communion. Sacrifice in ancient Judaea could take various forms—the weekly offering of twelve shewbreads, symbolic of the Tribes of Israel, the burning of incense and spices, as in the days of Noah. The *Akedah* (binding of Isaac) represented a sophisticated break from pagan rites that commanded human sacrifice. Afterward, a red heifer could expiate the sins of an entire people; a goat, those of the high priest. At Passover, a lamb was to be offered as a burnt holocaust. Persons who could not afford sheep or goats were forced to sacrifice pigeons or doves.[9] These were purchased at stalls proximate to the sacrificial altars, much the same as crosses, candles, and rosaries are peddled in or near cathedrals today.

For Jesus to have physically attacked the money changers, who were fulfilling a needed function and were little more than conduits to the high priests, would have been a denial of the economic and social realities of his day. Such action would have contravened the prophetic teaching which declares: "Their holocausts and their victims shall please me upon my altars" (Isa. 56:7). It contradicts the concluding message of the Oberammergau play which proclaims "praise be to the lamb who was slain," "saviour of all sinners."[10] It is out of keeping with his otherwise peaceful nature. As Rabbi Krauskopf noted:

> It would certainly have been a strange proceeding for a leader, far-famed for his gentleness and forbearance, for a Prince of Peace, for an exultantly proclaimed "King and Deliverer of his People" to inaugurate his messianic reign with starting a riot among the people, with openly and fiercely attacking the priests and teachers of Israel, with laying violent hands on the bodies and properties of people peacefully pursuing their lawful trades—and all this in one of the courts of Temple grounds, at a time when pilgrims were streaming to the Sanctuary for the celebration of their festival of liberty, at a time when the Roman garrison in Fort Antonia, almost within earshot of his voice, was keenly on the alert for the slightest outbreak among the revolution-suspected people.[11]

If Jesus did attack the money changers, he was sparked not so much by the existence of sacrifice as by the corruption in a system which placed obstacles between man and god. Professor Brandon and T. S. Kepler both have pointed out that many scribes shared Jesus' concern about Temple graft which filled the pockets of the Sadducean families of Boethus and Annas.[12] The Talmud also contains a warning from rabbis to "you sons of Eli, who have dishonoured the

Temple of the Lord" (Pesahim, 57). The lesson intended by this action was not that Jews were inherently avaricious or usurious (canards which are still believed), yet that is what the Gospels seem to suggest. In their zeal to re-create the scene, the villagers at Oberammergau have gone beyond Jesus' denunciation of the "den of thieves." Till recently, Daisenberger's heavy-handed script had Christ rail against the "servants of Mammon." To which one of the merchants responded in true Shylockian fashion: "My money! Ah, my money!"[13] Though such lines have recently been dropped, the merchants still agitate the crowd with cries of fidelity to the laws of Moses. Then these pseudo-Arab curs slink offstage to press the Sanhedrin for the elimination of their enemy.

The portrayal of the Sanhedrin, both in the Gospels and at Oberammergau, and its implementation of the *Halakhah* (Jewish law) present even greater problems. This "council court" was a 71-man body, drawn from the leading religious and lay figures of the day. Called into being shortly after the Roman conquest of Judaea, it served simultaneously as the chief legislative body and high court of the Jews. At a local level, a *Bet Din* or court consisting of three rabbis and priests adjudicated cases of divorce, inheritance, adoption, and the like. Towns with more than 120 inhabitants had the right to appoint a small Sanhedrin of 23 judges to pass on criminal cases. Ultimately, cases on appeal, those involving a definition of *Halakhah,* blasphemy, false prophets, or idolatry were brought before the Great Sanhedrin, which met in the *Lishkath Hagazith* (Chamber of Hewn Stones), a precinct within the inner courts of Herod's Temple.[14]

The Gospels offer little description of the hall of the Great Sanhedrin or the makeup of the body which tried Jesus. We are told simply that "the chief priests and elders gathered together in the court of the high priest, who was called Caiphas and took counsel how they might seize Jesus by stealth and put him to death."[15] For staging, the Oberammergauers were left to their own, which is how they came up with a Latin decalogue and outsized menorah. In one instance, at least, the villagers were correct, for the members of their Sanhedrin sit in a semicircle, as outlined in the Mishnah, Sanhedrin 36b.

The members of the high court who appear onstage are shallow imitations of Caiaphas and Annas. Reading gospel denunciations of scribes and Pharisees who constituted the bulk of the Sanhedrin, it is difficult to imagine how it could be any other way. Jewish leadership, which produced the likes of Philo, Hillel, Gamaliel, Jochanan ben Zakkai, Joshua ben Hananiah, and Akiba ben Josef in the intertestamental period, conforms instead to the vicious diatribe in Matthew 23, where scribes and Pharisees are marked down as a brood of vipers and serpents, killers of prophets, whited sepulchers of hypocrisy, blind fools. With the help of money-grubbing merchants, the Sanhedrin arranges to bribe Judas. It despatches temple police, strangely attired in studded leather vests and peaked helmets and carrying halberds common to sixteenth-century Europe, to arrest Jesus in Gethsemane on the night of the first day of Passover. The Sanhedrin interrogates Jesus, physically abuses him, and condemns him to die for blasphemy on the same night. It presses a noble, detached Pilate for the death of the pretender, orchestrates the mob against Jesus, belittles his suffering during his crucifixion, and stands guard against his possible resurrection. All of this villainy, acted out onstage at Oberammergau, supposedly is faithful to the Gospels. With few exceptions, it is nonsense.

The New Testament presents a confusing picture of Jesus' arrest. The very existence of a Temple guard is questionable for the obvious reason that the Romans who had so much trouble with people in this imperial outpost would not invite additional mutiny by permitting the existence of such a force. The Gospels differ among themselves whether it was an armed multitude sent by priests or a cohort of Roman troops accompanied by some Greeks and scribes who made the arrest. The most logical suggestion is that of Professor Winter who argues that a *decurio* (a unit of ten Roman soldiers commanded by a captain) executed the arrest order. They were joined by Temple officers whose presence was necessary to pick Jesus out from among his apostles.[16]

The synoptic Gospels (Mark 14:12, Matt. 26:17–29, and Luke 22:7–20) also indicate that Jesus celebrated the feast of Passover, and with it the Holy Eucharist, before he was arrested. Once the Passover festival began (in Jewish law, holidays commence at sunset), he could not have been arrested. Not only would such action have contravened the very meaning of Passover, which symbolizes freedom in every generation, it would have violated the very Halakhah which the Sanhedrin was bound to uphold. The Torah specifically forbids occupation with worldly matters, including criminal cases, after sunset ushers in the Sabbath or a festival (cf. Exod. 12:16; Lev. 23:7; Num. 28:18). The Talmud also prohibits capital trials on the eve of a Sabbath or festival (Sanh. 4:32a).

How then could Jesus have been arrested on Passover? The answer, as supplied by Professor Joseph Klausner and others[17] is that he was not arrested on the eve of the Passover. We are left without any reason for a First Seder-Last Supper, but as Klausner says, "We thus escape the impossible supposition that the Sanhedrin examined Jesus during the night of a Festival or (according to Luke) on the first day of the Feast of Unleavened Bread."[18] Klausner's suggestion that only the Book of John, which speaks of Jesus' arrest the day before Passover (John 13:1), is correct is appealing, but it flies in the face of Christian tradition which places Jesus' arrest on the night between Holy Thursday and Good Friday. There is one talmudic *baraitha* (teaching) which seems to support Klausner's thesis, for it speaks of a certain Yeshu who was detained forty days before being hanged "on the eve of the Passover" (Sanh. 6:43a). But even Klausner rejects this reference as unhistorical and "lacking in accuracy."[19]

Let us agree, for the moment, with Klausner that Jesus was not arrested on Passover. It seems evident that he was arrested during the night. He was, with his apostles, stopped at "a country place called Gethsemane" (Matt. 26:36 and Mark 14:32), actually a wooded grove below the Temple Mount. There, he admonished Peter that the latter would deny him two or three times (Matt. 26:34 and Mark 14:30) "this very night" before the cock crowed. The guards who made the arrest carried with them "lanterns and torches" (John 18:3). Though Jesus had prayed in the Temple many times, the guards still required Judas to single him out by a kiss in the dark. All of this should indicate that Jesus was apprehended and brought before the Sanhedrin at night, another impossibility, for the Talmud commands that capital charges be tried by day (Sanh. 4:35a).

There are those who still debate whether it is legitimate to apply talmudic standards to the trial of Jesus. The Talmud, a thirty-five-volume compilation of religious and secular information, including historical, medical, agricultural data and allegories, was assembled by Jewish scholars over a period of seven hundred years (200 B.C. to 500 A.D.). Its core, the Mishnah, was codified by Judah ha-Nasi at Bet Shearim sometime near the end of the second century. One of its sixty-three tractates, Sanhedrin, deals specifically with the operation of law courts, and it is to this lengthy tract that most historians, including Professors Klausner, Sandmel, Cohn, William Wilson, and Brandon have turned in an effort to demonstrate the legal incongruities of the gospel story. Of the ancient Sanhedrin's commitment to talmudic procedure, Brandon writes, "Those leaders were curiously punctilious in observing the laws of evidence."[20]

Other scholars like Dropsie College's Solomon Zeitlin and Paul Winter contend it is invalid to apply talmudic rules which were agreed to long after the death of Jesus. Winter maintains that the talmudic ordinances were based on principles of rabbinic-Pharisaic exegesis formulated in the Diaspora. The class that dominated before the destruction of the Temple were the Sadducees, aristocrats who cleaved strictly, if torturously, to the letter of the Torah. Though ancient sources make reference to a formulation of Sadducean law, no such book of decrees exist and we are thus left without any guide to ancient legal procedure.[21]

The claim of Sadducean control of Jewish institutions may be accurate, but it is misleading. The Sadducees constituted only a fraction of Judaea's population. The Pharisees, whose name derives from the Hebrew for numbers, were by far more numerous and more representative of the outlook of the masses. Their teachings did become the core of Diaspora Judaism. It is Diaspora Judaism which has been punished for the "crime" of deicide. If Diaspora Judaism has been held accountable, it is only logical to insist that the accusers consult the Pharisaic code which has governed the Jews for the past eighteen hundred years.

In fact, the Mishnah was not the revolutionary departure from Sadducean traditions that some have argued. Of the Pharisaic sages who formed the basis of the Talmud, Robert Seltzer has written that the traditional rabbinic view holds they are "the direct continuation of the scribes mentioned in connection with Ezra in the mid-fifth century B.C.E., a professional class that preserved, interpreted and applied the oral traditions that supplemented the written biblical legislation."[22] Winter allows that Jewish law, no matter how differently interpreted, had its roots in common-law precedents. Louis Jacobs, who has commented that such differences between Hillel and Shammai threatened to divide Judaism into two *Torot,* also concedes that many of the basic rules of Halakhah and the early strata of the Mishnah may have been formulated long before the final codification of the Talmud.[23] Rabbi Arnost Zvi Ehrman of Ramat Gan actually detects a host of "ancient *halakhot* and even *mishnayot* from the time of the Second Temple" in the critical tractate Sanhedrin. These include restraints upon the activities of the king acting as judge (dating from the time of Alexander Jannaeus more than a century before the time of Jesus), restrictions of marriage in the priesthood, relations between Zealots (Kannaim) and Aramaean women, and the right of criminals to expect a portion of the world to come. Most significantly, Dr. Ehrman declares, "The whole order of the four capital cases certainly—by its very nature—dates from Temple times."[24]

If we were left with the strict Sadducean application of the Torah demanded by Zeitlin and Winter, we would still not be without guidelines in evaluating the trial of Jesus. Writes Father Roland De Vaux, "The process of a trial can be reconstructed by piecing together all allusions in other books of the Bible, and by making use of passages which represent

God's disputes with men as a formal trial, especially in Job and the second part of Isaias."[25] Even under the Sadducean rules, it is clear that justice was to be meted out in public (Deut. 21:19, Amos 5:10, 1 Kings 7:7). An action would be instituted by a private person (Deut. 25:7, Job 9:19) and the king or his judges would convene a hearing at the gates of the city or at a sanctuary (Exod. 21:6, 22:7; Judg. 4:5; Isa. 7:16, Jer. 26:10). During arguments, the judges were seated (Dan. 7:9–10; Isa. 16:5). The accusation was presented orally by the accuser, who stood to the right of the accused (Job 21:35–36; Isa. 65:6; Dan. 7:10). The accused was given the right to speak (Deut. 17:4; Job 13:22; Isa. 41:21). Witnesses were then called (1 Kings 21:10,13; Mic. 1:2; Prov. 14:25; Isa. 43:9,10,12; Jer. 26:17). Proofs of fact were introduced before the judges (Exod. 22:12; Amos 3:12; Deut. 22:13–17). False witnesses were condemned to the punishment that would have befallen the accused (Deut. 19:18–19; Dan. 13:62). For a death sentence, the law required at least two witnesses for the prosecution (Num. 35:30; Deut. 17:6; 1 Kings 21:10; Dan. 13:34). When everything was thoroughly examined, the court declared the defendant guilty or innocent (Exod. 22:8; Deut. 25:1; 1 Kings 8:32; Prov. 17:15). Sentence would be pronounced while the parties remained standing before the judge (Isa. 3:13; Ps. 76:10; Isa. 50:8; Deut. 19:17). In case of capital offenses, the witnesses must accept responsibility for throwing the first stone, if the defendant were condemned to death (Deut. 13:10; 17:7).[26]

Whichever legal system, Sadducean, Pharisaic, or Roman, is applied to the trial of Jesus, the morass of impossibilities offered by the Gospels, yet faithfully rendered onstage at Oberammergau, is overwhelming. Roman provincial law required that the arresting military officer deliver a prisoner over to a local magistrate who would prepare a charge sheet before presenting him to the procurator. The Book of John (18:12, 13) implies Jesus was turned over to a subordinate of the high priest to secure exactly such a charge sheet. Yet there is no further mention of this procedure in John or any of the other Gospels. Instead, the interrogation of Jesus takes place at the high priest's "house" (Luke 23:54) at a time when, by talmudic standards, the Sanhedrin could only sit legally in the Chamber of Hewn Stones (Sanh. 10:86b) or, applying the archaic rule of Torah, at a holy place ("the master of the house shall come near unto God," Exod. 22:7). In this case, at least, there should be no question of the antiquity of the talmudic rule, since after the Roman destruction of Jerusalem in 70 A.D., there was no more Temple, no more Sanhedrin.

If the meeting place of the group that judged Jesus is in doubt, so is its makeup. The Book of Mark alone tells us that "all the priests and the Scribes and the elders" assembled for this predawn convocation (Mark 14:53), but the Christian theologians Bo Reicke, S. G. F. Brandon, and Paul Winter dispute the likelihood of calling a full plenum for every occasion.[27] If even one member of the Sanhedrin were absent, the trial would be illegal, as the Talmud required the presence of all seventy-one for a case involving a false prophet (Sanh. 1:2a). Such unanimity is also implicit in those passages of Deuteronomy (17:7; 21:21) which deal with cases of false prophets.

Like the Torah, talmudic law specified procedures to be followed in capital cases. Heralds were to go through the streets shouting that so and so, son of so and so, had been charged with a crime. "Whoever knows anything in his favor, let him come and state it" (Sanh. 6:43a). Witnesses were to be examined separately. When they entered a room, "awe is installed into them" (Sanh. 2:29a). They were warned that hearsay evidence was inadmissible. Every effort was made to emphasize the seriousness of a capital, as distinguished from civil, case. Once judgment had been executed in a capital affair, the witness was told, there could be no restitution, for a person could not be brought back to life. The witness would be responsible not only for the blood of the accused but also for "the blood of his potential descendants until the end of time" (Sanh. 4:37a). The judges then examined the witness with a number of searching queries, requiring specific answers related to dates, places, and proof of guilt. Involved as the process was, it was merely an elaboration of the biblical injunction against giving false witness (Deut. 19:18).

If the accused were found innocent, he was discharged. If he was to be condemned, the Talmud required a day's recess, during which the judges were to practice moderation in food and drink, discuss the merits of the case, and possibly uncover points in favor of the accused (Sanh. 5:40a). Capital cases which carried with them an unfavorable verdict could only be decided, upon reflection, "on the morrow" (Sanh. 4:32a, 35a). Such talmudic rules again were probably of an ancient, possibly Hashmonaean origin, for historians note a disinclination after the fall of Jerusalem for the remnants of Jewry, whether in Judaea or Mesopotamia, to implement capital punishment.[28]

In Jesus' case, it is apparent that no legal code was followed. There were no heralds soliciting witnesses in the Gospels or at Oberammergau. Though Matthew and Mark speak of many who came forward to bear false witness (Matt. 26:60–61 and Mark 14:55–59), the only specific information they supplied to the Sanhedrin was that Jesus predicted he would rebuild the Temple in three days, a distortion of his promise of resurrection. The priests recognized the falsity of such testimony but did not invoke the threat of punishment outlined in Deuteronomy 19:18. Instead, judgment was rendered on the spot, without a moment's reflection. In Matthew 26:65 and Mark 14:63–64, the high priest tears his garments and shrieks that Jesus has blasphemed. The scribes and other priests then spit upon him, slap him in the face, blindfold him, and dare him to make a prophecy.[29]

Among the several capital crimes listed in the Torah is reviling of God (cf. cursing as defined in Lev. 24:15–16 and 1 Kings 21:10), an act punishable by stoning. The Talmud restricts this form of punishment to anyone who utters the ineffable name or Tetragrammaton, YHWH (Sanh. 6:56a). From what is recounted in the Gospels, Jesus neither reviled God nor did he speak the divine name. According to the Book of Luke (23:66–71), when he was asked if he were the Christ, he said: "If I tell you, you will not believe me, and if I question you, you will not answer me, or let me go. But henceforth, the Son of Man will be seated at the right hand of the power of God." When pressed again, he answered, "You, yourselves say that I am." In Matthew (26:64), his response is, "Thou has said it. Nevertheless, I say to you, hereafter you shall see the Son of Man sitting at the right hand of the Power and coming upon the clouds of heaven." Only in Mark (14:62) does Jesus declare: "I am. And you shall see the Son of Man sitting at the right hand of the Power and coming with the clouds of heaven."

There is no way that any of these statements could be equated with what constituted blasphemy in ancient Judaea. The closest Jesus came to uttering the name of God was when he employed the euphemism "Power." Even then, he was not guilty of reviling God, as some have suggested. We have already noted that others in this age had arrogated to themselves the title of messiah without incurring the wrath of the established priesthood. As Haim Cohn says, "No Pharisee would ever count as blasphemous or otherwise improper an assertion of divine authority."[30] At worst, Jesus' impiety commanded corporal punishment, not death. The Mishnah quotes the sages as stating that one who employs substitutes for the ineffable name "is the object of an injunction, but not punishable by death" (Sanh. 6:56a).

Rabbi Krauskopf deemed the entire proceeding as outlined in the Gospels incomprehensible. Of Jesus, Krauskopf wrote, "He is condemned to death for irreligious actions and for blasphemous sayings; there is not in the whole compendium of the talmudic law, an enactment, a decision, a decree that could even by the farthest stretch of an orthodox imagination construe as heresy or blasphemy anything that Jesus ever did or said."[31] Since Jesus had not uttered the name of God, Krauskopf tried to determine what other sin he may have committed. To claim descent from the House of David would not have been seriously considered, for the Sanhedrin knew better than anyone else the genealogy of people in Judaea. His promise to rebuild the Temple in three days could also be ridiculed, as it had taken forty-six years to complete the structure. Miraculous cures can now be attrib-

uted to Jesus' talent for counseling the hysterical or use of
herbs learned from the Essenes. There has never been a
prohibition within Judaism against healing the sick on the
Sabbath.[32] Declared Krauskopf, "There is not one word of
truth in all these trumped-up charges against the rabbis."[33]

If Jesus were guilty of anything, Krauskopf wrote, it was
that he had spoken disrespectfully of the rabbis—"a guilt
that was one of the commonest and most harmless occur-
ences in those days of free speech."[34] Some Pharisees within
the Sanhedrin may have regarded his words as rash fantasy,
but the leaders need not have done so. Sedition and slander,
incitement to idolatry, were all punishable by death under
the codes of the Torah (Deut. 17:12; 18:20) and Talmud
(Sanh. 10:86b–87a). The Talmud speaks of a rebellious
elder who refused to abide by the decrees of the Bet Din and
was executed before a festival (Sanh. 10:89a). There is even
a spurious reference to a *mesith,* seducer from the faith,
named Ben Stada who some have attempted to identify as
Jesus. That Jesus was not "a rebellious elder" who could be
sentenced to death is evident to Haim Cohn who points out
the precedent applied only to (*a*) Sadducees who were (*b*)
ordained scholars, and Jesus was neither of these.[35]

The probability is that a small clique of Boethusean
priests, representing the most extreme faction of quietism in
ancient Judaea, conspired to eliminate Jesus. In part, they
were prompted by the same fear that religious reformers
from Muhammad to Martin Luther have inspired in established priesthoods. Jesus constituted a threat to their vested
positions because "the whole multitude was in admiration of
his doctrine" (Mark 11:18) and "were very attentive to hear
him" (Luke 19:47, 48). Moreover, his roots in Galilee, the
site of a bloody uprising in 4 B.C. and the center of Zealot
agitation may have caused some to see in him a potential
leader of sedition. Mark suggests there was a recent insurrection in which Barabbas may have played a role. John (11)
relates the fears of the high priest "if these things continue,
the Romans will deprive us of our official positions and of
our statehood." Professor Winter insists: "He was no revolutionary prompted by political ambitions for the power of

government; he was a teacher who openly proclaimed his teaching. He never announced the coming of his own kingdom, but preached the kingdom of God that comes without observation."[36] Since the imminence of the divine kingdom could be twisted to mean a threat to Rome, the "Quisling appointees of the occupying Romans" (as Swidler and Sloyan refer to the high priests)[37] delivered him up to Pilate.

In the Gospels, Pilate emerges as a reluctant participant in what seemingly is a minor affair in his domain. In Matthew and Mark, the entire sequence from Jesus' appearance before Pilate to his public condemnation and scourging covers no more than twenty verses (Matt. 27:11–30 and Mark 15:1–19). Luke interpolates a scene before Herod Antipas, but cleaves to the same basic structure (23:1–31). In John, however, Pilate's earlier indifference is transformed into active partisanship on behalf of Jesus. No less than four times does the Roman procurator attempt to convince "the Jews" that Jesus is innocent (John 18:38–39; 19:6; 19:12; and 19:15), and each time he is rebuffed.

As Professor Klausner has noted, all the stories of Pilate's opposition to the Crucifixion are "wholly unhistorical."[38] They emanate from late sources which attempted to minimize Roman responsibility, as Christianity took root within the Gentile world. In reality, Pilate was "a man of blood," to whom "the killing of a single Galilean Jew was no more than the killing of a fly."[39] Among the Roman officials—Fadus, Cumanus, Felix, Festus, Albinus, and Florus—sent to govern Judaea in the first century, Pilate's reputation for brutality stands out. It was he who introduced the ensigns of Caesar into Jerusalem. When the Jews reacted by blocking all entries into the city, he first ordered the people "cut to pieces," then backed off. When the Jews tried the same civil disobedience to prevent confiscation of Temple funds for construction of an aqueduct, he had them beaten from the streets. Josephus informs us that "many of them perished by the stripes they received, and many of them perished as trodden to death by each other."[40] There is an oblique reference in the Book of Luke to the slaughter of Galileans "whose blood Pilate had mingled with their sacrifices"

(Luke 13:1). The most trenchant indictment of this man came from Philo who called him "naturally inflexible, a blend of self-will and relentlessness," a vindictive man with "a furious temper" who indulged in bribery, insult, theft, repeated executions without trial, in short "ceaseless and supremely grievous cruelty."[41] Eventually, this obstinate tyrant was recalled to Rome to stand trial for his abuse of power.

Even within the parameters outlined by the synoptic Gospels Pilate should emerge as the archetype villain he truly was. This was done in the medieval Passion at Towneley, England. Early on, Pilate announced to the audience that he intended to kill Jesus, but that in order to derive more pleasure from the act, he would feign sympathy for the accused. Said the Roman governor:

> I shall fownde to be his freynd utward, in certayn.
> And shew hym fare cowntenance and wordys of
>   vanyte;
> Bot or this day at nyght on crosse shall he be slayn,
> Thus agans hym in my hart I bere great enmyte.[42]

Such a portrayal of Pilate is furthest from the minds of the Oberammergauers. As the Passion unfolds onstage, Pilate is one of the few characters shown to possess compassion. He may be pompous, even disdainful of Christ at first, but like his aides Sylvus and Claudius, his offstage wife Procula, and the centurion who commands the troops during the Crucifixion, Pilate is solicitous of Jesus, contemptuous of the rest of the Jews. When the priests come before him demanding Jesus' death, the original Daisenberger script called for him to dismiss their charges as "the fruit of the most fanatical imagination."[43] Then the procurator that Klausner calls "a man of blood" states, "No Roman can condemn a man to death for such talk as this."[44]

Following his initial questioning of Jesus (including the "what is truth?" exchange), Pilate informs his aides, "Under no circumstances will I yield to the accusations by the high priests, but will do my utmost to save this Jesus."[45] Yet when he learns Jesus hails from Galilee, Pilate is almost relieved, for now he can turn him over to Herod Antipas. This is the same Pilate who only recently had massacred a number of Galilean pilgrims, and who until that very day had been the enemy of Herod. But we are to believe the procurator turned Jesus over to a puppet king to prosecute on grounds of lese majesty.

When Jesus returns from Herod, it is again Pilate who speaks on his behalf before the high council and mob. At one point in the original Daisenberger text, the Roman asks, "Is your hate against this man so deep and bitter that he cannot satisfy you by the blood from his wounds?"[46] Pilate again declares he cannot condemn Jesus to death, but does permit him to be scourged, in the hope that this would placate the Jews. In Pilate's final dramatic appearance, when he offers the Jews a choice of prisoners to be set free according to his or their custom,[47] Daisenberger has the Roman governor denounce the "despicable fickleness"[48] of people who cheered Jesus only days before. Then, as he presents the crowd the choice between a debased and bloodied Jesus and Barabbas, the disgusting robber, Pilate would plead anew with the men of Judaea: "Look well at these two. The one mild of countenance, dignified in his bearing, the picture of a wise teacher—one whom ye yourselves have honoured long, not one evil can be laid to his charge, and already he has been humiliated by the most grievous chastisement. The other an ugly, savage creature, an accused robber and murderer, a horrible picture of a perfect villain. I appeal to your reason and human feelings. Choose! Whom will ye that I release unto you, Barabbas or Jesus, called the Christ?"[49]

It is a fascinating scenario and one which is cut out of whole cloth. Professor Brandon was especially exercised by the Barabbas incident as recounted in the Gospels, noting that the governor, "for some unexplained reason," had become convinced of the innocence of Jesus and the "malevolence of the Jewish authorities." Pilate therefore agreed to release a prisoner (Barabbas) who only recently had caused Roman deaths in an insurrection. Concluded Brandon, "the whole account is patently too preposterous and too ludicrous for belief."[50]

Actually, the number of historical and legal incongruities associated with Pilate in the Gospels and Oberammergau would, in themselves, justify a lengthy monograph. Dr. Klausner and Haim Cohn relate just a few: (1) no Jews, not even the high priests, would be permitted at a hearing traditionally held in camera in the Praetorium;[51] (2) Pilate could not waive jurisdiction over to Herod because Roman governors were not only competent but under an obligation to adjudicate the case of any man suspected of treason against the emperor or making preparations for an insurrection;[52] (3) even if Pilate had considered turning Jesus over to the tetrarch Herod, it would have been impossible to squeeze this action within the given time frame, as the two men did not share the same palace;[53] (4) under Roman law, a prisoner could not be flogged before sentence of death had been handed down, because scourging was an essential and inseparable part of the crucifixion punishment;[54] (5) the so-called *privilegium paschale* (custom of freeing prisoners at Easter) was never recorded in Jewish history but was a phenomenon of the late Roman Empire, limited to the emperor alone, and not applicable to prisoners accused of capital offenses or treason;[55] (6) according to the code of Justinian (9.47.12) "vanae voces populi non sunt audiendae" (vain voices of the people may not be listened to), and nowhere in Roman history do we find a court "truckling to the imprecations of the masses";[56] and (7) there is the problem of washing of the hands, a Jewish, not Roman, expression of nonparticipation in a bloody deed, for "no Roman governor would ever commit the folly of washing his hands in public before 'multitudes' of natives and demean himself to make a solemn declaration of his innocence, as if they were his judges."[57]

Echoing Klausner, Winter suggests that the gospel writers deliberately transmuted Pilate from an insolent, cruel provincial dignitary to a sensitive figure to curry favor with Roman authorities. In the era before Constantine, when their families were being cast into the circuses, "exponents of Christianity did not, on occasion, shrink from blatant falsification in their endeavours to persuade a hostile ruler that some of his predecessors had been favourably disposed toward the church."[58] In the process, all guilt for the death of Jesus was projected upon a Jewish mob, Jewish guards, Jewish priests.

Oblivious to apostolic motivations, the villagers of Oberammergau insist they have been faithful to the Gospels, and no less an authority than Reinhold Niebuhr conceded the scenes with Pilate and the Sanhedrin rest "solely on the Biblical narratives."[59] The villagers argue that they need the "good cop" Pilate as opposed to the "bad cop" priests for dramatic effect. Bürgermeister Zwink told me, "I say the dramatic elements cannot emerge from the Passion play when Pilate says, 'All right, kill Jesus.' He must say, 'No, I do not want Jesus' death.' "[60] The notion of a reluctant Pilate appealed to Reinhold Niebuhr who fifty years ago termed Oberammergau "perfect drama." Pater Rümmelein, who toned down some lines for the 1980 text, adds: "John's Gospel shows that Pilate wanted to free Jesus and that some of the Jews wanted to have him killed. It is the same in the Passion play. The other Gospels—Luke, Mark—also show that people wanted to have Jesus killed. So Pilate gave in and sentenced Jesus. There is no difference between the Gospels and the play. Oberammergau has always followed the Gospels."[61]

The villagers' commitment to Holy Writ is admirable. But, as Professors Parkes, Klausner, and Sandmel have all noted, such sources often are too cryptic or vague, inconsistent and unhistorical. Holy Writ may also be cited selectively and tendentiously. An author may choose the relatively benign gospels of Mark or Luke as his point of departure, or he may select Matthew and John, both of which stress Jewish responsibility for deicide. It was to the latter base that Othmar Weis and Alois Daisenberger grafted their own fantasies of ancient dialogue and action. The danger, as Tom Driver has warned, is that when the Crucifixion story is played out by amateurs for mass audiences, distortions of one kind or another are inevitable.[62] At Oberammergau, historical distortions are evident in costumes, props, customs (e.g., Mary Magdalene implies that her trip to the tomb is in accord with some unknown Jewish tradition), and chronology. Distortions are manifest in treatment of a new covenant, the behavior of the Pharisees and Sanhedrin, the character of Pilate, and ultimately the relationship between Jesus and his Jewish people. Long ago, Rabbi Krauskopf protested, "While Christians have a perfect right to ascribe to Jesus whatever miracles and supernatural happenings they please, they have no right to do this at the cost of falsifications of Jewish History, of mistranslations of Jewish scriptures, of misinterpretations of Jewish laws and institutions."[63] Instead of illustrating that greed, tyranny, and collaboration were at the heart of what Haim Cohn calls "a perversion of justice,"[64] Oberammergau perpetuated the stale canard of Christ-killing. In its own way, the village has contributed more to hatred than reconciliation.

6

Hymn of Reconciliation or An Anti-Semitic Play?

At least one prominent Christian journal regretfully concedes that "authentic presentation of Christ crucified is necessarily a stumbling-block to Jews, and foolishness to Gentiles."[1] Still the villagers in Oberammergau persist in the delusion that their Passion is "a hymn of reconciliation."[2] So declared Anton Lang, the Christ of 1910 and 1920, Alois Lang, who played Jesus in 1930 and 1934, and village historian Hermine Diemer. As late as 1970, Dr. Karl Ipser wrote in his foreword to the playbook that the villagers "erect the cross against hate, for the sake of peace and reconciliation."[3]

The theme of reconciliation was at the heart of Joseph Cardinal Ratzinger's sermon in Oberammergau before the premiere on May 18, 1980. "Passion plays must be an event of penance and reconciliation," said the cardinal whose archbishopric includes Oberammergau, "for Christ has died to reconcile us with God and men." Cardinal Ratzinger reminded his listeners that none should seek to assign responsibility or guilt for the death of Christ, since such questions were anachronistic. Apart from original sin, Christianity knows no concept of collective guilt. Moreover, the *Cate-*

chismus Romanus, the official basis of Catholic teaching, emphasizes that Jesus died for the sins of all mankind, that his death, then, was necessary for salvation.

Christ's message from the cross was one of peace, and that particularly related to the Jewish people. "We know," said Cardinal Ratzinger, "that a chain of anti-Semitism belongs to the darkest chapters of Christian history." The Oberammergau Passion, however, had "nothing in common with anti-Semitism, the idea of which arose as a result of the Crusades and several host desecration legends." Neither the authors (Weis and Daisenberger) nor the performers had anything in common with German national anti-Semitism of the past century. Cardinal Ratzinger called upon "our Jewish friends" to cease looking for elements of bigotry in the Passion, for preachments of hate are "foreign to the historic origin and the spiritual content of the play."[4]

The cardinal's position is echoed by spokesmen in the village. Pater Rümmelein maintains, "The question of guilt is not asked in the play. All spots that might offend Jews have been eliminated, and *nobody* will say, after seeing the play, 'Oh, these Jews killed Jesus.'"[5] Bürgermeister Zwink is even more positive. "We believe in good relations between Jews and Christians," he told me in his office four years ago. "The Jewish man is the same for me as another man. The message of the play is a religious message. Ninety percent who come here would say it is good, lovely. They see the history of the Bible from the entry to Jerusalem to the Crucifixion. I think it would be good if Jews came to the Passion play to see themselves."[6]

The issue of anti-Semitism has been revived every decade since Oberammergau acquired worldwide celebrity. Individual perspectives depend very much upon background or religious loyalties. A legion of Christian apologists have come forward to exonerate the Passion. In 1890, William Stead made no reference whatever to anti-Semitism in his lengthy commentary on Oberammergau. Rather, he compared the brutality of Caiaphas to a contemporary, Constantin Pobedonostsev, Russian procurator of the Holy Synod, who was then "raging in his orthodox zeal against the sectaries who dared to obey Christ in their own fashion."[7] Forty years later, the principal journal of American Baptists declared, "A normal Christian believes that the telling of the story of Jesus as winsomely as possible is perfectly compatible with whole-hearted appreciation and good-will toward the Jews as a people."[8] Reinhold Niebuhr dismissed suggestions that the play evidenced medieval anti-Semitism as "far-fetched."[9] Harold Kuhn attended performances in 1950, 1960, and 1970, followed the German text "carefully," and "did not ourselves feel the material to be negative toward the Jewish leaders as some regard it to be."[10] John Stoddard, J. B. Priestley, Hans Christian Andersen, W. A. Darlington, Sarah Howe, Janet Swift, John Jackson, Vernon Heaton, none of them detected anti-Jewish elements in the Passion. In fact, one critic suggested in 1960 that charges of anti-Semitism smacked of "mccarthyism [sic]."[11] Another, Harold Brown, accused Jews of being "excessively sensitive or deliberately perverse." For Brown, the charge that the Oberammergau Passion was anti-Semitic was "a racist ruse."[12]

Jewish critics have always found the play insulting. Back in 1900, Rabbi Krauskopf wrote, "If all that was enacted last summer in the Passion Play at Oberammergau be true, we have no right to continue as Jews."[13] In 1930, Esther Moyerman, editor of a Philadelphia Jewish journal, likened the play to "a harsh and ancient religious libel which belongs to the Dark Ages."[14] Moyerman's peers in Chicago also scored Oberammergau for "promoting anti-Semitism and spreading the gospel of not brotherhood, but 'Down with the Jews.'" Said New York's *Jewish Tribune*, the religious consciousness awakened only a burning hate for Jews, "for the Passion Play's greatest aim was to exalt Christianity by pushing Judaism into the mire; to exalt the Christian by splashing mud upon the Jew."[15] Decades have passed, and the Second Vatican Council has formally lifted the onus of deicide from the Jewish people, yet late into the 1960s, the American Jewish Congress could still complain about "the continued demonstration of an apparently unconquerable bigotry by the residents of Oberammergau."[16]

Jews have not been alone in their criticism. A number of prominent Gentiles—Deems Taylor, Cynthia Bourgeault, Tom Driver, and Eric Bentley—have detected anti-Semitism in the production. An "offended" Eric Bentley said, "Even to those who could not read the text, the anti-Semitic attitude of the production would have been quite obvious."[17] Writing for *Christian Century*, Driver stated flatly, "The play *is* decidedly anti-Semitic, and its interpretation of the crucifixion and the events leading to it is harmful not only to Christian-Jewish relations, but to proper understanding of the Christian gospel."[18] Driver labeled the Daisenberger Passion an "anti-Jewish play" which "serves to propagate anti-Semitism, a modern disease as loathsome as the 17th century plague which struck fear into the hearts of the Oberammergau forefathers."[19] His journal seized upon this metaphor, for *Christian Century* editorialized six years later, "The village escaped that plague, but since has been spreading another—anti-Semitism."[20]

Over the years, the organized Christian hierarchy also has pointed out that anti-Semitic elements in the Passion conflict with resolutions adopted by the World Council of Churches in 1948 and 1961, the National Council of Churches in 1964 and 1968, the Department of World Mission of the Lutheran World Federation (1964), the House of Bishops of the Protestant Episcopal Church (1964), the Vatican's *Nostra Aetate* Declaration, and the Guidelines and Suggestions for Implementing the Conciliar Declaration for Vatican II (1974).[21] In March 1968, the Secretariat for Catholic-Jewish Relations of the National Conference of Catholic Bishops (including Msgr. George Higgins, Msgr. John Oesterreicher, and Rev. Edward Flannery) warned against "carelessly written or produced" Passion plays which might "become a source of anti-Semitic reactions."[22] Two years later, a group of American scholars, including Markus Barth (Pittsburgh), Father Raymond Brown (Saint Mary's, Baltimore), W. D. Davies (Duke), W. R. Farmer (Perkins, Dallas), James Sanders (Union), and Dean Krister Stendahl (Harvard), examined the Oberammergau text and found that it "perpetuates the age-old Christian attitude which contributed to the holocaust of the thirties and forties of this century."[23]

Frankly, it is difficult to imagine how the Oberammergau Passion could avoid some anti-Semitic taint. The seventeenth-century text did not, as we have seen, spring sui generis from the earth. Its roots are in medieval tropes and cycles performed from Monte Cassino to Wakefield. It reflects the change in emphasis wrought during the era of the Crusades, when Christ was transformed from savior to sufferer. It also shares a penchant for Jew-baiting with earlier forms of literature. As Leon Poliakov has noted, "There is virtually no genre—fabliau, satire, legend, or ballad—in which Jews are not present or are not described with ridicule or hatred, often with the help of that scatological touch so popular at the period."[24] The stage especially became an instrument of anti-Jewish warfare, because, as Salo Baron relates, it offered opportunities to playwrights and actors "to vent their anti-Jewish spleens."[25] Such dramas, like charges of sorcery, ritual murder, usury, well-poisoning, and host desecration proliferated in German-speaking areas because of "the deeply-rooted antiJewish feelings" of the populace.[26] Exactly such bigotry disturbed Sister Louis Gabriel who denounced the 1970 Passion, saying, "In this monumental thriller of hate, evil, betrayal and discord, for every minute of six hours spectators know who are the good and who the others are."[27]

This Manichaean apposition was evident in all Oberammergau productions right up to 1980. *And here it must be emphasized that we are talking about pre-1980 Passion plays. Extensive revisions have been accomplished by Pater Rümmelein, but it is the traditional Daisenberger Passion which impacted upon generations of spectators and which must be evaluated.* From the moment the chorus tramped onto the stage for the first time and the Prologue pronounced "God's curse" upon the "oppressed race" from Zion,[28] damnation of the Jews was a theme that cropped up repeatedly in the Daisenberger text. When Adam was enjoined to earn his bread by the sweat of his brow, when Vashti was rejected, when Joab was cursed for his "false brother kiss," when Cain was driven to raving by his conscience, and when the Jewish mob accepted responsibility for Christ's death, shouting, "His blood be upon us and our children," the lesson was clear.

The Gospels may have provided the seedbed for such theology, but medieval religious drama, "that incomparable vehicle for propaganda," provided what Poliakov termed the most assiduous cultivation of anti-Jewish sentiment.[29] God's curse upon the Jews was clearly pronounced in a thirteenth-century Orleans sepulcher play. Three monks stood before the Marys lamenting the good shepherd "whom no guilt stained." Then they spoke:

> THIRD MONK: Alas, sinful race of Judaica, whom a dire madness makes frenzied! Detestable people!
> FIRST MONK: Why condemned ye to an impious death the Holy One with savage hate?
> SECOND MONK: O race accursed.[30]

At Chester, an angel would appear before Mary and tell her that "Jews should be put behynde, for it passes out of their kinde through Christ at his cominge."[31] At Oberammergau, Jesus informed his apostles, "As I said unto the Jews, whither I go, ye cannot come."[32] This statement, drawn from John 13:33, left no doubt that for Jews alone, there was no hope of salvation.

Wanhope, despairing of God's mercy, was all that was open to Jews, a people described in medieval literature as false, perverse, disloyal, wicked, felonious swine, or "devils from Hell, enemies of the human race."[33] Another French Passion, *La Vengence et destruction du Hierusalem*, shows them after the Crucifixion, stricken with blindness and stubbornness.[34] Oberammergau spared few, if any, of these epithets. The spectator in Bavaria was melodiously informed that Jews were "a fiendish brood," "that murderous horde," "this evil band," a "murderous league," inhuman knaves, bloodhounds, fools who had come "up from nethermost Hell."[35] Scarcely a "wicked wile" known to man was not intoned against them during this hymn of reconciliation.

They were scored for their vanity, for proclaiming themselves God's chosen people, for their blindness and obstinacy in cleaving to the archaic faith of Moses, for hardening
their hearts against Jesus, for uttering lies and conspiring
against him, for spite, envy, and brutality.

Whenever possible, Oberammergau reinforced the popular stereotype of Jewish avarice. When merchants squealed
over their lost ducats after Jesus overturned their tables in
the Temple, people in the audience nodded, knowingly.
When the merchants appeared before the Sanhedrin to
protest the inconvenience, money was still their object.
Whether 1900 or 1980, when Jesus is finally apprehended,
the money changers stayed onstage long enough to make
certain that everyone understood that their spiteful attitude
stemmed from love of lucre. Such images, wrote Wilm Sanders, were "painful continuations" of medieval cliches
which treated all Jews as usurers. They were, he added,
"Not well founded in the Bible."[36] Sister Louis Gabriel
went further, stating there are no speeches of "evil-doing,
conspiring, haggling Jewish merchants in the Gospels." The
scenes involving the merchants were nothing but polemic,
for which there was not a trace in all four Gospels.[37]

Significantly, the one apostle to betray Jesus conformed
to the stereotype of the moneygrubbing Jew. Judas complained about money as soon as Mary Magdalene anointed
Jesus with a spikenard of oil at Bethany. "The money might
have been better spent," he lamented. "What a loss for the
poor and us."[38] He continued to whine about scant provi-
sions as Jesus and the other disciples prepared to enter
Jerusalem. When his protests were waved aside by Jesus,
Judas fretted: "I see it now, there is nothing in prospect but
to live in continual poverty and misery."[39] Greed made him
amenable to the offer of the merchants to betray his master.
He readily accepted the thirty pieces of silver tendered by
the Sanhedrin, the price supposedly fixed for a slave by the
code of Moses.[40]

That Judas repented his actions, upon seeing Jesus debased, is irrelevant. His remorse came too late. After two
soliloquies in which he cursed the synagogue and likened

himself to the "pest-stricken . . . scum of mankind,"[41] he committed suicide. One verse in Matthew (27:5) and three in Acts (1:18–20) were translated into an act, replete with prologue, chorus, tableau of Cain, and a five-minute death speech. Until 1910, Judas was accompanied to his death by a number of demons, "groundlings" who delighted in his actions. After his "death shriek," the demons nibbled at his innards, then carted his body off to Hell.[42] The sickening scene was reminiscent of *Le Mystère de la Passion*, another medieval drama where Jews were urged by devils to "kill him and hate him just as we do." When Judas betrayed his master, the demons howled with glee.[43]

Rabbi Krauskopf was particularly disturbed by the portrayal of Judas in 1900. "Everything that is vile in human nature is pressed into that one character of Judas Iscariot," he wrote.[44] Traditionally, the role went to a physically unattractive villager, one with a hooked or bent nose. Onstage, only Judas of all the apostles carried a moneybag in his girdle, the symbol of Jewish greed. Only Judas wore a black outer robe. His face was haggard, his eyes furtive, and he moved in "a snakelike glide across the stage."[45] In 1980, however, I found Martin Kratz's Judas one of the few genuinely tragic performances in the Passion.

No matter how Judas is portrayed at Oberammergau, he is a symbol—of the Jewish people and their willingness to betray Christ. According to Salo Baron, "It did not require too much imagination to view his personality as typical of the whole Jewish people, whose heart was supposed to be filled with rancor and the desire to betray its Christian hosts."[46] Gentile converts to Christianity in the early Middle Ages noted the presence of many prominent figures named Judah (Judah the Galilean, Judah Maccabee, Judah Aristobulus, Judah the Essene, Judah ha-Nasi) in Jewish history and concluded that the name was practically synonymous with that of Jew. The personal name and the ancient Jewish homeland (Judaea) derived from the same root (Yehuda) and even sounded the same (Iudaeus) in Latin. Christians simply fused the identity of the betrayer upon the entire Jewish people, much the way people today refer to Uncle Sam, John

Bull, or Ivan. The identification worked in two ways. When Judas appeared in a portrait like the Last Supper or onstage at Oberammergau, his inner garment was yellow, the color worn by Jews in medieval and Nazi ghettos. His red hair, or, as in the case of the Corpus Christi pageant, red wig, customarily distinguished the devil in other plays. Thus Judas, symbol of the Jewish people, was the devil personified and the Jews servants of Satan.

Judas may have been the primary symbol for the Jews, but he was not the only one represented at Oberammergau. The Daisenberger text contained another, almost unnoticed, libel of Jews in general. As Jesus made his way slowly down the Via Dolorosa toward the end of the Passion, he buckled under the weight of the cross and collapsed near the door of a shop. At that point, the shopkeeper spoke, "Away from my house. Here is no place for thee to rest!"[47] The man's name was Ahashuerus. He represented not the ancient Persian king but the spectral figure in Christian legend, the Wandering Jew. At times his name was Cartaphilus (beloved of God), Buttadeus (God smiter), Malchus (after the soldier who struck Jesus in Gethsemane), or Ahashuerus. For his denial of Christ, his lack of mercy, he was doomed to roam the earth until the second coming. The Roman destruction of the ancient Jewish state, coupled with periodic expulsions of Jews from European lands, gave the tale efficacy. It has cropped up, with some variations, from Utah and West Virginia, to Germany and the Ukraine. The consistent element, however, has been eternal damnation for the Jew.[48]

Surrogates like Judas, Ahashuerus, and the *Händler* were still insufficient to carry the guilt for Jesus' death. The Daisenberger text made certain that no Jews escaped reprobation. High priests, Sadducees, Pharisees, rabbis, scribes, guards, and common folk all were (and to a certain extent still are) cursed for the sin of deicide. The interaction of these groups onstage at Oberammergau approximated the worst anti-Semitic fantasies of Eduard Drumont or Julius Streicher.

From the outset, Caiaphas made it clear that two religious forces were diametrically opposed, and that the Jews represented hauteur, spite, and violence. In lines now muted, but recited until 1980, the high priest declared: "Now we shall see who will triumph! He with his followers, to whom he preaches without ceasing of love—a love that included publicans and sinners, and even Gentiles—or we with this multitude filled with hate and revenge that we are letting loose against him."[49]

In scene after scene, the Jewish establishment conspired, with or without the merchants and Judas, to finish off "this enemy of Moses and Israel." In the original text, the rabbi proposed to seize Jesus and cast him into a prison. Another councillor, Joshua, suggested spying him out, then over-coming him bodily.[50] If it could not be done legally, Ezekiel recommended some action be carried through "by force of will." Nathaniel suggested staging a riot. To which the ubiquitous rabbi responded, "As a last resort, a hand can always be found that in the dungeon's silence will rid the Sanhedrin of its enemy."[51]

The goal of the conspirators has always been death. The wicked Nathaniel (an Oberammergau invention, as much as any character from Zefferelli's *Jesus of Nazareth*) was the first to paint the way. In the opening scene, when the traders were chastised, he incited them to revenge, declaring, "This man full of deceit and heresy must perish."[52] That line is now gone, but thereafter the chants "Er muss sterben!" and "Ans Kreuz mit ihm!" are repeated so many times that even a small child can understand the perfidy of the Jews.

The scene following the Sanhedrin's payoff to Judas was, and is, especially grotesque. The Temple watch had been dispatched with Judas to arrest Jesus, and the elders dis-cussed what they should do with the Nazarene upon his return. One suggested he be cast into the darkest dungeon, laden with chains, to remain buried alive. Caiaphas rejected that idea, saying Jesus might break his fetters through magic. The high priest continued:

> CAIAPHAS: Hear then, the High Priest. Is it not better that one man *die* than the whole nation perish? *He must die!* Without his *death*, there is no peace in

> Israel, no security for the Law of Moses—no hour of
> peace for us!
>
> RABBI: God has spoken through his High Priest. Only
> by the *death* of Jesus of Nazareth can and must the
> people of Israel be saved.
>
> NATHANIEL: The word has been burning on my
> tongue—now it is spoken. *He dies*—the enemy of
> our Fathers!
>
> ALL (excepting Joseph and Nicodemus): *He must die!*
> *He must die* for our safety.
>
> ANNAS: By my grey hairs, I will not rest until the blood
> of this deceiver washes out the shame.[53]
>
> > > > [Italics mine.]

The Gospels, at least, waited till Jesus allegedly blas-phemed before the Sanhedrin. Not so, Oberammergau. Without so much as a hearing, let alone trial, the judges of Israel supposedly decreed Jesus' death. Unbelievably, in the Daisenberger script action continues onstage for another ninety lines, during which members of the Sanhedrin chant, *"He must die! He must die!"* no fewer than *six* times.[54] Even in the sanitized 1980 version, where several of the schemes and screams have been deleted, it is a sickening act and one for which there is no testamental precedent.[55]

The scene of Christ's formal interrogation before the Sanhedrin was equally appalling. The Gospels (Matt. 26: 59–69; Mark 14:55–65; Luke 23:63–71; John 18:13–24) are rather laconic about what transpired. The Daisenberger script, however, elaborated on the cruelty of the high priests. After Jesus offered his prediction of the Son of Man sitting on the right of the Power of God, the Oberammergau text con-tinued:

> CAIAPHAS: He hath blasphemed! What further need
> have we of witnesses? Behold now you have heard
> the blasphemy. What think you?
>
> ALL: *He deserves death!*
>
> CAIAPHAS: He has been unanimously declared guilty
> of *death.* Yet not I, nor the High Council, the divine

law itself pronounces the sentence against Him. Ye masters of the law, I summon you to answer. What says the holy law of him who is disobedient to the authority instituted by God?

JOSHUA: Whoever is proud and will not obey the commandment of the Priest, who serves at the same time the Lord, thy God, according to the judgment of the judge, *that man shall die* and thou shalt blot out the evil from Israel!

CAIAPHAS: What threatens the law to the Sabbath breaker?

EZEKIEL: Keep my Sabbath, for it is sacred to you! Who profanes it shall be guilty of *death*. Who does work on that day, his soul shall be cast out of the people.

CAIAPHAS: What punishment does the law decree to the blasphemer?

NATHANIEL: Tell the children of Israel: A man who curses his God shall bear his punishment, and he who slanders the name of the Lord shall *die!* The whole community shall stone him, be he a native or a stranger! Who slanders the name of the Lord shall be put to *death.*

CAIAPHAS: Thus the judgment is pronounced over this Jesus of Nazareth, pronounced according to the law. Fathers of the people of Israel! It is now your due to speak the final sentence about the guilt and punishment of this man!

ALL: He is guilty of blasphemy. He has deserved *death.*

CAIAPHAS: Lead him away.

SELPHA: So, come Messiah! We will assign to Thee Thy palace.

BALBUS: There Thou shalt receive the homage, due to you.

ALL: Yes, away with him. *He shall die. We shall not rest until he is put to death.*

ANNAS: God grant that soon the hour will come that will deliver us for ever from our enemies.

ALL: God grant it![56]

[Italics mine.]

The Sanhedrin could not be moved, even when Judas appealed to them to release his master. Their crassness was revealed anew when the grief-stricken betrayer pitched the thirty pieces of silver back at them. The nonplussed members of the high court simply discussed how the blood money might be put to use and agreed that it would be used to buy a potter's field.[57] They persevered after Jesus' execution as they drove him through the streets to Pilate's house. Caiaphas exhorted his minions, "Rest not until he is blotted from among the number of the living." His peers responded, "We will not rest! We demand his *death*, his blood." And the accompanying mob mocked Christ, shouting, "*Death* to thee, thou false prophet."[58] As with practically all the scenes above and below, the 1980 version keeps the action intact, with only a line or two deleted or muted.

In the lengthy scene at the Praetorium, the priests tried unsuccessfully to persuade Pilate that Jesus constituted not merely a blasphemer but a political threat to Rome. "By our laws, he deserves *death*," they all declared. "Therefore we must insist that he pay the decreed penalty of *death*," said Annas. When Pilate demanded a private audience with Jesus, Joshua, peeved by the delay, added, "All has been examined. The law itself condemns him to *death*." After Pilate shunted them off to Herod, they still shouted, "He is guilty of *death*. He must *die*. And today too!"[59] In the 1980 text, references to death have been removed, but Annas still affirms, "Even if a thousand obstacles stood in our path, the blasphemer shall receive His deserved punishment."[60]

At least the decrepit puppet king is portrayed with a spark of mercy. Herod feared that Jesus was the reincarnation of his old nemesis John the Baptist. Jesus' haggard appearance put such fears to rest. The court enjoyed a few moments of mockery with this famed miracle worker. Throughout the scene, which has been abbreviated in the 1980 version, the priests pressed for confirmation of "the sentence of the Synagogue." Said Nathaniel: "The law demands his *death*." Herod, however, adjudged Jesus king of fools and presented him with a royal mantle. The priests protested, "Not this— he is worthy of *death!*" Nathaniel pointed out that Jesus was a blasphemer. "And as such the law declares him worthy of *death*," all the priests responded. As they continued to chant, *"To death with him! To death with him! He must die!"* Herod refused to execute "so exalted a king." The priests offered him one last chance: "Speak the *death* sentence, as the law decrees." But he instructed them to take their bloody cause back to Pilate.[61]

Once more before Pilate, the members of the council shouted, "To *death* with him!" When Pilate offered to have Jesus scourged, Annas declared, "That is not enough." When the governor reminded the priests of his custom to release a prisoner, they shouted, "Release Barabbas. This one to the cross!" The disgusted governor reminded them that they were not the people. "The people will speak for themselves." As the priests scattered to round up a mob, the Roman guards took Jesus off to be scourged.[62]

Even today, the flogging is an unforgettable scene, and one which cannot help but rouse anger toward those responsible. Jesus, stripped to the waist, is tied to a post while the guards lash at him with ropes. The beating is unconvincing, but not so the crowning of the "pitiable king of the Jews." The guards laugh as they press the crown of thorns into Jesus' scalp. When blood flows from his brow, spectators in the great hall at Oberammergau groan audibly.[63]

Subsequently, the stage is filled with hundreds of people, assembled from all directions by the priests. One Catholic commentator said of the "howling, bloodthirsty, arm-waving mob," "Never have I seen anything so convincing and terrifying."[64] In the traditional Daisenberger text, the people engaged in an exchange with the chorus as they swarmed before the Praetorium. The black-draped chorus tried to reason that Jesus should be set free, but the people shouted, "To the Cross with Him! To the Cross with Him! His blood be on us and our children!"[65]

That antiphonic prelude was deleted from the 1980 production. There were even a handful of women and children (no more than twenty-five out of six hundred persons on stage) who stood off to the right and quietly protested what was taking place.[66] But other than these slight cosmetic changes, the current text is faithful to Daisenberger. What follows is the most vicious anti-Semitic vignette in the Passion. Nathaniel, Annas, Ezekiel, and Caiaphas all adjure the people to respect the laws of Moses, to cast off the teachings of "the tempter," and the people reply, "Long live the High Council! Long live our teachers and priests!" The emphasis, however, is not so much on life, once more, as on death:

ANNAS: And may the Galilean *die!*

CAIAPHAS: Come, let us hurry to Pilate.

NATHANIEL: Let us demand his *death.*

PEOPLE: Away to Pilate! The Nazarene shall *die.*

CAIAPHAS: He corrupted the law. He despised Moses and the Prophets. He blasphemed God.

PEOPLE: To *death* with the false prophet! The blasphemer must *die!* Pilate must have him crucified.

CAIAPHAS: He will pay for his misdeeds on the cross.

PEOPLE: We shall not rest until the sentence is spoken.

CAIAPHAS: Children of Israel! Yes, you are still the true descendants of your father Abraham. Thank God that you have escaped from the indescribable doom which this deceiver wished to bring on you and your children.

ANNAS: Only the untiring efforts of your fathers have saved you from the abyss.

PEOPLE: Long live the High Council! Let the Nazarene *die!*

CAIAPHAS: The governor will give you a choice between this blasphemer and Barabbas. Let us insist on the release of Barabbas.

PEOPLE: Let Barabbas go free! Let the Nazarene *perish!*

ANNAS: Praise be to you, and our fathers, who have heard our prayers!

PEOPLE: Pilate must consent! We insist on it!

CAIAPHAS: Remain steadfast!

THE HIGH PRIESTS AND COUNCILORS: This day will give us back our honour and freedom to the whole of Israel.

CAIAPHAS: Be impetuous in demanding the judgment.
PEOPLE: We demand the conviction of the Galilean!
SERVANTS AND SOLDIERS: Rebellion! Insurrection!
PEOPLE: The Nazarene must *die!*
CAIAPHAS: Show courage! Hold out undaunted! our
just cause protects us.
PEOPLE: Let Pilate speak the *death* penalty.[67]

[Italics mine.]

The frenzied mob presses toward the Praetorium, while
Roman legionnaires armed with spears form a file before
them. Pilate finally appears, bedecked in a white toga. Jesus
and Barabbas are brought before him:

PEOPLE: Judge Him! Sentence Him!
PILATE: See what a man!
HIGH COUNCIL: To the cross—
PILATE: Cannot even this pitiful sight win some com-
passion from your hearts?
PEOPLE: Let him *die!* To the cross with him!
PILATE: So take him and crucify him, for I find no guilt
in him.
CAIAPHAS: Governor, hear the voice of the people of
Jerusalem. They join in our accusations and demand
his *death.*
PEOPLE: Yes, we demand his *death.*
PILATE: Lead him down and let Barabbas be brought
here from prison.
ANNAS: Let Barabbas live. Pronounce the *death* sen-
tence on the Nazarene.
PEOPLE: To *death* with the Nazarene.[68]

[Italics mine.]

When Pilate reminds the mob of his practice of releasing a
prisoner, they shout, "Let him *die,* the false messiah, the
deceiver." When he asks them if they wish their king, they
respond, "Away with him! Free Barabbas." When he asks
what should be done with the king of the Jews, they shout
three times, "Kreuzige ihn! Kreuzige ihn!" (Crucify him!

Crucify him!) When, with hands outstretched, Pilate protests that Jesus has done no wrong, the people repeat three more times, "Kreuzige ihn! Kreuzige ihn!"[69]

Pilate instructs one aide to prepare the death sentence and another to bring him a bowl of water. In the traditional text employed at Oberammergau, he said, "See, I wash my hands. I am innocent of the blood of this just man. It will rest upon you." The priests and people responded as in Matthew 27:25: "We take it upon us. His blood be upon us and upon our children!" Pilate ordered Barabbas freed at the city limits, then repeated, "I have no share in this blood-guilt. Let it be as I have cried aloud: it falls upon you and upon your children." And once more, lest anyone but the deaf fail to comprehend, the priests and people screamed: "Good! Let it fall upon us and upon our children!"[70]

Pater Rümmelein deleted the second affirmation from his 1980 edition, as he had done away with the exchange between mob and chorus. Even with those changes, however, the scene still contains twenty-five references to death or crucifixion. While theologians may debate whether those who condemned Jesus were a crowd (Matt. 27:20; Mark 15:8, 11) or "mob" (Luke 23:18), it is evident to all who attend Oberammergau that the Book of John (chaps. 18, 19) is correct in blaming Jews. For once Pilate's decision has been pronounced, Caiaphas still declares, "Victory is ours! Rejoice, our faith is saved!" Annas urges his brethren, "Hurry, so that we can return home in time to eat the Passover lamb." What Sister Louis Gabriel has termed the "worst scene" in the play concludes with the people shouting, "Oh joyful day! The enemy of Moses is overthrown! So it will be with all who despise the law. He deserves death on the cross. Now peace will return to Israel."[71]

Daisenberger did not ignore the Jews' malice on the way to Golgotha. We have already alluded to the figure of Ahashuerus, the Wandering Jew. As Jesus proceeds along the Via Dolorosa, however, he is accompanied by priests who reproach the Roman guards for treating him so gently. The people, too, continue to denounce him, shouting, "Up to Golgotha! To the cross with him! To the cross! Let him bleed on the cross! Hail Israel! Your enemy is cast down! His death is our salvation! We are free! Long live our fathers, death to the Galilean!"[72] All of this takes place before the eyes of a tormented Mary and the women of Jerusalem.

The scene at Golgotha is worse.[73] As the curtain opens at center stage, the two robbers are already tied to the T-shaped crosses. We hear the sound of hammering offstage but are spared at least having to witness this action. The executioners raise the third cross, above which is a sign inscribed "Iesus Nazarenus Rex Iudaeorum." Unlike the two robbers, however, Jesus is suspended to the cross by nails that can be seen protruding from his hands and feet.[74] John Stoddard described the Crucifixion in the following manner: "The realism in all this is terrible. Apparently we see the bloodstained nails piercing both hands and feet. The crown of thorns still wounds his forehead; his garments are still marked with the blood of the scourging; and most trying of all, when the centurion's spear pierces his side, what seems to be real blood spurts forth and leaves a crimson stain."[75]

Through it all, the priests do not betray a shred of remorse. They are more upset by the inscription above Jesus, which they consider an affront to their people. They stand by and jeer, awaiting the satisfaction of seeing his bones broken and his body thrown into "the pit of the malefactors."[76] Informed that the curtain veiling the Holy of Holies in the Temple has been torn in two, the priests must leave before the executioners carry out the bloody rite of breaking legs. In the traditional text, Caiaphas rages: "This has this wretch done, through his magic art. It is well that he is out of the world; otherwise he would throw all into disorder." The priests and Pharisees amen: "Cursed be the ally of Beelzebub."[77] Rümmelein, at least, spared us this and a reprise where the priests return to view the body of Christ, which they want torn by wild beasts. When they learn the body is to be turned over to Joseph of Arimathaea, the rabbi proclaims in true "Oil Can Harry" fashion, "The traitor to the synagogue! He has deceived us again!" To which Annas adds, "And spoiled our triumph."[78]

As the "angry men" go off, a handful of Christ's followers

go about taking his body down from the cross. It is an ever so slow process. The two Marys stand downstage, consoling one another. As I looked about the theater, I noted that few were listening to what they were saying. All eyes, it seemed, were riveted upon the men who were moving tenderly at the cross. Two ladders (eight and fourteen feet high) were raised in front of and behind the cross. The men who climbed these ladders first draped the crucifix with a large, white sheet. Then, as they removed the nails, people in the audience moaned again. Finally, the battered body of Jesus was taken and laid on the lap of the Virgin. It was an excruciating scene.

Withal these dramatic caricatures and blood-filled lines, sensitive, intelligent people have emerged from the great hall at Oberammergau and concluded, "In this play, there is nothing offensive to Jews."[79] Advocates have long praised "its civilizing power,"[80] "the evangelical purity of the play."[81] After three missions to Oberammergau spanning thirty years, W. T. Stead of the *Review of Reviews* concluded in 1910: "The play is good, as wholly good as any mortal institution can be. It is good for the players, good for the audience, good in itself."[82]

A fairer evaluation was offered in 1900 by Oberammergau's own parish priest Joseph Schroeder who criticized the play, saying, "Its blind hate is the immediate motive for the whole Passion of our Lord."[83] Conniving priests, money-grubbing merchants, a weak-kneed Judas, and a blood-thirsty, howling mob should have made debate over the nature of the Passion rhetorical. The Daisenberger text, as originally performed, and even with its substantial emendations, has always been offensive to Jews. It could, as Dr. Alois Fink, head of Bavarian Radio, declared in 1970, properly be labeled "anti-Judaism."[84] More recently, Bruno Bettelheim wrote, "A better case can be made for Oberammergau being nothing but an expression of what was there all the time, and what people wanted to see and hear. My guess is that nobody who is not inherently an anti-Semite would go and watch this performance. Oberammergau was performed for centuries before Hitler created the Holocaust. But it is an expression of virulent anti-Semitism and as such it should be objected to."[85] Whatever term (anti-Judaism, anti-Semitism) is applied, it is difficult to disagree with Tom Driver that the Passion has been "positively harmful to the curious and the faithful who journey to see it."[86] The question is to what extent harm has been done. And that will be explored in chapter 7.

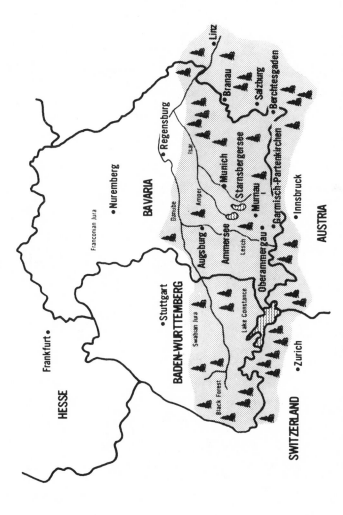

Map of Bavaria. Drawing by author. Redrawn by the Media Center, Youngstown State University.

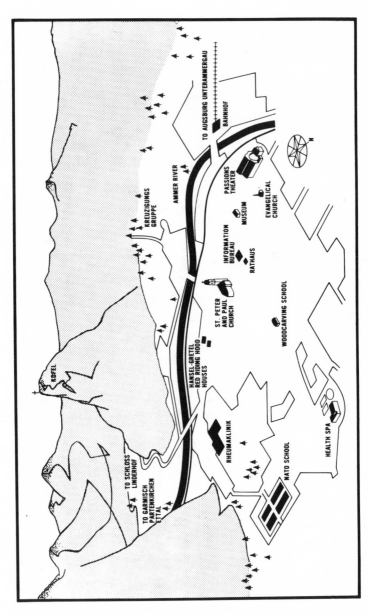

Map of Oberammergau. From the Gemeinde Oberammergau. Redrawn by the Media Center, Youngstown State University.

Oberammergau from a distance. Photo by author.

Dome of Ettal monastery. Photo by author.

Oberammergau's parish church. Photo by author.

Outside the Oberammergau Passion Hall. Photo by author.

The Oberammergau theater stage. Photo by author.

High priest with horned headdress. Drawing by Jonathan
Friedman and the Media Center, Youngstown State University.

One of the *Lebende Bilder:* Adam and Eve expelled from the Garden of Eden. From *Passion Oberammergau* (1980). Reprinted by permission of the Gemeinde Oberammergau.

Jesus and the high priests before Pilate. From *Passion Oberammergau* (1980). Reprinted by permission of the Gemeinde Oberammergau.

The scourging of Jesus. From *Passion Oberammergau*
(1980). Reprinted by permission of the Gemeinde
Oberammergau.

Jesus and Barabbas. From *Passion Oberammergau*
(1980). Reprinted by permission of the Gemeinde
Oberammergau.

Pressing thorns into flesh. From *Passion Oberammergau* (1980).
Reprinted by permission of the Gemeinde Oberammergau.

The Crucifixion. From *Passion Oberammergau* (1980).
Reprinted by permission of the Gemeinde
Oberammergau.

7

The Impact of Anti-Semitism

Give me that man that is not passion's slave, and I will wear him in my heart's core.
— Hamlet to Horatio, act 3, scene 3

Social scientists agree with Shakespeare that men are creatures of emotions, drives, and instinct. The most obvious, hunger and sex, constitute only a minor part of human behavior. According to Erich Fromm, man is driven principally by his "rational and irrational passions"—his needs for love, solidarity, freedom, and truth, as well as his ambition, greed, anger, and desire to control, submit, or destroy. "These passions move and excite him," writes Fromm. "They are the stuff from which not only dreams, but all religions, myths, drama, art are made—in short, all that makes life meaningful and worth living." Motivated by such passions, people even risk their lives.[1]

Emotional responses may be triggered in a number of ways. Some psychiatrists argue that man is aroused by isolation, pain, neurochemical or hormonal changes.[2] Others maintain that the brain is in a state of constant excitation, actively seeking a release of nervous energy. Konrad Lorenz, the German psychologist, distributes instinctive energy a little differently, parceling it out to various neural centers in the body, where it wells up till it explodes "spontaneously," without a stimulus.[3] Most authorities, however, agree that there must be an external factor before passions are aroused. Such stimuli may be verbal or visual. And the response may, in a social sense, be positive or negative. A number of examples come to mind where passions have been aroused by words alone. Almost thirty years ago, Dr. Alfred Kinsey and his associates noted differences in erotic responses of men and women to sadomasochistic stories.[4] Polemical writings through the ages have inflamed people against one another. In the twentieth century, dictators and demagogues have learned to exploit the media to their own ends. As Lorenz states, "Demagogues are well versed in the dangerous art of producing supranormal dummies to release a very dangerous form of militant enthusiasm."[5] On an individual basis, people may react in a variety of ways to flattery or insults. As for the latter, Anglo-Saxon law operates under the contradiction that while words alone do not constitute a justification for violence, it is possible that in extraordinary circumstances (when racial pejoratives are flung against blacks, Jews, or Italians) a person may "see red" and be excused his intemperate reaction.

Visual stimuli certainly awaken a wide range of responses. The 1969 U.S. Surgeon General's Report, Albert Bandura, Lawrence Donner, and Richard Walters have all noted how television's coverage of urban riots, assassinations, skyjackings, and other acts of terror has prompted a "monkey-see, monkey-do" imitative behavior, not only in this country, but across the world.[6] Labor Day or Easter telethons have mobilized the collective conscience of Americans on behalf of paraplegic children. In their living rooms or darkened theaters, people laugh at a pratfall, weep at the death of E.T., and grow angered at an injustice acted out before them. Anyone who ever attended a World Series finale, a soccer championship, or even a Little League playoff can attest to the validity of Irving Goldaber's contention that competitive games arouse aggressive behavior not only for the participants but for the spectators as well.[7] Since men cheered on their favorite gladiators or lions pitted against Christians, people have "vicariously vent[ed] their own strong emotions through identification with actors on stage."[8]

The play at Oberammergau has always affected its own cast. From the moment of selection, actors literally became the characters they portrayed. Hans Christian Andersen noted how the woodcutter Schauer, who played Jesus in 1860, could not eat or speak till he had spent time alone on the hillside.[9] Several others who portrayed Christ have fainted on the cross, overcome with exertion and nervous strain. One, Joseph Mayr, is reputed to have "died of a broken heart" after being passed over for an encore of the role in 1900.[10] Before each performance, the villagers, true to their "solemn duties," congregate in the parish church at 6:30 A.M., to pray for spiritual guidance. After the closing tableaux and final strains of the orchestra at the last performance of summer, all stand together, hands clasped, moved to tears.

Such genuine emotion was communicated to, and shared by, the audience. At the turn of the century, the evangelist Adelina Patti reported how she sat "spellbound, fascinated, still as a statue except when shaken by sobs and convulsed by weeping." Oberammergau was, to Ms. Patti, "the most wonderful scene I have ever beheld in my life."[11] In his day, W. A. Darlington searched the exiting crowd and found not one person who was not "deeply and whole-heartedly engrossed in the action that was going forward."[12] Villagers told of a scientist who had lost his entire family in a railway accident. He came to Oberammergau, bent on suicide, but left the theater with "an encouragement for living." Local legend also told of two bishops who despised one another so much, they never spoke. Because of a shortage of rooms, they were forced to share an attic overnight. After the play, they walked home, "hand in hand like two small boys who have decided to be friends."[13]

Dr. Charles Waltner, former chief of Woodside Psychiatric Hospital in Youngstown, considers such emotional identification normal and adds that feelings induced within a viewing audience depend upon environment, education, and sense of immediacy.[14] If carried too far, however, this identification could have drawbacks. In 1900, Rabbi Krauskopf related, "I had heard that some had been so wrought up by the play as to become temporarily insane, and run about town haunted by wildest hallucinations."[15] Villagers who held the roles of villains were ostracized like modern-day sin-eaters. Andreas Lang, who played the character known simply as "Rabbi," met with two actual rabbis in 1900 and told them that two English women had refused to lodge in his home because he had "persecuted Christ." In like manner, visitors shunned, even refused to touch Gregor Lechner who played Judas over two decades. Lechner told Krauskopf that he did not want his son to follow him in the role. "God forbid," said Lechner. "I love my child too much to bring the same sufferings upon him which I and my father before me have been obliged to endure."[16] It was well that the younger Lechner declined the role, for in 1922 a spectator actually tried to shoot Guido Mayr (Judas) on stage.[17]

Spectators' responses today may not be quite as extreme as they were sixty years ago, but they reflect the "edifying" impact of the play nonetheless. A group of Austrian students who attended the 1970 performance (before major editorial changes were attempted by Rümmelein and when the bulk of anti-Semitic material was intact) told Annemarie Weiss that they found the play to be "a religious experience." A young couple, who had been there in 1960 and planned to return in 1980, called the Oberammergau Passion "moving and beautiful."[18] A Danish pastor called it "striking." The leader of a Presbyterian church group from California found it "overwhelming." Others used words like "wonderful," "fascinating," "impressive," and "mysterious."[19] One visitor, reflecting the feelings of a college professor who had said earlier "that was as good as a week's retreat,"[20] declared after viewing the 1970 play, "I have had dinner with Jesus."[21] Few of those polled after the 1960 or 1970 performances expressed anti-Jewish sentiments. For the most part, they did not interpret the scenes before Pilate as conferring eternal damnation upon Jews. Annemarie Weiss was repeatedly told, "We take over the responsibility. We are fully equal in responsibility. I accept the damnation. We learned that in school." Practically all agreed that Jesus had to die for men's sins or else "we would have been lost."[22]

The same sentiments were expressed by members of my

Oberammergau tour group after attending a performance of the Passion in June 1980. When the last triumphant notes of the chorus had sounded, the audience held back momentarily, wondering whether applause was appropriate. About half did applaud. The others declined, out of what seemed to be reverence. Afterward, the Marquadts from New York enthusiastically told how the play had been a religious experience for them. They were also thrilled by the inclusion of Old Testament scenes which they interpreted to be a link between Judaism and Christianity. The Kelly sisters from Australia also came away with no ill feelings toward Jews. "Christ had to die on the cross," they told me. "He died for our sins." The schoolteachers likened the Oberammergau production to "religious drama . . . like Handel's Messiah." The Beagles and fourteen-year-old Alex Tanner saw more drama than religion in the Passion. The most negative expression I heard from anyone came from Mr. Zielinski who said, "It was pretty much what I expected." None of these people were angered or upset by what they had seen.[23] Nearly all agreed with the statement offered earlier by Franz Mussner that "the Jewish process against Jesus should not be regarded as character crippling."[24]

Most of the emotions unleashed above were of a positive nature. They may reflect a growing sensitivity among Christians to their relationship with Jews, a greater education. More likely, they are the product of the civilized world's revulsion at the Holocaust. Before World War II, the Daisenberger text employed at Oberammergau was just as likely to trigger a wave of negative passions directed specifically against the Jews.

It would be nice to believe that only certain personalities are prone to aggression or violence. Thus the entire Nazi period could be written off as an aberration. But as Anthony Storr, Clyde Kluckhohn, and Rollo May have all pointed out, human aggression is ubiquitous.[25] Fromm refines that statement somewhat, saying "vengeful" aggression is worldwide, to the ninth generation among Yakuts, longer in the case of revenge directed by Christians against Jews.[26] Normal men and women are also, to a certain degree, guilty of some form of paranoia. Worn down by stress or frustration, they welcome scapegoats and project these figures "into a mythological world, inhabited not by human beings, but by demons, ogres and witches whose evil practices can only be combatted by equal malice on our part."[27]

Irenäus Eibl-Eibesfeldt has called man's ability to transform his opponent into a "devil" more serious than the invention of weapons. "In the last analysis," the German psychologist writes, "it is this capacity to switch off pity that makes him into a cold-blooded murderer." Thanks to their highly developed intellect, people can convince themselves that their enemies are not merely objects of fear and mistrust, but monsters or vermin which "not only may, but must be killed."[28]

Stanley Milgram's experiments have demonstrated that it is not difficult to prompt a supposedly normal man to violence.[29] It is even easier to incite a group. Demagogues have always appreciated man's astonishing readiness for collective aggression."[30] What the ancient Greeks termed *enthousiasmos*, Konrad Lorenz calls *Begeisterung* (militant enthusiasm). Citing a Ukrainian proverb, Lorenz says, "When the banner is unfurled, all reason is in the trumpet." A *heiliger Schauer* (holy shiver) passes over the individual. He soars above everyday life, ready to abandon all for the satisfaction of a specific, momentary emotion. Instinctive inhibitions against hurting or killing are cast aside, and honorable men may feel "absolute righteousness even while committing atrocities." All that is necessary is the presence of the hated enemy and a sense of immediacy, a real or imagined threat. It is the kind of phenomenon noted at athletic contests where riots occur because, writes Ashley Montagu, many spectators are "not merely vicariously but actively engaged in worsting their man's opponent."[31] Adds Sol Levin, onetime head of the Department of Psychiatry at the Northeast Ohio College of Medicine: "There is a decided similarity between aggressive behavior in a pogrom and sporting events. You are dealing with open aggression which tends to loosen boundaries. If someone starts it, even the meekest, mildest man will shout, 'Kill him! Kill the enemy!' What I call a war behavior. Then the man wakes up and asks, 'Did that happen to me?' It's almost as if he were in an hypnotic trance."[32]

Montagu suggests that sporting events may serve as a healthy outlet, catharsis, for the universal rage of man, but Dr. Irving Goldaber, whose Miami-based research center focuses upon crowd and spectator behavior, takes a different view. "Demagogues are sophisticated in hype," Goldaber told me, "but not in defusing emotions. What if it goes over the top—a kidnapping of a racehorse, the killing of an athlete? The only way you can tell if the behavior is harmful is after the fact, if there is an incident. Then you can say, 'Look, I told you so.' "[33] Once collective action has begun, Hans Toch informs us, it acquires a momentum of its own. People without grievance may be drawn into the mob or pack, lured by a desire for adventure or the need to belong. Whether the aggressive behavior takes the form of a demonstration, riot, or massacre, it succeeds if it has the sanction of peers or history. Wrote Toch, "The Ghost of Riots Past hovers like a friendly specter over each new outbreak; it provides historical sanction, and it furnishes vivid images of how and why to proceed."[34]

The spoken or written word have long been instrumental in fomenting violence. To have enemies, says Gordon Allport, one must have labels, linguistic tags which build fences between people. This antilocution, verbal assault, facilitates the transition from one level of prejudice to another and culminates in physical attack.[35] Novels, short stories, or newspaper items reinforce hostility, but actually seeing hated stereotypes played out on film or in the theater is even more disturbing. Art, wrote Morse Peckham, is a Circe. "It can turn men into beasts."[36] According to Dr. Levin, "The more sensory channels that get filled, the more easily one can identify the enemy."[37] In a more flowery fashion, Dolf Zillmann concurs, stating, "Communications involving concepts that relate to the individual's acute emotional state potentially reiterate arousal-maintaining cognitions."[38] Zillmann's words ring especially true for Oberammergau:

In the case of annoyance, this means that films that feature provocation and retaliation, annoyance and anger, mistreatment, hostility, aggression and violence are unlikely to disrupt the maintenance of annoyance and anger even if they are otherwise involving, because they tend to remind the viewer of his or her own feelings. In other words, they simply do not let the viewer forget about the mistreatment he or she has suffered and/or the reprisals he or she may have contemplated, but was unable to carry out.[39]

Consider, then, the impact of Passion plays in past centuries upon audiences which were neither literate nor privy to papal encyclicals dealing with ecumenism. Constantly exposed to homilies about the treachery, greed, and satanic influence of Jews, they brought with them to the theater a religious zeal not unlike that of today's football fan. Theirs was a world of good pitted against evil. The evil ones were responsible for the bloodied crucifixes which hung in churches from Europe to Latin America. Many Christians brought with them a "pathological absorption in the physical wounds of Jesus."[40] Now the Jewish merchants, priests, and mob responsible for these hideous torments were reveling before them onstage.

While conceding difficulty in ascertaining the extent or quality of influence of bigoted sermons and religious dramas, Salo Baron declares, "The masses could not long remain unaffected by their influential opinion molders."[41] Leon Poliakov likened the vigor of feelings provoked by Passion plays to the same boxing matches mentioned by Montagu or "better still with the political celebrations favored by the monolithic parties."[42] The comparison with sporting events or rallies appeals also to Dr. Goldaber, who offers that people have come to Oberammergau for some specific need: "The event becomes an enabling agent to fulfill that need. Just as spectators at a sporting event, they come as latent actors. An emotional frenzy can be reached once they are legitimized as actors. And like spectators at a sporting event, when you have a crowd that is anticipating a physical experience, it will have a physical experience."[43]

Historically, such frustrations have not remained pent up. Writes Leon Poliakov: "The violence of these remarks (and we must remember that they are being spoken on a stage!) remains painful and difficult to accept in our own day. Imagine the effect they must have had on the childlike and unsophisticated mentality of the men of the medieval period! In a total identification, the crowds lived Christ's agony intensely, transferring all their rage to his tormentors, with a real massacre often following the depicted one."[44] After Passion play performances, Jewish populations, even in large cities, were not safe. Pogroms took place in Freiburg (where anti-Jewish scenes were banned in 1338), Frankfurt (where authorities instituted special measures to protect Jews in 1469), and Rome (where all Passion dramas were banned in 1539 because they were followed regularly by the sacking of the ghetto along the Tiber).[45]

There is no recorded instance of a mob swarming into the streets of Oberammergau looking for Jews to kill. For one thing, they would have had to travel miles before they would have found one in this part of Bavaria. Only rarely, and for short periods, have Jews ever lived in the village. It is also true, as Hans Lamm, *Rosh Kehillah* of the Munich Jewish community told me, "We are not living in the Middle Ages any more. Some water went down the Hudson and the Isar rivers since then. Did the pogroms or Holocaust start with Oberammergau? I think that nobody came out of the play as an anti-Semite if he was unprejudiced before, and vice versa. Nobody became a Jew-lover when he was an anti-Semite before. It's a show, an experience. Whether it's a religious or dramatic experience depends upon the religious attitude of the person who sees it." Lamm also quoted a Jewish friend who told him, "Were I no Jew and understood no German, then I would leave the great building and the little village clearly inspired after the seven hour performance."[46]

Others have not been so charitable in their evaluations. Rabbi Krauskopf found Jewish friends who told him that if they were not Jewish the play would have led them "to hate the Jew ever after." Thirty years later, the *Christian Century* agreed, "The Passion Play drips poison." The editors of this prominent Protestant journal warned that the emphasis upon Jesus being beaten, hammered with nails and dangled on the cross may "excite glands" of some spectators to "go out and get the Jews." The *Century* considered the Passion inflammatory and likened it to atrocity stories from World War I which were designed to work up hatred of men in the trenches. Said the *Century*, "No drama which incites pogroms should be put on in the name of Jesus."[47]

The *Christian Century*'s comments were addressed not to a medieval mentality but to people in the twentieth century. While much water had indeed washed down the Isar and Hudson, hostility toward Jews had not abated. "The masses of adults are mentally developed to a point lower than a normal fifteen-year-old child," lamented the *Century*'s editors in 1930. More ominous, "Half of the 682 million nominal Christians in the world today cherish a primary and naive hero and villain tale of the crucifixion."[48] The mass of Christians in the world in 1930 required a simple scapegoat, one whose villainy they could readily identify. Even before Adolf Hitler, human aggression, paranoia, and projection fixed upon this contemporary horror in the form of the Jew.

A strong argument might be made that the general level of intelligence has not increased since the *Century* made its observations. Certainly the persistence of anti-Semitic images in the United States and France, despite the Holocaust, is depressing. More disturbing is the recent revelation by the West German government that as many as 18 percent of the people in "free" Germany look back upon the Nazi period as "the good old days."[49] Negative aspects of bonding, noted by Eibl-Eibesfeldt, Toch, Milgram, and others, are still very much in evidence at Oberammergau where in 1970 Hans Zander likened the "animal group psychology of spectators" to "penguins."[50] People go to Oberammergau disliking Jews and come away liking them less. Ernst Maria Lang conceded as much, saying, "Anti-Semites come as spectators and are reinforced in their ways."[51] A few are even brave enough to vent traditional anti-Semitic feelings. One told Annemarie Weiss:

> The Jews are damned. In the moment when they crucified the Christ, the Lord repudiated them. They can entreat him what they want—you see what they endured in the concentration camps. It didn't help them at all; the Jews are damned. They can pray all day, fast and plead, but the Lord God doesn't hear them. They are damned. They have no resting place on earth. They haven't recognized Christ. Even today they don't convert. They still wait for their messiah. You can turn a Jew around, however you want, but a Jew is a Jew.[52]

Not only has anti-Semitism the sanction of peers and history, the prerequisites for violence noted by Toch, until 1965 it carried the tacit blessing of the church. Vatican II relieved Jews of the charge of deicide, but it has taken more than fifteen years for changes in theology to seep into Oberammergau. As Msgr. C. M. Genewein of the archbishop's office in Munich told me, "It certainly takes a long time to change that. Jesus was killed by the Lord for the sins of man. That's what the church says. The people in the villages say certainly still—it's the Jews. But we make efforts to tell them again and again—Holy Friday, Easter—it was not the Jewish guilt that killed him, but the guilt of all of us." Allowing that anti-Semitism has been a problem for the church, Monsignor Genewein added, "I have no explanation for anti-Semitism. I have no explanation for Nazism. How was it possible in a people to establish Hitler and his gang. I have no explanation for Marxism. I think something like that must be inborn, a potential to, let's say, get perverse. Maybe the temptation of hatred and *Macht* (power) can make something like that."[53]

For over three hundred years, Jews have been portrayed at Oberammergau as the *Volk der Gottesmörder*. Even in 1980, thirty-five years after Auschwitz, the revamped play offered (*a*) avaricious Jewish money dealers bent on gaining revenge against Jesus; (*b*) spiteful Pharisees and rabbis who emphasized the breach between the code of Moses and Christianity; (c) horned high priests conspiring to eliminate Jesus by extralegal means; (d) constant reference to a new covenant and the exclusion of Jews from salvation; (e) choral interludes where Jews were referred to as deceitful, blind, greedy, corrupt, or inhuman; (f) a noble Pilate; (g) a Jewish mob shrieking twenty-five times for the death of Christ; and (h) heartrending scenes of flogging, humiliation, and crucifixion.

How harmful these images may be is still being debated. There frankly is no way of telling how many hundreds of thousands of visitors to Oberammergau before or after the Holocaust carried anti-Semitic feelings home with them as lasting souvenirs of the Passion play. In 1900, Rabbi Krauskopf expressed concern over such silent backpacking, saying, "I know of nothing that could have rooted deeper among these people, the existing prejudice against the Jew, and spread wider the world's hatred of him than this Passion Play of Oberammergau."[54] Douglas Hare minimizes the impact, since the production is normally staged only every ten years.[55] Professor Swidler, on the other hand, considers Oberammergau part of "the whole warp and woof of Christian anti-Semitism." "It is no more a problem in encouraging anti-Semitism than many other things," he told me, "rather it reflects mainline anti-Semitism."[56]

Whether one subscribes to Rabbi Krauskopf's view, it is reasonable to assume that most visitors to Oberammergau were possessed of normal human emotions, including rage, hate, and aggression, which could be stimulated by the written word or acted scene. According to NEOUCOM's Sol Levin: "We all have basic hostility, aggression, which we learn to deal with in a reasonably sublimated way. Any number of events, however, can channel rage with moral blessing. As long as people need to feel comfortable and need to satisfy their own murderous rage, they are looking to channel rage away from themselves or their own family, what I call the leapfrog effect. The Jews, by virtue of their supposedly knowing more, killing Jesus, their wealth, became universal scapegoats. If you have a climate where there is tremendous rage, related at an interpersonal level, anything like this, a common event that people can use becomes the focus of destruction toward the minority group. It can be contagious, as in Nazi Germany."[57]

Youngstown's Charles Waltner, who endured Hungarian fascism before immigrating to the United States in 1941, likens the Oberammergau Passion to a thermometer. "It is not the cause of fever, but rather measures fever," says Dr. Waltner. Interestingly enough, Dr. Waltner, like Professor Levin, allows that the "thermometer" may also serve as an instrument of pain. This was particularly so during the Nazi epoch, when the Passion ("a byproduct of anti-Semitism") was useful in dehumanizing Jews. Adds Waltner: "If people are frustrated, angry, have lost what they believed belongs to them, are despairing of the future, they look for a scapegoat, one who can defend themselves least. There are periods of relapses in man's behavior, when just like an individual there could be cultural paranoia. The German experience was that with Bismarck, the Kaiser, and the military, they were losing constantly. Then came the Versailles treaty. Their own personal security was involved. Rather than accepting their own responsibility, there was a feeling that they could not succeed because of an external conspiracy. Along came the messiah—Hitler."[58]

More than anything else, the Nazi phenomenon confirms the actual danger of theater like Oberammergau. The Nazis did not have to invent the Passion play. Rather, as Drs. Waltner, Levin, Swidler, and Goldaber have attested, they welcomed it as part of an existing propaganda apparatus. "As a world citizen, an American, a Jew, a human being, we know it institutionalized anti-Semitism," says Irving Goldaber. "Although we cannot *yet* point to a particular incident of violence as a result of the play, we know that it reinforced general, cultural anti-Semitism, placing the anti-Semitic legions in the front row."[59] To which, Yale's Dr. Robert Jay Lifton, author of *The Broken Connection*, adds: "Yes, of course, the famed passion play at Oberammergau could have significantly intensified anti-Jewish images and feelings. I understand victimization as stemming from what I call 'rival immortality systems,' and here the Jewish 'rival' is perceived as evil, and of course the source of the murder of God's human embodiment."[60]

No hymn of reconciliation, Oberammergau has always been an exhortation to revenge. The play, in part, symbolized animosity built up over two thousand years against Jews as Christ killers, usurers, well-poisoners, blood polluters, capitalists, and Bolsheviks. Given proper exploitation, it could serve to channel pent-up aggression. All that was needed was the proper stimulus and director. For Germans in the 1930s, this was provided by Adolf Hitler.

8

The Tercentenary: The Passion Play as Nazi Propaganda

That a Passion play could reinforce anti-Semitic prejudice or generate potential violence was freely admitted by the villagers of Oberammergau in the preface to their 1950 playbook. "Sometimes," they wrote, "in earlier times and at other places, it has happened that spectators were stirred to take sides against Judas or the Jews." That could not happen at Oberammergau, however. Such behavior could only stem from a misunderstanding of the Passion, which "stands aloof from history and worldly conflicts and has no part in the internecine strife of nations."[1]

The integrity of the Oberammergauers and their Passion was put to a test during the Nazi era. The village planned a tercentenary celebration for 1934. Beginning with Whit Monday, May 21, through September 23 of that year, eighty-four performances would be given. Concerned that certain aspects of the new German regime might repel their regular clientele, authorities assured Western journalists there would be no departure from the traditional text or production. As the *New York Times* reported, "The representations will be dominated by a Christian, primarily Roman

Catholic spirit, and any heterodox influence will be kept out."[2]

It was repeatedly denied that the Nazi government had made any attempt to modify the text or thrust of the Passion. In July 1933, six months after Hitler took power, Josef Raab of the municipal council told the press, "We don't believe that the new movement in Germany will have any such effect. Why should anti-Semitic principles induce any hostility toward this great Biblical story? We shall go ahead with our plans for next year's tercentenary presentation undeterred by political disturbances." Benedikt Stückl, manager of the Passion play theater, who was to play the role of Nathaniel, added: "We shall none of us feel the least reluctance about playing our Jewish roles. Politics passes such things as our play on one side, just as do international hatreds. In 1922, people feared that war hatreds would keep the Americans and the British away from our play. On the contrary, the play proved one of the greatest influences in reconciling the people after the terrible slaughter." Anton Lang, the Christ of 1900, 1910, and 1922, Prologue in 1930 and 1934, summarized the feelings of villagers, saying, "Tell my many kind friends in America who often write me that the spirit of Oberammergau is unchanged."[3]

In its first year, the Nazi regime was occupied with more important matters than the Passion at Oberammergau. This was, after all, the period of *Gleichschaltung*, the smashing of independent bodies which might oppose nazism. Newspapers, trade unions, schools, and law courts had to be purified. By July 1933, when Herr Raab, Lang, and Stückl were reassuring their friends, Hitler had succeeded in dissolving all political parties in Germany but his own. At the same time, Franz von Papen achieved a concordat with the papacy, relieving twenty-one million Catholics of self-doubts generated long before by Bismarck's *Kulturkampf* while simultaneously promoting passive, superloyal behavior which some have labeled the "Gehorsam Mentalität."[4] When the Oberammergauers were completing their rehearsals in the spring of 1934, Hitler was planning to act against a threat from within his own movement. In April, he secured the backing of the *Wehrmacht* against the *Sturmabteilung* (Brown Shirts) headed by his old crony Ernst Röhm. On the night of June 30–July 1, when Oberammergau was celebrating its feast of reconciliation, some four hundred German leaders, including Röhm, Otto Strasser, General Kurt von Schleicher, and Gustav von Kahr, were executed in a purge known as the Night of Long Knives.[5] The death of eighty-seven-year-old President Paul von Hindenburg in August 1934, removed the last obstacle before Nazi hegemony. The passing of "the father of the fatherland" was observed in a dramatic tribute at Oberammergau.[6] More significantly, Adolf Hitler could now fuse the positions of president and chancellor into that of führer, absolute leader.

The fate of Oberammergau was not completely ignored by the Nazi hierarchy during those early years. Disclaimers from village spokesmen notwithstanding, Josef Goebbels had made it clear that all forms of art must conform to the political system. In June 1934, Goebbels reminded members of the German Theater Association meeting at the Dresden State Opera that "art and politics spring from the same essential core, and the rules of their trade are, in principal, the same." For nearly a century, said Goebbels, German art had been victimized by experimentation. Now, however, the German people had achieved their own revolution, with its unique dynamic and sense of justice. That revolution gave art a new significance. It altered the relationship of people to art, and vice versa. Art, he declared, "is a child of the times." There could be no deviation from what the revolution determined as legitimate, for if art does not conform to politics, "it may influence politics."[7] The same message, demanding conformity with the philosophy of nazism, was repeated by Goebbels at a Strength through Joy meeting in Berlin in November 1937.[8]

Hitler, too, had more than a passing interest in art, or more specifically Oberammergau. In a speech to the Reichstag on March 23, 1933, he emphasized the need for a "thorough moral purging" of the nation. The education system, theater, cinema, press, must reflect "realities" of an era when "blood and race will once more become the source of artistic intuition."[9] Art, racial values, and politics constituted the main themes in Hitler's address for Party Day in September 1935, when the Nuremberg Laws were promulgated.[10] Not surprisingly, then, Oberammergau occupied a special position in his cultural perspective. Georg Lang, the Passion's producer in 1934, noted how Hitler had attended the last performance in 1930 and was "most enthusiastic in his comments."[11] In fact, Hitler called the Passion an "Anschauungsunterricht für Rassenunterschiede" (an instruction for racial distinction).[12] As late as July 5, 1942, Hitler said of Oberammergau:

> One of our most important tasks will be to save future generations from a similar political fate and to remain forever watchful in the knowledge of the menace of Jewry. For this reason alone it is vital that the Passion Play be continued at Oberammergau; for never has the menace of Jewry been so convincingly portrayed as in this presentation of what happened in the times of the Romans. There one sees in Pontius Pilate a Roman racially and intellectually superior, there he stands out like a firm, clean rock in the middle of the whole muck and mire of Jewry.[13]

It is not difficult to understand why the Passion appealed to Hitler. Like the Bavarian villagers, Hitler was provincial, raised in a relatively small mountain town. Trained as a Catholic, he imbibed anti-Jewish rants in church, long before his celebrated introduction to political anti-Semitism in Vienna at age eighteen. A fanatical devotee of Wagner, Hitler shared some of his hero's enchantment for "the sublimely mournful ritual of the Holy Passion."[14] The spectacle of hundreds of persons onstage, choral chants, and thunderous orchestral passages resembled Wagnerian opera. The betrayal of Jesus by Judas was nothing less than the *Dolchstoss* (stab in the back) perpetrated by Jews against Germany in 1918. And then there was the relationship between Mary and Jesus. Hitler revered his mother and could readily identify with the touching scenes at Bethany, where Jesus took leave of the Virgin, or when she followed him along the Via Dolorosa, and finally at Golgotha. He was Jesus, Klara Polzl Mary, when on the cross Christ proclaimed: "Mother, see your son! Son, see your mother!"[15] But he would not submit to the Jews without a struggle. As he shouted in one of his early speeches:

> I say my feeling as a Christian points me to my Lord and Saviour as a fighter. It points me to the man who once in loneliness, surrounded only by a few followers, recognized these Jews for what they were and summoned men to the fight against them, and who, God's truth! was greatest not as sufferer but as fighter. In boundless love as a Christian and as a man I read through the passage which tells us how the Lord at last rose in his might and seized the scourge to drive out of the Temple the brood of vipers and adders. How terrific was his fight for the world against the Jewish poison after 2000 years, with deepest emotion I recognize more profoundly than ever before in the fact that it was this that he had to shed his blood upon the cross. As a Christian I have no duty to allow myself to be cheated, but I have the duty to be a fighter for truth and justice.[16]

There are those, of course, who dismiss Hitler's references to Christ as platform rhetoric. Of point 24 in the original Nazi party program in 1920, which spoke of "positive Christianity," and repeated declarations in 1933 that the government "regards Christianity as the foundation" of Germany's national life,[17] Ferdinand Friedensburg says, "In the beginning Hitler liked to simulate a certain degree of Christian mentality and respect for the church."[18] In reality, though, Hitler was so committed to de-Jewing Christianity, that his attitude soon approximated "Christophobia."[19] Not only did the Nazis hate Jews for killing Jesus, wrote Maurice Samuel, they also hated them for bringing Jesus into the world. An ideology which subscribed to pagan symbolism and Nietzschean morality could only be what Richard Rubenstein called "dialectically negated, heretical Christianity."[20] In practice, Hitler's contemptuous treatment of the bishops' conferences at Fulda, his suppression and arrest of church figures who opposed his regime, invalidated his identification with Christ.[21] As Franklin Littell states, "In theological terms, Nazism was the true—if illegitimate offspring of a false relationship between the Christian church and the ethnic bloc or nation."[22]

Even allowing that Hitler's public expressions of faith were cynically inspired, the fact remains that he built upon a hatred of Jews which had been taught first by the church catechism. In a dinner discussion with two bishops, the Nazi leader explained he was merely putting into effect what Christianity preached and practiced for two thousand years.[23] The identical point was regretfully conceded by Gregory Baum of Saint Michael's College, University of Toronto, who recently wrote:

> While it would be historically untruthful to blame the Christian Church for Hitler's anti-Semitism and the monstrous crimes committed by him and his followers, what is true, alas, is that the Church has produced an abiding contempt among Christians for Jews and all things Jewish, a contempt that aided Hitler's purposes. The Church made the Jewish people a symbol of unredeemed humanity; it painted a picture of the Jews as a blind, stubborn, carnal, and perverse people, an image that was fundamental in Hitler's choice of the Jews as the scapegoat.[24]

Christian anti-Semitism was a tool by which Hitler could manipulate the feelings of the German masses, and in this process Oberammergau acquired new importance. But apart from Hitler's personal interest in the Passion play, Nazi officials could not afford to detach themselves entirely from the village's 1934 production. The nation's reception of four hundred thousand foreign visitors would reflect upon its ability to accommodate much larger crowds coming to the Olympic Games in 1936. A successful pageant would cloak the regime with an aura of respectability. Tourists would be impressed not only with the sense of continuity but also with the cleanliness, order, and utility of the new Germany.[25] The Passion's simplistic assaults upon Jews as enemies of civilization served to justify anti-Semitic programs and might even win friends for nazism. It simply was too important as a device of propaganda to be left to the staging of Bavarian amateurs. Finally, the play always generated income, perhaps as much as a million dollars in a given season. In a small but significant way, then, Oberammergau could be a boon to the sagging German economy.

Far from keeping its hands off the production, the government did everything possible to promote the tercentenary. Because the U.S. dollar was down in ratio to German currency, American visitors were informed they could purchase tickets to the play at a 40 percent saving over the 1930 price. Housing costs in "homes furnished to the height of Bavarian luxury" were also down, 60 percent. The Nazi government was subsidizing a special railway ticket that granted a 33 percent rebate for trips to Oberammergau from all parts of Germany.[26] The Hamburg-American and German-Lloyd steamship lines took out two-page ads in *Travel Magazine,* replete with etchings of the sun beaming onto the stage where stood a subdued Christ. The steamship companies reminded readers that these would be the only performances of the Passion until 1940.[27] A similar half-page ad in the *Times* (London) coaxed people to "come to Germany and see for yourself" this land of "wondrous beauty and infinite variety." Travelers were especially urged to "visit Oberammergau's colorful spectacle and reverent representation." The Cook's Agency, which was responsible for the promotion, advised its readers that they could save 27–33 percent on registered marks (traveler's checks purchased before entering Germany).[28]

The German government especially coddled foreign drama critics. Throughout Oberammergau's rehearsal period, such writers were granted free access to the village, where trappings of nazism were deliberately downplayed. On the eve of the premiere in May 1934, the government arranged for a first-class train to take representatives of the British, Scandinavian, American, and Dutch press from Munich to Oberammergau. The Nazis must have done a good selling job because most of the reporters who traveled to Oberammergau came away impressed with the pristine nature of the Passion. *Commonweal's* Edythe Helen Browne found the play "different in particulars" but was more transfixed by the spell of the village, its downy beds, the taproom of the Alte Poste Hotel, and the outdoor frescoes.[29] The same Bavarian charm dulled the observations of the *Times* correspondent, who adjudged the 1934 text "completely free of political distortions." The *Times's* critic found some evidence of the Nazi regime in town—a salute now and then, a swastika flag at the *Stadthaus*—but offered that "a more peaceful and friendly place could be hard to find in Europe."[30] A like observation was offered by the *New York Times's* Frederick Birchall who found Oberammergau "a mighty pleasant place, rejoicing in the purest air and most picturesque surroundings in all the mountain country around."[31] G. E. R. Geyde noted a few men in brown shirts who greeted one another with the Nazi salute. There were portraits of Hitler in some shop windows, even a swastika or two attached to cars.[32] But, observed the second correspondent for the *New York Times,* "There is no other Bavarian village of the size in which the signs and symbols of the German Nazi revolution are so inconspicuous as in Oberammergau just now."[33]

Far from organizing boycotts, Western churchmen, educators, and journalists urged the faithful to attend the Passion. At a time when former inmates of Nazi concentration camps were already revealing the "deliberate instruments of torture and terrorism" operative at Oranienburg, Hohnstein, Lichtenburg, and Dachau,[34] authorities in Oberammergau could report they were "very satisfied" with advance bookings.[35] America was expected to send 50,000 visitors. In Canada, the National Education Council announced that 2,000 students and teachers under the direction of McGill University Chancellor E. W. Beatty would attend a performance in August. In Britain, the archbishop of Canterbury expressed the naïve hope of 15,000 of his countrymen who would make the pilgrimage when he prayed "that a great gathering may assemble at Oberammergau to receive for themselves the deep impression which the passion play cannot fail to give and with its inspiration to hasten the time when, forgetting the misunderstandings of the past, the nations may live together in mutual understanding and good will."[36]

To speak of goodwill and Daisenberger's text in the same breath is, as we have shown, a contradiction. To believe that the Oberammergau Passion in 1934 would prove impervious to Nazi influence borders on fantasy. A discerning critic would have observed that in April 1933, Alois Lang (Christus in 1930) attributed delays in cast selection to political changes taking place in Germany. Said Lang, "Our former parish councils have been dissolved as a result of the National Socialist victory, and must be reformed in accordance with the new principle of 'equalization' so that their party representation will correspond to the votes cast in the Reichstag election."[37] When the new council finally got around to choosing members of the cast, the selection took place under the supervision of Hermann Eisser, the Bavarian state minister that Hitler had appointed high commissioner for Tourist Traffic. Puffed the *Völkischer Beobachter* of these proceedings: "Under the influence of the National Socialist victory, the vote was held for the first time not in the customary secrecy, but rather openly so that each voter could openly and manly express himself for or against a candidate."[38]

In a town where the Bürgermeister Raimund Lang had been a Nazi party member since 1932, the assignments parceled out for 1934 were significant. The director was Georg Johann Lang, Daisenberger's grandnephew, a dour-faced individual who became one of the first Nazis in Oberammergau and served Goebbels's propaganda ministry willingly until the end of World War II.[39] One year after the tercentenary, Lang would direct Anton Lang (the most fa-mous Christ of this century) in an anti-Jewish drama called *The Harvest*. At a time when the Nuremberg Laws were denouncing sexual relations between Jews and non-Jews as bestial, Oberammergau repeatedly depicted the "betrayal" of an Aryan girl by a Jew.[40]

With the exception of Judas and Pilate (portrayed by Hans Zwink and Melchior Breitsamter respectively), the major roles at Oberammergau in 1934 went to individuals whose loyalties were unquestioned. Alois Lang, the forty-two-year-old wood-carver selected as Christ, joined the Nazi party in 1939. Eight of his 12 apostles also were members of the NSDAP, including relatives Johann Lang (who joined the party in 1933) and Andreas Lang (a party member after 1938). Anni Rutz, the young typist who played Mary, was a member of the *NS Frauenschaft*. The *Dekorateur* (stage manager) Eduard Lang had joined the NSDAP in 1933. The families of Hubert Mayr (Peter) and Hugo Rutz (Caiaphas) counted Nazi party members since 1933. So too the Bier-lings, Preisingers, Bohns, Frimbergers, Funks, Heinzellers, Streibls, Zwinks, and Otts. Of 714 persons who took part in the play, 152 were party members before May 1, 1937, the date arbitrarily selected by Allied officials after World War II to define pure Nazis. The figure takes on added significance when it is understood that more cast members joined the party after that date and that many of the 700 onstage in 1934 were simply children used in tableaux or mob scenes.[41]

After the war, the Nazis in Oberammergau would maintain they had been "bullied" into joining the party. Josef Raab, a self-styled "passive" member of the party since 1938, ex-plained that his own membership had been forced onto him (*a*) to retain his post as administrative inspector in 1937, then (*b*) to keep his son in an academic *Gymnasium* in 1940.[42] Alois Lang claimed that he resigned his post as town coun-cillor in 1933 rather than accede to an ukase ordering him to become a Nazi. Before a denazification panel in Garmisch in 1947, Lang portrayed himself as a foe of Hitler, a benefactor of the few Jews who lived in Oberammergau. Because of his alleged opposition, the Nazis withheld licenses to operate a hotel-cafe for several years. Confronted with perpetual poverty, Lang reluctantly joined the party.[43]

Lang and Raab were typical of most Oberammergauers. Far from being sympathetic to nazism, the people claimed after the war that their village was known as the *Schwarze Dorf* (the black village or village of black sheep) because so few Nazi leaders come out of Oberammergau during the twelve years of Hitler's rule. When Nazi party meetings were called, the Bürgermeister "always" had to send messengers from house to house commanding people to attend. Even then, the *Ortsgruppenleiter* had to open such meetings to members of the women's labor service to give them a semblance of good attendance.[44] Hans Maier, director of the 1980 Passion, recalls that members of the Catholic students league refused to join the Hitler Youth and were slow in registering for military service.[45] People "hated" the greeting "Heil Hitler" which supplanted the traditional "Grüss Gott" or "Guten Morgen." "The fact is," Bürgermeister Raab wrote Allied authorities in 1946, "that in no rural district were party institutions as badly received as in Oberammergau. In Oberammergau live only opponents of Nazism."[46]

The tale of a village of living saints would be commendable, if true, but unfortunately it is not. The baser instincts of the Oberammergauers were already revealed in 1922 when Anton Lang, the gentle Christ for that year's hymn of reconciliation, informed Ferdinand Reyher that World War I had destroyed "the old joy" in making the Passion. "France will never be satisfied until Germany is destroyed," said Lang. "We hope no French will come. If they come, we must take care of them. There is too much hate against France." Noting how Germany's national catastrophe had become an obsession for its people, Reyher concluded, "The new hate of all Germany for France was packed into those words."[47]

Four decades and one world war later, Tom Driver detected the same hostility in Oberammergau. Wrote Driver, "What is present is something older and deeper than Nazism—a Bavarian, if not a German racial consciousness supported by a conservative religious culture. The pity is that the Bavarian seems hardly able to distinguish between his religious feelings, his anti-Jewish prejudices, and his racial and cultural pride."[48] Like so many other Germans, the villagers want to dismiss the Nazi period from their memories as an embarrassing, ugly page in history. Some declined to join the party. None was sent to concentration camps. The bulk responded to nazism with the same fervor that marked the rest of Bavaria. In the first elections held after the Nazi takeover, the NSDAP won five seats of ten on the village council.[49] Such support only increased during the remainder of the Hitler epoch. According to Walter Behr, chief of the Theater Control Section for the U.S. Military Government of Bavaria from 1946 to 1948, "The whole village of Oberammergau had one of the highest percentages of Nazi followers."[50] Of twenty-five hundred townspeople, some have estimated the number who were active Nazis at as much as 60 percent.[51]

Given such a background, it should not surprise that contemporary political ideology did seep into the Passion play. In 1934, the community of Oberammergau commissioned the poet Leo Weismantel of Obersinn, Rhön, to create a five-act play which was to be performed on alternate days with the Passion. In his "Oberammergauer Gelübdesspiel," dramatizing what happened during the plague year, Weismantel had the people pray:

> We come to thee, o Lord—
> In holy dresses which thy son had borne,
> In the dresses of those who have betrayed and hated Him.[52]

Those lines were also incorporated in the preface of the 1934 playbook. Even before that, however, the reader would learn that "the German people and its tribes" had been spared the dreadful misery not only of plague but of "Bolshevism, this pestilence of abandonment of the race created by God." And further, "Instead of the imminent ruin we experience the fortune of a new life which unites us all in our race. Is there any time more favorable than these days of the suppression of the antichristian powers in our fatherland to remember the price the Son of God Himself paid for His people, the people who adhere to Him and to His banner."[53]

The denunciation of Bolshevism reflected Hitler's crusade for "real Christianity" against "a Bolshevist culture, against an atheistic movement, against criminality," expressed at Coblenz in August 1934.[54] Remarkably, though, Oberammergau's racial slurs were consistent not merely with the tenets of nazism but also with prevailing church thinking in Bavaria. Cardinal Erich Faulhaber had said at Advent in 1933, "From the church's point of view, there is no objection whatever to racial research and race culture." The cardinal, whose diocese included Oberammergau, did advise that love of one's own race must not lead to hatred of another.[55] In 1938, Faulhaber would offer words of sympathy to Munich Jews, victims of the *Kristallnacht* pogroms which left their synagogues in ruins and many of their number in jail. In 1933, however, he paved the way for later torment by making it clear that modern Jews were cut off from divine blessing. Said Faulhaber: "After the death of Christ, Israel was dismissed from the service of Revelation. She had not known the time of her visitation. She had repudiated and rejected the Lord's Anointed, had driven Him out of the city and nailed Him to the cross. Then the veil of the Temple was rent, and with it the covenant between the Lord and His people. The daughters of Sion received the bill of divorce, and from that time forth Assuerus wanders, forever restless over the face of the earth."[56]

There were other changes in the 1934 production, all of them attributable to "current tendencies" in Germany. Wrote the *New York Times*'s Frederick Birchall, "Subtly, though unmistakably, there is a new note in the presentation. As is, perhaps, natural in a Germany newly made over, it is a note of virility and strength." Where Anton Lang had portrayed Christ as a character of meekness, humility, and infinite patience, Alois Lang wished to create bolder illusions of a prophet-leader. Like Hitler's Jesus, the fighter in the Temple, Lang told reporters he wished to emphasize his savior's heroic side, his strength in adversity. Pilate, too, underwent a transformation. According to Birchall, "Never has Pilate seemed more scornful of Caiaphas and his fellow priests Annas and Nathaniel. Pilate stands out pleading with the persecuting hierarchs, an Aryan who is their noble foe." Even worse, noted Birchall, "Never have Oberammergau's Jewish mobs been more virulent, never have the Pharisees and scribes who invoke the mob been more vehement than this year."[57]

If in peaceful times, among relatively stable people, the Passion can reinforce or inflame anti-Semitic impulses, one can only imagine its impact upon Germans and others disposed to treat Jews with contempt fifty years ago. The *Times*, like Birchall, found the tercentenary to be an epic of sustained enmity of money changers, bitterness of Pharisees, and scenes dominated by the theme of vengeance, but commented dryly that the play was a tragedy from "which a spectator may take away what he is by temperament equipt to discover in it."[58] The people of Oberammergau may offer all the disclaimers and anti-Nazi protests they can muster, but a truer picture of their temperament emerged on August 13, 1934. On that date, Adolf Hitler returned to the village, not as a simple citizen as in 1930, but with Hindenburg now dead, as the führer, Germany incarnate.

As the *Völkischer Beobachter* described it, "The village of passion players and woodcarvers experienced a great, joyful surprise. Totally unexpected, the Führer, Reichschancellor Hitler came to Oberammergau." Hitler had come from Munich early in the morning by auto, with his personal adjutant Sepp Dietrich, Gruppenführer Bruckner, Oberführer Schaub, and Art Academy Professor Adolf Ziegler. Shortly before 8 A.M., when most of the audience were still filing to their seats, he entered the theater from the second doorway to the left. As soon as the people recognized him, "They shouted in spontaneous enthusiasm a thousandfold heil to the Führer until the great play began." During the first half of the performance, Hitler supposedly followed the play "with deep emotion." At intermission, Bürgermeister Lang stepped onto the stage and solemnly offered the village's appreciation to Hitler. Lang also instructed the spectators to follow the play in silence, since the führer had come for the sole purpose of "edifying our holy Passion Play."[59]

Now, as people bolted from the theater to get a glimpse of Hitler in the street, "joy burst forth everywhere," "an indescribable jubilation." Houses were decked out in "the shining red of the Swastika flag." Uniformed Hitler Youth strutted about, singing the German national anthem, the "Horst Wessel Lied," the "Lied of the Saar." Members of the *Bund Deutscher Mädchen* gathered every conceivable mountain flower to strew in the path of the modern savior. Police, gendarmes, and firemen formed a wall to restrain the crowds. "The press of humanity was so great it was hardly possible for his crowd to proceed."[60]

Hitler went on to the Hotel Wittelsbach, operated by an old Nazi chum Max Streibl, to eat lunch. The crowd followed and filled the small square, shouting in unison: "We want to see our Führer on the balcony, for only a minute!" For two solid hours, "the enthusiasm for Hitler exceeded all bounds. The shout of Heil had no end." Shortly before 2 P.M., Hitler returned to the Passion hall and was greeted once more with "endless jubilation." As the play resumed, the first speech of the Prologue was also disrupted by cheers. And when the play ended, the same scene of joy was re-created, especially when Hitler went on the stage to congratulate members of the cast.[61]

Even allowing for the natural hyperbole of the *Völkischer Beobachter*, this account seems far more likely than that offered by Bürgermeister Zwink when I spoke with him in 1980. Thirteen years old in 1934, Zwink recalls "Mr. Hitler" as "the man of the state." His visit supposedly caused no more than a ripple of excitement. "We said Hitler is here, but no more. In the morning, there was some 'Heil Dir! Heil Dir!' But it was just another person in the hall."[62]

Imperturbability is not a trait which would normally be ascribed to Oberammergau. Photographs taken at the time reveal the obvious elation of Passion play principals on the visit of the führer to the village. Other photos show *Jugend* celebrations, Nazi winter sports carnivals, and party gatherings in an elite Nazi *Kaserne,* with representatives from Berlin present.[63] To demonstrate its loyalty to Hitler, Oberammergau sent three hundred of its men off to fight his war. Nearly one hundred died on battlefields. Of the rest who became prisoners of war in Russian, American, French, or British compounds, only nine listed their rank as *Soldat* (common soldier). Either out of pride of achievement or puffery, the others were *Leutnant* (lieutenant), *Zwangs SS, Unteroffizier* (petty officer), *SS Unterscharführer* (another noncommissioned officer), *Ober Wachtman* (sentry), *Feldwebel* (sergeant), *SS Ob-Schutzmann* (SS policeman), or *Grenadier* (a rather pompous way of referring to an infantryman).[64]

Fealty at the front was more than matched at home. In the last years of the war, the boardinghouses and hotels of Oberammergau housed factory workers who had been bombed out in Augsburg. Many came to work in BMW blockhouses or the new Messerschmitt research and development laboratory camouflaged and nestled by the hills. Some Nazi leaders still fantasized that wonder weapons—rockets, jet aircraft, super tanks—would change the course of the war. Failing that, elite units of the SS would fight a thousand years in the redoubt (Etchdall) of the Allgau and Bavaria before surrendering. One such Panzer unit arrived in Oberammergau at the end of April 1945. Apparently the villagers who had lived through the conflict in their "sheltered haven, untouched by shattering air raids,"[65] did not welcome the thought of Götterdämmerung. With American forces at the outskirts of town and real machine-gun fire sounding, the inconvenienced residents prevailed upon the Panzer unit to capitulate.[66]

There was one more, unwelcome, group of wartime visitors. They were the thousands of Hungarian, Ukrainian, Greek, French, Latvian, and Jewish slaves who also worked in Oberammergau's factories. They had not asked to be there. Dragooned from their homes, marched over mountains from Garmisch and Oberau, they were housed in a *Lager* (camp) of fifteen plywood and tar-paper barracks. For months, the foreigners labored next to German civilians in

the concrete factories which were festooned with the führer's proclamations, anti-Semitic cartoons, and anti-Allied
propaganda posters. They wore motley collections of prison
uniforms, were poorly fed and cared for. Some died of disease, brutality, or broken spirit. Some ran away and paid for
their impetuosity. One group of young boys from Ravens-
brück were betrayed by the monks of Ettal to the SS in the
second week of April 1945. By way of contrast, the village
asked no questions of SS Lieutenant Georg Kurt Mussfeld,
responsible for killing Jews in Lublin during the war.[67]
Strange to tell, as late as 1946, no one in Oberammergau
would admit to knowing about concentration camps, or
Dachau only seventy-five miles away, or genocide. Men-
dacity was Oberammergau's final tribute to Adolf Hitler.

9

The 1950 Revival

Oberammergau emerged from World War II, in the eyes of one observer, "seedy and dejected."[1] There was no paint or plaster for buildings in need of repair, no linen or cutlery to replace that which had worn out. Some thirty houses and hotels had been requisitioned by elements of the U.S. Army, which established a European Command Intelligence School in the scenic community. The army supposedly made over one hotel into a brothel for officers. In the process, people were displaced from their own homes. Alois Lang, for example, was forced to live in a barn, behind his family's famed hotel which served as divisional headquarters.[2]

Oberammergau's problems were complicated by the continued presence of Germans who could not return to their bombed-out homes in other towns and perhaps as many as ten thousand displaced persons, part of nearly two million Nazi slaves found in the West when the war ended.[3] For the most part, UNRRA, which was charged with their rehabilitation and repatriation, preferred to make use of elite lodges or *Kasernen* in Bavaria. In Oberammergau, however, the refugees were confined under guard to the former labor camp barracks. The DPs had better clothes, sufficient blankets. They could also obtain passes to go into the village.

But as elsewhere in Germany, food rations proved to be inadequate and a source of friction between the villagers and outsiders.

In this pastoral region, food supply should not have been a problem. The villagers created a thriving black market which traded religious wood carvings for such luxury items as American cigarettes, chocolate, and liquor. A bottle of gin would buy a superbly carved Madonna of the largest size. Yet the basic Christian instruction to share with those less fortunate was, as Willard Heaps noted in 1946, "noticeably absent." Said Heaps, "The 'foreigners' receive only the minimum Bavarian food ration and are unable to supplement it with produce purchased from local farmers, as are the natives." None of these people seemed interested in sharing their stores with their hungry countrymen in other parts of Germany, particularly the north, on whom they placed blame for the war.[4]

Oberammergau was defiant and bitter. Its worst hostility, however, was reserved for the displaced persons. Elsewhere in Germany, refugees had gone on rampages, destroying property and beating civilians. The situation had deteriorated to the point where by the fall of 1945 U.S. authorities felt compelled to call back into service twenty-two thousand German police and issue arms to them.[5] The fear of retaliation was present in Oberammergau. As Jim Elder, then a teen-aged survivor from Hungary, recalls: "They expected to be punished very severely. But after a few weeks, fear turned to outright hostility. There was quite a bit of that directed toward the DPs. They were resentful because every day we could walk into the town hall and get an ID from UNRRA, then get the bread. Later, you could always get an MP to help you out or make your own ID. One day, I was soaking my feet in the river, with my buddies. A bunch of Germans came by. They said, 'Dirty Jew!' I shouted back, 'Goddamned Germans!' We got into a fight. That I would dare talk back to this outstanding Bavarian citizen. We got the shorter end of the stick. We still were not well physically."[6]

In this, too, Oberammergau was no different from the rest of Germany. In Bavaria and Franconia, people lamented: "What a mess the *Führer* made—he hounded away our good Jews and now we have instead all these bad Jews."[7] On July 5, 1945, Gen. Lucius Clay summarized the German attitude in the following manner: "No general feeling of war guilt or repugnance for Nazi doctrine and regime has yet manifested itself. Germans blame Nazis for losing war [*sic*], protest ignorance of regime's crimes and shrug off their own support or silence as incidental and unavoidable."[8] There never would be a time of national self-abasement. Within the year, Clay would report evidence of Germans repeatedly circumventing occupation laws as they gained new confidence.[9] There were even complaints of a reemergence of the right wing in Bavarian politics by September 1945.[10]

Waffling, ambiguous policies of the U.S. military contributed, as much as anything, to a revived German arrogance. The Allies were supposedly committed to denazification, as a secret communique to War Secretary Stimson expressed it in July 1945, an "unrelenting policy of uprooting Nazi influence in Germany."[11] For the Soviets, this meant executing perhaps as many as 250,000 Germans, sending another 500,000 to prison by the end of 1946.[12] In the American Zone, denazification was quite a different story. Gen. Joseph T. McNarney, Eisenhower's successor as occupation chief, could tell a radio audience that denazification was "well-advanced" by December 1945,[13] but the fact is that the program was by that time little more than a joke.

While McNarney was patting himself on the back, his deputy Clay was recommending that arrests be limited to "active members of organizations being tried by the International Tribunal, dangerous security suspects, and those individuals against whom specific evidence is available as to their participation in war crimes."[14] With thirteen million registrants in the American Zone, three million of whom were potentially chargeable, the U.S. had neither the capacity nor resolve to pursue each case as strenuously as it might.[15] Denazification simply eroded till it went out of existence. On March 5, 1946, American officials approved a law distinguishing between major and minor offenders, the latter to be dealt with swiftly and to be given no more than probationary sentences.[16] Five months later, the military government amnestied those persons born after January 1, 1919, "except fanatics in leadership."[17] Another amnesty was extended at Christmas 1946, to those disabled by war and those who had made little profit from affiliation with nazism.[18]

In March 1948, Undersecretary of the Army William Draper instructed Clay that *all* denazification proceedings were to be completed by the end of the year. The Soviet military threat, coupled with congressional criticism of the "persecution" of our new-found German friends, impelled Secretary Royall to this decision. General Clay did not have to be pressured. He had already urged the creation of a clemency board.[19] By January 1949, only three hundred Nazis remained in prison in the American Zone and Clay could say of German panels which reviewed many cases, "They may not have cleaned their own houses thoroughly, but they at least removed the major dirt."[20]

Originally, the Americans wanted to do more than punish Nazi sympathizers. They wanted to "reclaim" Germany's population from "Goebbels' cynicism."[21] To achieve this lasting spiritual and moral reform, a reorientation program was entrusted to the Psychological Warfare and Information Control Divisions of SHAEF. Through their Education, Cultural Affairs, and Religious Affairs branches, these units monitored Germany's postwar cultural rebirth. All personnel and facilities in radio stations, libraries, newspapers, theaters, and schools were screened before being issued operating licenses. Wrote General Clay in 1945, "We were particularly careful to remove Nazis from information and entertainment media which would exert an increasing influence on the German people."[22] Clay's pronouncement was premature, for his own Education Branch revealed that 60 percent of the German schoolteachers employed after the war had been Nazis.[23] It simply was impossible to revive German culture without utilizing some former Nazis. And

most of these had suffered no greater deprivation than Georg
Johann Lang who was fined two thousand deutsche marks
(two hundred dollars) by a Garmisch tribunal in 1946.[24]
Denazification was a travesty, reorientation a failure.
American policies vis-à-vis German economic recovery
were little better. In an interview with CBS's Larry Leseuer
in December 1948, Clay rhapsodized about the emotional
uplift wrought in Germany by the European Recovery Plan,
currency reform, and the restoration of local autonomy.[25]
There is no question that the postwar economic miracle
changed the destiny of free Germany. But already in 1946,
Clay had made it clear that the revival of local industry and
culture would, if necessary, supersede even American economic interests. In a note to Hildring, dated February 16,
1946, the American commander recommended reopening
breweries in Bavaria, even if such action generated negative
"psychological values" at home.[26]
All of this—the cold war, ego conflicts among generals,
the slovenly nature of the bureaucracy—worked to the advantage of the Oberammergauers. The villagers were cog-
nizant of the inefficient workings of denazification. They
also appreciated the American commitment to German cultural and economic rebirth. In Oberammergau that meant
the Passion play. Already in the summer of 1945, the village
"buzzed with rumors" that the Passion, which had not been
given in 1940, might be staged in 1946. Bürgermeister Raab
approached U.S. authorities in town and was encouraged
when Maj. Charles Heyl, commanding officer in Oberammergau, sent along a request for clearance to OMGUS headquarters in Munich on September 14, 1945. Ever sensitive to
the Nazi issue, Raab's application was accompanied by a
letter of reference from Oberammergau's parish priest.[27]
The records contain no statement of a formal rejection at
this point. It may be that the villagers themselves recognized
the difficulty in performing the Passion with one leading
candidate for the role of Christ (Alois Lang) under temporary
ban by denazification officials and another (Otto Haser) still
in a Russian POW camp. More likely, the request was
deemed impolitic or presumptuous coming so quickly on

the heels of war. Raab's application was probably turned down for failing to supply the more than eighty licensing forms necessary to the Theater Control Division.

When the required forms were submitted, it was not Raab but Melchior Breitsamter who sought permission to stage the Passion in 1950. Beginning with March 1946, Breitsamter patiently and meticulously filled out the military government *Fragebogen* (statements of activity and desirability) as well as Information Control personnel and business questionnaires. Breitsamter—Pilate in 1934 and Annas in 1980—listed his occupation as *Sagewerker* (worker in a sawmill). To the question had he suffered racial or religious persecution, participated in the resistance, or had his freedom curtailed under nazism, he responded no. A review of his *Fragebogen* indicated that his income actually trebled (up to seventy-five hundred deutsche marks from twenty-five hundred) during the war. Breitsamter admitted to "normalen Mitgliedsbeitrage" in the DAF, NSV, and NS *Reichskriegerbund* since 1936. He had also voted for Hitler in the November 1932, elections. But unlike Bürgermeister Raab, the Langs, and many others, he had never been a member of the Nazi party. Now all he wanted was to carry on the three-hundred-year-old tradition of performing the religious "Übungsspiel."[28]

A counterintelligence investigation into Breitsamter's background revealed that he had been favorably disposed toward the Nazi party in its early days, that he believed national socialism to be the right thing for a divided and tottering Germany. After a few years, however, he changed his mind, especially after witnessing the persecution of the church and Jews. Breitsamter claimed that he had been warned by an *Ortsgruppenleiter* to cease speaking out against the Nazis. His eldest son apparently shared his views, for when Melchior junior was drafted into the Waffen SS, he spent some time in a punitive company for failing to carry out certain orders of his superiors.[29] When Melchior senior became convinced that Germany was being ruined by nazism, he became "a stout opponent of the regime." In the spring of 1945, he was one of those who came out actively against the Nazis and helped convince Panzer forces near Oberammergau that further fighting was senseless.[30] On the basis of such information, Lt. H. Peter Hart, acting chief of Counter Intelligence in Munich, concluded there was no evidence of Nazi activity on the part of Breitsamter. Therefore, there was "no CI interest." Lieutenant Hart's findings were countersigned by Robert S. Martindale, civilian chief of the Intelligence Section.[31]

Breitsamter's denazification clearance under the classification "White B" and the approval of his license seemed assured. The application was sailing along smoothly through occupation channels till it came to the desk of Erich Adler, intelligence officer for the Information Control Division in Munich. Adler was one of the few people to recognize the unregenerate nature of Oberammergau and its Passion. In interviews with Breitsamter, Adler learned that the applicant himself felt that press attacks against Oberammergau because of its political attitude during the Third Reich were justified. Despite Oberammergau's expressions of religious piety, Adler concluded that an "exceedingly large percentage" of party members in town still demonstrated a willingness to identify with the Nazi regime.[32] "There was never any pressure brought upon the individuals to join the party," he said, "and they did so entirely on their own free will, either because of a belief in the goals of the NSDAP or because of greed for money and other advantages." Moreover, "most of the persons who really count in the Passion Plays had teamed up with the NSDAP." Of these, "the most important players have not been denazified as yet." The 1945 election of Josef Raab, an early applicant for Nazi party membership, as Bürgermeister, was symptomatic of the attitude in the village.[33]

According to Adler, Breitsamter's emergence as representative of the play was nothing more than a ploy to obscure Oberammergau's political background. "The whole village," he wrote, "has been most anxious to transform its only presentable non-Party member, who had been prominent in the Passion plays in the past, into a fighter against Nazism and fierce opponent of the regime since its early

days." Such a tale, though convenient, was "not valid by
subject's own account." For the above reasons, then, Adler
recommended that the license be refused at least for one
year, until denazification proceedings throughout Bavaria
were concluded, or Oberammergau showed "a spirit more
worthy of its fame than it has done so far."[34]

Unfortunately, Adler was not sustained by his superiors.
On April 1, 1947, Ernest Cramer, chief of Media Intelligence
for the Information Control Division in Munich, reversed
the recommendation. Cramer had tried, without success, to
ascertain the names of possible cast members, their party
affiliation, *Spruchkammer* status, and the like.[35] In sessions
with Raab, Breitsamter, and a new Bürgermeister, Heinrich
Zunterer, Cramer was informed that the selection process
made it impossible to supply cast names before January
1949, at the earliest. From these meetings, it became clear to
Cramer that Breitsamter was "the responsible person in
name only." If licensed, Bürgermeister Zunterer, a man who
dominated the discussions, would probably "attempt to run
the complete show."[36]

Zunterer did not concern Cramer. His political record was
clean. Rather, Cramer fretted that the Passion play might
come under the sway of persons known for their voluntary
cooperation with the Nazis, particularly members of the
Lang family. His final recommendation was that a license
be granted, with the stipulation that all actors secure a
Spruchkammer clearance. The play director and any other
policy-making officials would, however, require special
ICD approval. Said Cramer, "This must be done to assure
that persons like Georg Johannes Lang, the former director,
a 1933 party member, or Wilhelm Lechner, director of a
school, a 1930 party member, will not regain positions of
influence."[37]

Cramer's recommendations sailed through the Theater
Control Section within two weeks. Munich Bureau Chief
Walter Behr sent along his okay to the chief of the Information Control Division on April 15. Behr, too, expressed
concern that participation by former Nazis might provoke
"adverse publicity in the world press." Against this possi-

bility, Breitsamter, Zunterer, and Raab had agreed to use only persons cleared by denazification tribunals. Significantly, though, specific references to the Langs, found in both the Adler and Cramer memoranda, were absent from Behr's report.[38]

There would be no more procedural snags. On April 29, 1947, R. C. Martindale, chief of the Intelligence Branch for ICD, recommended that a license be issued to Breitsamter.[39] The license was approved by Lt. Col. Anthony Kleitz, chief of ICD, four days later, and countersigned by Maj. R. D. Halpin for the administration on May 6.[40] Breitsamter was notified directly by Behr on May 9.[41] By January 1948, all names of potential players submitted to the Information Control Division had been cleared and were "free to work as actors."[42]

Where Eric Adler had cautioned against the possible return of Nazi sympathizers, and specifically the Langs in 1947, the reality was that most of the main performers in the 1950 play had party links.[43] Georg Johann Lang returned from an Allied detention camp to direct the hymn of reconciliation in 1950 and 1960, saying cockily, "We have a clear conscience. We have to fulfill a pledge and there is nothing offensive in our play."[44] Alois Lang, lightly rebuked by a denazification court the same day twenty-two guards from the Mauthausen concentration camp were hanged, assumed the role of Prologue in 1950.[45] Eighty-eight-year-old Anton Lechner returned to his role of Annas. Hugo Mayr once more was Caiaphas. The new Christ was thirty-seven-year-old hotelier Anton Preisinger. One of those who supposedly had been "forced" to join the Nazi party (in 1932!), Preisinger had been adjudged "a follower" and fined by a denazification court in 1947. Reminded of his background in 1950, Preisinger dismissed talk of nazism as "a lot of nonsense" and added, "People should stop talking about these things."[46]

If occupation authorities had merely been duped into approving an anti-Semitic revival, it would have been bad enough. Incredibly, the Oberammergauers, having won permission to stage the Passion, demonstrated more *chutz-*

pah by returning to the Americans for a loan! Anni Rutz, the Virgin Mary in 1934, released a trial balloon on the question of money during an interview with Western journalists in December 1948. The village, she said, might need as much as DM 1 million ($350,000) for theater repairs, refurbishment of scenery, and costumes. "Frankly," said Ms. Rutz, "we are counting on widespread good will, sympathetic understanding and help, as well as our own efforts to make the play possible." Some money would be raised from lectures and wood-carving tours. "But the rest will have to come from an advance of funds by the American Military Government and from contributions from religious groups and friends who remember our play from other years."[47]

Almost immediately, the Oberammergau Passion Play Committee, its director (Georg Lang), and Bürgermeister Raimund Lang (another old Nazi returned to office) issued denials of need.[48] Just as quickly, they reversed themselves and began appealing to the military government in Garmisch for financial aid.[49] On April 4, 1949, a formal loan application in the exact amount suggested by Ms. Rutz was forwarded to the Office of Finance Adviser for OMGUS Bavaria. Only now, the Americans were told the needed million deutsche marks would be used for street repair, extension of the water supply system, and construction of dwellings for refugees, in addition to renovation of the Passion theater.[50]

On the surface, there was nothing extraordinary about the application. The Oberammergauers were merely abiding by Article 28 of Military Government Law 63, which permitted communities to borrow "in anticipation of future revenues." Priority would be given to public health projects, waterworks, sewage disposal, hospitals, power plants, and schools. Hence the reference to street and water projects in the Oberammergau proposal. Article 28 also required a community to obtain a separate guarantee from a German bank. The Bayerische Gemeindebank of Munich informed the Bavarian Ministry of Interior that it would underwrite the loan at 6½ percent to September 1950.[51] In short, everything seemed in order when the loan application was forwarded from the Bavarian Ministry to the American authorities.

There were some problems, however. Oberammergau's expressed solicitude toward refugees was touching, if insincere. The original loan proposal drafted by the community in October 1948 made no reference whatever to housing of displaced persons. The item was added to curry favor with the Americans.[52] If anything, animosity against the DPs increased between 1945 and 1949. Mimeographed materials issued by the Passion Play Committee emphasized that the refugees constituted the biggest headache for the villagers. One circular allowed that it would be contrary to Christian tradition to turn out those "who had lost all their property and homes through the war." At the same time, there was a greater need—to ensure sufficient room for visitors to "this Christian play." Oberammergau called upon the Americans to evacuate houses, hotels, and ECIS school. Far worse, in a move that evoked images of wartime deportations, it called upon German authorities to "remove" as many as ten thousand refugees from Oberammergau, Garmisch, Schongau, and Unterammergau to "elsewhere in Bavaria." To the eve of the 1950 premiere, Oberammergau natives grumbled, "If it weren't for the refugees . . ."[53]

The Oberammergau application contained a more obvious defect than sham humanitarianism and that was its size—DM 1 million. U.S. officials were moving very cautiously on grants during this period, approving first the applications of gutted cities, which Oberammergau was not. Even then, the repayment period normally extended over thirty-one years and not the two years in which Oberammergau promised to repay the loan. The audacity of Oberammergau's application is demonstrated by a comparison with some of the projects which were approved in the spring of 1949: the city of Nuremberg was granted a loan of DM 400,000 to construct a gas plant; Fuerstenfeld received DM 600,000 to extend an electric power plant; Augsburg obtained DM 770,000 for hospitals and water repair; and Wurzburg received DM 820,000 for a housing project. These towns were anywhere from ten to fifty times larger than

Oberammergau, had been leveled by Allied bombardments, and yet were asking for much less.[54] Munich itself was seeking only DM 6 million to safeguard the power supply, repair and reconstruct a public transportation system, motorize city garbage collection, engage in street cleaning, and prevent further deterioration of public buildings.[55]

Not surprisingly, the Oberammergau application was turned down on May 19, 1949, by Maj. Gen. George Hays, deputy military governor in Berlin. The rejection had nothing to do with Oberammergau's treatment of refugees or the nature of the Passion. General Hays was principally concerned about the size of the loan application. He worried that at the rate authorities were receiving municipal applications for rehabilitation funds, the entire DM 1 billion targeted for such purposes in the U.S. Zone would soon be exhausted. After citing the needs of railway and power companies, private enterprise, and capital investment, Hays sidestepped the issue altogether, shunting the application to another committee of review being formed that spring by the military government.[56]

Oberammergau did not lack its advocates in the American administration. Over the next few months, Land Director Murray Van Wagoner, his assistant R. R. Lord, John Logan, and Blevins Davis of the Cultural Affairs Branch in Bavaria, continued to press higher-ups for approval. Writing General Hays, Van Wagoner stressed the "world-wide religious and cultural importance of the play." In 1950, proclaimed a Holy Year by Pius XII, "this great religious spectacle" might play a role "in the economic reconstruction of Germany through the acquisition of foreign exchange from visitors." Prewar Bavaria had generated an income of $40 million per year in tourism. Perhaps the Passion could "provide the spark needed to set the foreign tourist program in motion."[57]

Blevins Davis was even more direct. Writing Gen. Clarence Huebner, commander in chief of American troops in Europe, Davis complained, "Apparently we have given little more than moral support to this world famous project, which had its beginning three centuries ago." Davis had gone over every line entry in the Oberammergau budget

with "Baumeister" Raimund Lang and his assistant Benedikt Stückl. All of the items seemed reasonable, particularly
the figure of DM 60,000 which the community was propos-
ing for advertising. By way of contrast, German steamship
lines, railroads, and travel bureaus before the war had allot-
ted more than DM 2 million to promotion of the Passion.
Davis compared the production budget ($300,000) with the
cost of a Broadway musical. Union rules in the United States,
he noted, permitted only four weeks of rehearsal. In Oberammergau, the people had to give up work for more than a
year to fulfill their vow. Davis's letter continued: "I am convinced that this is an unparalleled opportunity for our country to firmly establish itself as an active force in the cultural
relations between Germany and the United States." The
Cultural Affairs specialist recommended that Huebner assign a contingent of "properly-trained" American troops to
Oberammergau to direct traffic, act as guides, and be sources
of information to all English-speaking tourists. Davis was
about to return to the United States (and just happened to
mention that he would be reporting to President Truman),
but he urged Huebner to meet with High Commissioner
John McCloy and implement his recommendations. He had
no reason to doubt that his proposals would be received
sympathetically. General Huebner had expressed interest in
reviving the play in earlier meetings. The general's support
was implicit in the comment made by Davis: "As you and I
agree, this is one of the greatest existing forces for good in
Germany and must be maintained."[58]

When interviewed recently, John McCloy minimized the
role of his office in this whole affair. "I do remember faintly
some discussion of it," he told me. "I talked with Adenauer a
little about it. Adenauer was not particularly sympathetic to
its revival because it had so many Nazi connotations—when
they used the Jewish scenes to show the fanaticism of the
mob." According to McCloy, one person who did push for
the revival was General Huebner's wife. "Mrs. Huebner was
interested in the thing. How or why, I can't say. She came
around once or twice. I certainly was not an active propo-
nent, but was prepared to go along with it. We wanted to see

it less political or biased. It had become more and more anti-Jewish as Hitler took over."

McCloy concedes that the Oberammergau project did fall within the general guidelines for the economic and cultural revival of Germany. "We were trying to reerect traditions, interest in public affairs, festivals," he said. "It was part of the aura of recovery. Some funds were coordinated with soldiers with the general thought of rebuilding a sense of community, for industrial and spiritual rehabilitation." McCloy insists that the monies did not come from his office or ERP funds. "It must have come from the military people, from their budget, for morale purposes. There was no institutional loan from the U.S. Government or World Bank. I'm sure they wanted to clear with me. I do recall it coming from military people. Bavaria was part of their bailiwick. I have the feeling it came out of profits from the PX, to subsidize for morale."[59]

On August 13, 1949, General Hays issued the following communication from Berlin: "Approval is granted for loan application of the City of Oberammergau, Bavaria, for 1,000,000 Deutsche Marks."[60] There are no other records available which shed light on the decision-making process. Oberammergau's loan was approved in this cryptic TWX because of a unique combination of factors: the town's historic and religious significance, its potential capacity to generate income, and American gullibility.

Their financial foundation secure, villagers in Oberammergau now plunged ahead with preparations for an estimated four hundred thousand visitors. Mutterings about refugees and housing inconvenience were temporarily muted, as in the nineteenth century, people bedded down in barns and kitchens. By the spring of 1950, the *New York Times* could report the village was "resplendent and gleaming." Wrote correspondent Kathleen McLaughlin: "Gay peasant-type cloths fluttered on tables set under wide umbrellas on the restaurant terraces. New curtains hung at the windows. Bed linen was immaculate and new cutlery gleamed on every table in inns and private homes."[61]

To guarantee the success of a venture they had underwritten to the tune of $300,000, American military authorities recommended Oberammergau as a rest and rehabilitation center for troops in Germany. Officials emulated Hitler, making available all kinds of special buses and trains. To make certain that everyone understood the play had the sanction of the Allied governments, high-ranking officials attended the initial performances. Thus John McCloy and Gen. Sir Brian Robertson, U.S. and British high commissioners respectively, attended the premiere on May 18, flanked by Federal Republic President Theodor Heuss, Chancellor Konrad Adenauer, Bavarian Minister-President Hans Erhard, several members of the Bonn cabinet, and four U.S. brigadier generals. Three days later, Gen. Thomas T. Hardy, C.I.C. of American forces in Europe, sat through the seven-hour performance with a group of officers from SHAEF headquarters in Heidelberg.[62]

Looking back, John McCloy says, "When I went we were watching pretty critically for any indication of a revival of Nazism. During the Hitler period, it had been Nazified— the mob rancor, Jerusalem as a fanatical pool against Christ. The feeling was there was a great need to clean up the play and script. We went there thinking much in terms of that. There were some changes. But still there was quite a remnant of anti-Semitism. Critics at the time commented that it still needed cleaning up. Generally there was a lack of enthusiasm dated to misuse by the Nazis. Adenauer who had been in the resistance was aware and was critical of that. In the middle of the play, he said, 'Das war zuviel.' [That was too much.] I had the feeling myself."[63]

Five years after the worst war in history, 500,000, not 400,000, persons traveled to Oberammergau to see the Passion. What they discovered was a village which emerged from a world conflict relatively unscathed, villagers who were unrepentant, even ungrateful. The 1950 playbook, for example, credited the revival of the play not to Breitsamter, Zunterer, or Raab but to the leadership of Bürgermeister Raimund Lang and his deputy Benedikt Stückl. Then, as now, there was not a word about American assistance.[64] The playbook did, however, reflect continuing bitterness toward displaced persons. As Joseph Maria Lutz noted, the village had been "flooded with refugees" who "took the best homes."[65]

Visitors found a community where the Bürgermeister was an ex-Nazi, the director of the Passion an ex-Nazi, Christ and most of the cast in hymn of reconciliation former Nazis. Despite a last minute recommendation from Willard Johnson of the Office of Religious Affairs of the U.S. High Commission for Germany that the anti-Semitic script be "revised drastically or rewritten entirely," the text audiences heard was practically the same employed in 1934.[66] It included the preface which predicted a time when all German tribes would feel like one people. And just as in 1934, the community of Oberammergau endorsed the following racist declaration:

> Time passed on and, after dreadful misery, saved the German people and its tribes from bolshevism, this pestilence of abandonment of the race created by God. Instead of the imminent ruin we experienced the fortune of a new life which unites us all in our race. Is there any other time more favorable than these days of the suppression of the anti-Christian powers in our fatherland, to remember the price the Son of God himself paid for His people, the people who adhere to Him and to His banner—does there exist any greater cause to perform the Holy Play entrusted to our community than to perform it in this year 1934 [sic] like a prayer of thanks with particular reverence and solemnity.[67]

Such sentiments must have appealed to more than Germans in an age of Stalinism, the Berlin Blockade, and Korea. But there was a special, bitter irony, even vindication for Germans in their utterance in 1950.

10

Profit from the Passion

Since its revival in 1950, the Oberammergau Passion has weathered a number of storms. The American Jewish Congress, American Jewish Committee, and Anti-Defamation League have all urged extensive revisions within the text. Failing that, these organizations have championed boycotts of the decennial performances. Such calls have been endorsed in America by editor Irving Howe, critic Alfred Kazin, Stanley Kunitz (winner of the 1959 Pulitzer Prize for poetry), playwright Arthur Miller, Lionel Trilling, Elie Wiesel, Maurice Samuel, Leonard Bernstein, Theodor Bikel, and George Steiner.[1] Their protests were endorsed in 1966 and again in 1968 by six of West Germany's leading literary figures, including Günter Grass, Heinrich Böll, and Ewe Johnson.[2] About the same time, Brian Epstein, manager of the Beatles, canceled plans to produce a "road company" version of the Passion in England and the United States.[3] Pater Stephan Schaller of Ettal, who labored unsuccessfully on a revision for 1970, publicly lamented: "In the 20th century, after the Third Reich, after Auschwitz, and especially after Vatican II, it appears necessary to examine this text and to eliminate passages which Jews regard as offensive and to thereby make it better and clearer."[4] In May of 1970, Bernt Englemann, president of Munich's

League for Human Rights, followed up on Pater Schaller's criticism by bringing suit before the city's public prosecutor against the Passion play's producers, charging that the "scarcely revised text" was more suited to Nazi propaganda than to Christian drama.[5] Englemann's suit failed, but as a result of the negative reactions that had been brewing for years, in 1980 Maj. Gen. R. Dean Tice, commander of U.S. armed forces in West Germany, instituted a ban on army-sponsored tours to Oberammergau. Thirty years after American occupation authorities made possible a revival of the Passion, General Tice found it "inappropriate and anti-Semitic [in] tone."[6]

Oberammergau's critics were hasty to point out they were not bent on abolishing the play. As the American Jewish Congress noted, "It has never been a question of seeking to suppress a celebration of the Passion of Christ. We oppose that kind of religious or artistic commitment which can find satisfactory release only in discredited libels against the Jewish people."[7] Had the above-listed parties pressed for a ban on all Passions, revised or otherwise, it is doubtful they would have been successful. The villagers evaded ecclesiastical and secular bans two hundred years ago, and they would have done so again. As both Bürgermeister Zwink and Spielleiter Hans Maier told me, "The play will never die out."[8] The main reason, quite frankly, is that this drama which denounces moneylenders, traitors, and religious profiteering is, ironically, the chief source of income for the village. Not mere anti-Semitism but cupidity distinguishes Oberammergau from its neighbors.

What originally were a handful of performances (four in 1810, six in 1811, sixteen in 1870, eighteen in 1871) in the nineteenth century grew to fifty-six in 1910, eighty-four in 1934, and one hundred by 1980. Capacity crowds of five thousand persons packed the theater, which was constructed in 1890 and remodeled in 1930 and 1950.[9] As the number of performances increased, so did the amount of revenue generated from the sale of tickets; playbooks and photos increased from $170,000 in 1890 to more than $15,000,000 in 1980.[10] What profits were left after expenses were distributed in the following fashion: one-third to the village poor, one-third to village improvement, and one-third to the performers.[11] For his role as Christus in the summer of 1880, Joseph Maier received $200.[12] Anton Lang, who proclaimed "our play is more than money; it is a vow, a consecration, a living ideal," earned a total of $3.37, enough to buy two pair of boots, for playing Jesus in sixty-eight performances in 1922.[13] Not only did villagers give up full-time employment for more than a year, but by performing on a stage open to perpetual rains, they risked impairing their health. Wrote Hermine Diemer: "Thus often what has been earned has to be spent again on doctor's bills."[14]

Oberammergauers have ever been sensitive to the charge that they perform the Passion for money, that they count their coin deliriously. But they attribute such charges to "the ugly snake of envy." Writing in 1950, when there was no disputing the link between the Passion and economic recovery, Dr. Eugen Roth defended the community against what he termed journalistic "harpies." The people of Oberammergau were not as materialistic as their neighbors in Bayreuth or Salzburg, he declared. The villagers were not saints, but they were motivated by the vow taken in 1633 and not profit. As proof, Roth offered Oberammergau's resistance to all "vulgar, venal" entreaties of "the opportunistic world." For more than a century, he said, "Oberammergau's spirit had repudiated all Judas-like temptations to sell soul and Saviour for thirty pieces of silver."[15]

Indeed, a good case could be made that Oberammergau has resisted the temptation to capitalize on its notoriety. In 1873, the villagers rejected a proposal to "remove the whole village" to Vienna as an attraction at the World Exposition.[16] At the close of the 1900 season, a New York company offered $5,000 to each principal who would participate in an Oberammergau-style production in the U.S. This too was refused.[17] At the same time, producers approached Anton Lang, then portraying Christ, suggesting that he act in a German translation of Charles Kennedy's play, *The Servant in the House*. Lang, offered a house, salary, and a bonus for the village, was told by Oberammergau's council that if he went to America, he would never play the lead role again. In 1910 Lang again was forced to cancel a private trip to Palestine following adverse comment in the German press.[18]

Apparently Lang learned his lesson, for in the midst of Germany's 1922 depression, he told a Western journalist, "Riches do not bring contentment and happiness."[19] In 1922 Hollywood's movie moguls dangled a large sum of money ($500,000) before the villagers for the rights to film a special version of the Passion. Though some of the younger residents in Oberammergau weakened, the traditionalists were adamant. Said one, "If this play is allowed to be filmed, I will go up to Ludwig's monument and with chisel and hatchet efface the inscription from it."[20] Others vowed to shear off their beards before participating in such a venture. Lang, who made clear his contempt for "the rubbish which for the most part is now fashionable on stage and screen in large cities,"[21] bluntly warned that if the movie proposal were approved, Oberammergau would have to get another Christus. In a letter to Janet Swift, the man who personified Christ declared, "The play has not been commercialized and never will be."[22] Ten years later, in the midst of the worldwide depression, Oberammergau again resisted the overtures of Cecil B. De Mille. In 1947, the townspeople turned down offers to perform in Düsseldorf.[23] Even today, Bürgermeister Zwink affirms, "Oberammergau is played in Oberammergau, not in Hollywood. Always. We have recorded the whole play for history, for our archive. In ten or twenty years we can see the cinema made in 1970. But Oberammergau is not going out. We don't want to go out."[24]

If Oberammergau has remained pure and untainted by financial enticements, how explain its nickname "das Sündige Dorf" (the sinful village) or the term "Oberammergauners" (swindlers) applied to its inhabitants by other Bavarians? Why was the village the subject of so many satirical cartoons in Munich newspapers showing Christ selling his locks by auction at the end of the season or Judas ridiculing the notion of any offer so low as thirty pieces of silver?[25] The fact is that economic need and not religious zeal has been the foundation of the Passion. Whenever the community was in financial trouble, its leaders discovered some reason for offering the Passion. In those rare cases where an excuse could not be found, the reputation of the community enabled it to peddle its wood carvings at rates far exceeding those in nearby towns.

When the prince elector forbade such religious performances in March 1770, the villagers reminded him of the continuity of their vow. But they also emphasized the material damage which would be done to them if the ban were enforced. In anticipation of ten thousand visitors, Oberammergau had already spent two hundred florins, printing up four thousand copies of the Passion text, repairing costumes, cutting and hauling wood. Though their application was rejected by Maximilian Joseph III "once and forever," the villagers proceeded with their play anyway and charged admission for the first time in 1770.[26]

In their application to Karl Theodor in 1780, the Oberammergauers again emphasized the economic advantages that would accrue not only to their village but "also for the rest of the whole country."[27] Between 1800 and 1810, economic deprivation and not disinterested religious zeal served as the motive for seeking permission to stage the Passion. Poor harvests and famine caused by countless invasions had reduced some to eating grass, snails, and bran. The closing of the Ettal monastery removed Oberammergau as a seat of a provincial court of justice. Wagon transports were taking merchandise into Upper Bavaria via different routes. The wood-carving activities of the Grodners had cut into another source of income. As Hermine Diemer put it, "From now on the passion play that had already saved Oberammergau from many a danger and plague was their last hope."[28]

In normal, prosperous times, the village would not permit any of its people to exploit their reputations. It apparently felt no compunctions about sending a fourteen-man contingent of wood-carvers and potters on a promotional junket to America during the inflationary crisis of 1923. This group, which included Anton Lang (Christ), Andreas Lang (Peter), and Guido Mayr (Judas), was sponsored by an American committee headed by New York attorney George Gordon

Battle.[29] The Oberammergauers were to offer exhibitions of their wares in New York, Cleveland, Cincinnati, Chicago, St. Louis, Philadelphia, Washington, Baltimore, and Boston between December 1923 and April 1924. Before they departed, Munich's Cardinal Faulhaber blessed them, saying their journey "in no way sought to profane the passion play." According to Faulhaber, the villagers were motivated by "lofty comprehension" and would decline every profit of a businesslike nature resulting from their fame.[30] A more candid view was offered by Anton Lang who told the *New York Morning Telegraph,* "If any large sum comes to us through our expedition, we want to see that money help the children of our country who are dying because they have not food enough to eat and clothes to protect them from the winter."[31]

At the very time, the Oberammergauers were turning down Hollywood's invitation to film the Passion as "a desecration," they accepted more than $100,000 in future orders and sales from Americans who packed their craft exhibits. When the advance group returned from the U.S. carrying a check in the amount of $10,000 toward the first receipts, the other villagers expressed "dissatisfication" with the American committee's financial statement because the orders were deemed too few. Within a year, reporters visiting Oberammergau could write that Anton Lang was "a lonely figure in his shop, casting placques which no one seeks."[32]

In 1932 Oberammergau could once more snub Hollywood because the 1930 Passion generated almost two million dollars in receipts. When people everywhere were begging for handouts, "The whole venture was a great commercial success. The [Passion play] committee was enabled to pay off a bank debt of nearly $400,000 and to carry forward a substantial balance."[33] In 1930 380,000 spectators came to Oberammergau. We have already seen how the Nazi government did everything in its power to attract an equal number, for political and economic reasons, in 1934. The income from the tercentenary performances came to more than three million deutsche marks. After individuals were paid, part of the surplus was used to build an outdoor municipal swimming pool, described as "the largest and best in Bavaria."[34]

In 1950, the net profit of DM 1.5 million ($500,000 after expenses) was used to refurbish the swimming pool and schools, to repair roads, regulate rivers, promote local craft and wood carving, and "meet the most urgent of community requirements."[35] Apparently there is no longer any need to speak of one-third of the revenue raised by the Passion going to the poor. There are no poor in Oberammergau. Of the anticipated $1.8 million in profit from the 1980 play,[36] the bulk was to go to road and bridge repairs, flood control (nothing more than a few stones planted every few yards in the Ammer River), the wood-carving school, and other local institutions. The latter include the swimming facility, an enormous lodge replete with two Olympic-sized pools, one with an artificial wave that "goes off" every ten minutes, and a modern hospital whose location in this small village is anomalous. Projected income from 1984 performances already has been earmarked for renovation of city hall and the construction of an indoor swimming pool with its own tidal wave.

Speaking before the people of Oberammergau at the opening of the 1980 season, Joseph Cardinal Ratzinger warned, "The impression must not arise that you perform the Passion play to fill your cashboxes. I urgently request you to pay attention to that fact and do everything to prevent such a falsification from occurring."[37] Unfortunately, protestations to the contrary notwithstanding, religion is big business in Oberammergau. It is Coney Island, Cedar Point, Disney World, but with a sanctimonious air. Oberammergau is a tourist trap which takes every conceivable form of currency and converts it at branches of the Bayerische Staatsbank, Bayerische Hypotheken-U.Wechsel Bank, Bayerische Vereinsbank, Bayerische Gemeindebank, or Deutsche Bank, while feigning religious piety. Thus in 1949, the Catholic church of Bavaria refused to identify itself with the play on the ground that the Passion was "an ordinary commercial enterprise and not entitled to Church support."[38]

Apart from the monies culled from the sale of tickets,

consider the following. All overnight accommodations are pegged to Passion tickets and are funneled through the office of the Bürgermeister. During the play season, there may be a rare room free in Murnau or Garmisch but none in Oberammergau. Every one of the quaint chalets becomes a guesthouse and/or cafe, with garrets reconditioned and meal tickets to specific inns issued by the central office. Every second afternoon, groups of wide-eyed Americans, Swiss, or Italians are disgorged from air-conditioned buses, and every second morning before eight the same tired, unwashed (many of the guesthouses have no baths, showers, or soap for the visitors) are piled into the same Cook's, Olson's, or Globus vans to make their return to Zurich or Munich.

It is all very efficient and lucrative. Few, if any, of the tourists leave Oberammergau without some memento of their pilgrimage. It may be an Alpine hat, an expensive pair of *Lederhosen*, knickers, or a mountain dress ($100), all of which will look silly back in New Rochelle or Van Nuys. It may be a pipe, a figurine, or even a life-sized crucifix ($1,500) done by Oberammergau's famed wood-carvers. Though the work is not much better than that done by similar craftsmen in Unterammergau two miles away, such a piece purchased in Oberammergau may carry a price tag two or three times as great.

Almost certainly the tourist will bring back a libretto published in any of a dozen languages for DM 5 ($3). Unlike the practice in conventional theater or opera, the Oberammergau Passion libretto is printed in only one language. Therefore, if people who cannot understand German wish to follow the action and translate simultaneously, they must purchase two texts. Hawkers selling a variety of books add to the confusion and irony of the opening scene of the Passion. While Jesus is chasing the money changers out of the Temple, their latter-day counterparts are making change in the audience.

No one is permitted to take pictures of the play while it is in progress. Although I have heard of no one being expelled from the theater for using his camera, the presence of uniformed guards at all entrances discourages such practice. As a result, the community has developed a monopoly in photographic mementos. A colorful picture book showing scenes of the Passion sells for DM 19.80 ($12.00), a package of forty-six slides for DM 56.00 ($36.00). The taped cassette or record version of the Rochus Dedler music can be had for DM 27.50 ($18.00). And while the Oberammergauers refuse to have their play videotaped or filmed for outside consumption, individuals may purchase a Super 8 movie of some scenes of the Passion and "curiorities [sic]" of the village for DM 75.00 ($45.00). It is all disturbingly reminiscent of the "last chance" souvenir stands in America's Luna Parks.

Apart from profit generated by ticket costs (averaging thirty dollars in 1980 as compared with twenty-four cents in 1910), the 500,000 tourists who came to Oberammergau in 1980 were expected to spend about $12 million in the shops, restaurants, and guesthouses, enough to sustain the villager for the next decade.[39] Ernst Zwink, defending the number of performances offered in 1980, argued that Oberammergau was merely responding to the demand of people who come from all over the world.[40] But when he was asked to explain the unusually high number of performances, Hans Schwaighofer, director and advocate of an alternate Passion play, rubbed his thumb and index finger together, saying, "If the people of Oberammergau were genuinely interested in fulfilling the vow, and only the vow, the play would be performed once, on the Passion Meadow, for free."[41]

Others have noted the tendency of villagers to "batten on" and "prosper exceedingly" from visitors.[42] Already in 1907, Katherine Roof denounced the practice of offering interim plays for "commercial advantage" and warned all but the blindest of optimists that "the spell of unconscious religious fervor was broken forever."[43] A contemporary, Rev. Robert Coyle of Denver, reported that some performers were actually charging twenty-five cents for autographs.[44] While this practice may have stopped, J. B. Priestley complained about the number of shop windows filled with crucifixes, saints, and martyrs, all at special Passion play prices. Wrote Priestley, "I told myself—no doubt because I was sleepy and cross—that this village was a durned sight too quaint and pious and old-worldly for my taste; it might have been invented by a tourist agency."[45] W. A. Darlington concurred, attributing Oberammergau's tacky commercialism to the influence of Cook's Tours.[46]

More recently, Oberammergau has been chastised for misrepresenting its so-called hotel space to tourists and engaging in "a notorious black market" in Passion tickets.[47] Townsfolk have been accused of selling everything from machine-tooled angels (foisted off as hand-carved artifacts) to toilet privileges.[48] In 1960, the shortage of hand-carved trinkets for the tourist trade was met with imports from Yugoslavia.[49] In the same year, the Passion guidebook extolled the virtues of Perutz Color Film, D-503 floor sealer for tiles, XOX biscuits, Edelweiss Dairy, Torpedo Typewriters, and Coca Cola. The most damning indictment of the village, which proclaimed it would "never play Judas" to its tradition, occurred early in 1936 when the Winter Olympic Games were held at Garmisch-Partenkirchen. For this occasion, the villagers combined their religious heritage with the spirit of the moment and produced carved figures of Mary Magdalene and the disciples in flowing robes—on skiis![50]

Even Oberammergau's staunchest defenders concede that *Kommerzialisierung* has gotten out of hand.[51] Like Priestley and Darlington, *Commonweal's* Richard Linn Edsall decried the "incredible number of stores selling postcards, texts of the play, knicknacks, stationery, pottery, all kinds of things sacred and profane—which makes you feel as if you were in a tourist-infested city."[52] In 1934, the *New York Times's* Frederick Birchall said the money "rolls in" and "the thing has become a gold mine."[53] More recently, Vernon Heaton, an apologist for the play, noted the "business acumen," "high individual profits," and "bandwagon tactics" common to Oberammergau.[54] In 1980, Bürgermeister Zwink commented, "The high standard of living is now causing trouble in trying to provide the necessary tourist accommodation during the festivals. No one is prepared anymore to move to the barn and rent his bed."[55] Theodor Geus summed up the problem for the *Frankfurter All-*

gemeine Zeitung, saying, the Passion "had lost much of its innocence." Added Geus, it was almost as if Jesus must die for the welfare of landlords and hoteliers or for the health resort which already with the profits of the Passion of 1970 should have been built and which will not develop after this passion season."[56]

The contradiction between those innocent Oberammergauers portrayed in the tableau onstage showing people swearing a vow in 1633 and today's mercenary villagers is obvious. Yet Dr. Hans Lamm, *Rosh Kehillah* of the Munich Jewish community, continues to speak on behalf of the villagers. Lamm told me, "It is big business, but that's no argument against it. Why do people go to Masada in Israel? No, that's a poor comparison. Religion, tradition, and theater are often intermixed. If Americans are stupid enough to come, 100,000 strong, then they have big business. The majority of Americans will not understand it. They will just enjoy it, like they enjoy Disneyland. There is no contradiction to have a religious experience and make money with it."[57]

More than ever, religion is big business, as the annual gross of such television personalities as Robert Schuller ($16 million), Oral Roberts ($60 million), Jerry Falwell ($50 million), Pat Robertson ($58 million), Jim Bakker ($51 million), Rex Humbard ($25 million), and Jimmy Swaggart ($20 million) attests.[58] Communities that lack for media personalities, but not from penury, have emulated Oberammergau and invented their own special reasons for staging a Passion play. Before World War II, religious pageants of this sort were staged in Roquebrune, France; Salzburg and Freiburg, Germany; Mexicantown (San Antonio); Bronxville, New York; Columbus, Ohio; and even Hollywood, California.[59] More recently, the plays have cropped up in Bruges, Belgium; Regina, Saskatchewan; Nova Fazenda, Brazil; Black Hills, South Dakota; Lake Wales, Florida; Strasbourg, Virginia; and Cambridge, Ohio.[60]

The proliferation of these Passions in Europe and the United States should be a matter of concern,[61] for it is difficult, as at Oberammergau, to tell where religious motivation ceases and avarice begins. Unlike Oberammergau, from which they draw their inspiration, many Passions perpetuate the ancient stereotypes of perfidious Jews hounding a suffering Christ. The Union City, New Jersey, play, for example, which was written in 1914 by Father Emile of Juville, was based on the seventeenth-century manuscript from Oberammergau. Despite criticism from the American Jewish Congress and the Bishops' Committee for Ecumenical Interreligious Affairs, more than four thousand persons packed Holy Family Church into the 1970s to see Jews portrayed as "short, fat, big-nosed brutish louts."[62]

The danger in this is that such pageants may be exploited for racist, not mere economic, purposes by unprincipled persons. One such case is the "Great Passion Play" performed for more than a decade in Eureka Springs, Arkansas. Until 1964, Eureka Springs was a dumpy little town perched in the northwest corner of Arkansas. The average family income was $900 per year. Practically every piece of real estate in town except a few old homesteads was for sale. Most of the stores on Spring and Main streets were vacant and could be rented for $25 per month. The Bank of Eureka Springs held approximately $500,000 in assets. Within eight years, the average family income increased to $7,100. Rentals downtown were impossible to obtain, even at eight times the 1964 cost. Deposits in the bank ran between $9 million and $12 million. A six-acre piece of real estate cost ten times what it had in 1964. A modern highway and ancillary roads were extended to Eureka Springs. And the guidebook produced by the Arkansas Department of Parks and Tourism devoted six pages of photos and publicity to "this fascinating city."[63]

What transformed this once obscure town was the vision of Rev. Gerald L. K. Smith. Awaking one night in California in 1964, Smith decided to re-create the Holy Land as it was in the time of Christ right here in America. It was not a novel idea. Carl McIntyre had tried in vain to do the same thing near Cape Canaveral a few years earlier. Smith's Jordan and Galilee, however, would be in the Ozarks. Drawing on monies raised through the Elna M. Smith Foundation (named for his wife), Smith succeeded in creating a sprawling religious complex in Eureka Springs. The center of his New Jerusalem is a Passion play theater which accommodates 4,400 spectators. Every day, every summer, the agony of Christ is acted out on a stage twice as large as that at Oberammergau. Next to the theater is a Bible Museum, with more than seven thousand volumes and a "Christ Only Art Gallery" featuring more than five hundred portraits of Jesus. Looming over the entire complex is a huge statue of Christ, with arms outstretched, seven stories of concrete and reinforced steel.[64]

The debt owed by Eureka Springs to Oberammergau was admitted by Smith himself. As he noted in 1973: "More than 100 people have stopped by in the last two seasons to tell us that they witnessed the original Passion Play in Oberammergau in 1970 and that it was easy for them to say that the production in Eureka Springs is superior. What a compliment. What an honor. Mr. Hyde [Robert Hyde, director of the Eureka Springs Passion] and his family went to Oberammergau to witness the 1970 opening of this historic Passion Play. He took a bronze plaque, and on this bronze plaque was engraved a greeting and a prayerful congratulation, and it was signed by Mrs. Smith and myself, together with the officers of the Foundation. This plaque now hangs in the city hall in Oberammergau."[65] Out of gratitude, Smith even renamed the hillock where his Christ of the Ozarks stands—Mt. Oberammergau.

Oberammergau taught Smith and others that there was profit in the Passion. The problem is that Smith possessed none of the grace of the Bavarians. A one-time follower of Huey Long, an associate of Father Charles Coughlin, Smith was, until his death in 1976, an unrepentant anti-Semite. From 1942, his *Cross and the Flag* publication spread libels against Jews, blacks, and Communists, who Smith believed were destroying the Holy Land (Palestine), polluting America's blood, and threatening its institutions. In 1944, Gov. Thomas Dewey called Smith a "rodent" and accused him of undermining the basic principles of the U.S. Constitution. In 1956, Richard Nixon referred to him as "a race-baiting merchandiser of hate." In 1969, the conservative *Man-*

chester Union-Leader denounced his "un-American, anti-Semitic rabble-rousing with all the indignation we can muster."[66]

Not surprisingly, then, Smith's Passion has been a traditional anti-Semitic spectacle, replete with kaffiyehed money changers, slinking, bearded priests, a blond, noble Pilate, and angry mobs. Months before the play opened for the first time in 1968, the Secretariat for Catholic-Jewish Relations of the U.S. Conference of Catholic Bishops warned against performing Passions which emphasized deicide. "It was utterly predictable," wrote the Anti-Defamation League's Arnold Forster and Benjamin Epstein, "that the script of the Smith Passion play in Eureka Springs would be based on the Oberammergau version, that it would include the line from Matthew (and others that have no Scriptural basis at all) and that it would be redolent with all the other ancient anti-Jewish overtones, including blood-thirsty mob scenes, that have stained the history of Passion plays through the ages."[67] The Reverend Lester Kinsolving, who viewed the Ozarks Passion in 1972, called it "an atrocity."[68]

Because his play held out the promise of jobs, tickets, food, housing, and knicknacks, Smith encountered little resistance when he came to Eureka Springs. Local high-school girls eagerly handed out literature on the Passion to tourists. Stores displayed posters. Smith's colleague, Charles Robertson, was inducted into the Eureka Springs Chamber of Commerce.[69] The economic boomlet generated for Carroll County (Smith claimed his center brought in $29 million by 1972) won endorsement of other projects from Senators John McClellan and J. William Fulbright, Congressman John P. Hammerschmidt, Secretary of Commerce Maurice Stans, Orval Faubus, and Winthrop Rockefeller.[70]

Although Oberammergauers may disclaim any responsibility for Smith, the ease by which this demagogue seduced a population and government officials demonstrates the danger arising from staging a Passion play. Oberammergau showed the way, and in an age of revivalism and reborn Christianity, more communities may discover the economic benefits to be derived from ministering to the religious needs of people on an annual, not decennial, basis. Bigots and hypocrites will be supplied with an excellent sounding board for their anti-Zionism or anti-Semitism. And the gullible, whether in Europe or America, will pay heartily for the privilege of taking home with them souvenirs of hate.

11

The Rosner Option

There is no possibility that Oberammergau will forgo its performances of the Passion. Whether because of the vow or big business, it simply will not happen. That being the case, could an alternate version, one less offensive to Jews, be staged? This question was first raised in the 1960s when outside attention and criticism were focused upon the village. Some people suggested that Oberammergau return to the eighteenth-century work devised by Ferdinand Rosner, while others clung to the traditional Daisenberger text. The ensuing emotional struggle, which resembled a political fight, divides the people of Oberammergau to the present.

The figure responsible for reviving the Rosner text is Hans Schwaighofer. A master sculptor, director of the *Holz-schnitzer* school, Schwaighofer received accolades for his performance as Judas in 1950 and 1960. Assigned to direct the Passion in 1970, he proposed that Oberammergau return to the baroque version. As Schwaighofer viewed it, the Daisenberger text, with its horned priests, bloodthirsty crowds, innocent Pilate, and theme of a new covenant, was an embarrassment. The problem was attributable not so much to Daisenberger or the villagers of Oberammergau (neither of which could be charged with hatred of Jews) but rather to Othmar Weis, who wrote at a troubled time, when there was "a tendency in poetry for anti-Semitism." Daisenberger merely removed a small portion of Weis's material. But from 1860 "the voices for a text alteration have never been silent."[1]

Schwaighofer was supported in his efforts by Pater Stephan Schaller, the Ettal priest charged with editing the Passion for 1970. Schaller was, perhaps, the leading expert on the Rosner play (he had written his doctoral thesis on the subject and would subsequently publish *Passio Nova: Das Oberammergau Passionsspiel von 1750* in 1974) and favored it over Daisenberger.[2] When Schwaighofer put his proposal to the village council in 1966, it was initially passed by a vote of one. In a subsequent plebiscite held in October 1966, which was boycotted by most of the Oberammergauers, the people voted to retain the Daisenberger text. Wrote Pater Schaller, "People had to choose between two evils. I have the opinion that Oberammergau chose the lesser evil, that is, to retain the traditional text and to purge it."[3]

Schwaighofer resigned his post as director for 1970, but Schaller labored over the Daisenberger text for two years, while villagers "watched his work with mistrust."[4] The council told him before he started that they would not approve new versions of the Prologue. Later, they altered his text in rehearsals. As Hans Zander noted, the play was "nimbly retouched," shortened a bit by the removal of "23 achs and ohs." Basically, though, the Passion was still "miserable." While some offensive passages had been deleted through the arithmetic principle of chance, Zander reckoned "about half the anti-Semitism remains," including the antiphonal exchange between chorus and mob dealing with the curse of God.[5]

Following the 1970 performances, Schwaighofer persisted in his effort to replace the Daisenberger version with Rosner. He no longer had the assistance of Schaller, who had been assigned to work on the fifteen hundredth anniversary of the Benedictine order. Schwaighofer did, however, find new allies. From the United States came Rabbi Marc Tanenbaum, head of the American Jewish Committee. For more

than a decade, Rabbi Tanenbaum has commuted to Oberammergau trying to convince village leaders to support
Schwaighofer's reform. Participating in a prestigious interfaith forum on the Passion held by the Catholic Academy of
Bavaria in Munich on November 19, 1978, Tanenbaum reminded his colleagues: "For millions of people, Oberammergau is the image of Christianity in Germany. For many
others, Americans and men of other lands, Oberammergau is
an example of what is happening in the new Germany."[6]
Tanenbaum and the American Jewish Congress endorsed
the Rosner version, which they said "uses allegorical figures
to depict the fight between good and evil, but avoids restat-
ing the charge of collective deicide against world Jewry."[7]
For Tanenbaum, the Rosner text was a traditional morality
play, where Jews figured only marginally in the conflict
between Jesus and Lucifer. "It is essentially a millennial
Passion play with the Children of Light versus the Children
of Darkness, Lucifer, and the seven deadly sins," he said
recently. "Rosner is less invidious dramaturgically. There
are no priests with horned hats, no vulturous Pharisees with
black beards and spittle running down. Jews are almost incidental. In the play, it is clear that Lucifer pressured them to
do what they did. The way it came out in actual production, I
felt a sense of relief."[8]

In Germany, Schwaighofer's call for Rosner was endorsed
by Carl Orff, the renowned classical composer, who offered
to write music to replace that of Rochus Dedler. In Oberammergau, too, Schwaighofer received support from a number of reformists headed by Deputy Mayor Helmut Fischer,
a lawyer who played the part of Christ in 1970. After some
discussion, an agreement was reached with Bürgermeister
Zwink, a Daisenberger traditionalist, to permit several trial
performances of the Rosner play under the direction of
Schwaighofer in the summer of 1977. Approximately six
hundred villagers participated in these *Rückgriffe*, which
earned favorable reviews from the press, the archdiocese of
Munich, and the Jewish community in Bavaria.[9] As Schwaighofer declared, "A Rosner text in the year 1980 signified no
risk for the people of Oberammergau, for the greatest part of

visitors, media, the press, Catholic parties, the Lutheran Evangelical party, and also of the Jewish organizations have informed us that that was the way for Oberammergau in 1980."[10]

Rabbi Tanenbaum was impressed by the commitment of Schwaighofer and Zwink to eliminate any taint of anti-Semitism, "to expunge the image of Nazism from Oberammergau." The night after the Rosner preview, a group of town leaders and members of the American Jewish Committee stayed up till 4:30 in the morning, discussing various problems. Tanenbaum reports, "Their commitment to change was total. We got the feeling that in a spirit of good will, they would clean up what problems existed in the Rosner text." Later, Tanenbaum was invited to offer lectures on anti-Semitism before crowds of several hundred villagers. "They were staggered by the information and the film strips," he says. Like Schwaighofer, Tanenbaum was confident that the town would stage Rosner in 1980.[11]

From a more detached vantage point, Munich's Hans Lamm wryly notes, "everybody" was for the Rosner version, "only not in Oberammergau."[12] After the 1977 season, the villagers were asked again to indicate their preference in a poll. Only two-thirds of those eligible to vote did. Of those, 60 percent answered all eleven questions posed in the plebiscite. And of those, half were for, half against reform. Generally, the majority were against switching to Rosner for 1980. The dispute over how to count the votes had to be turned over to the *Stadtrat*. There, the majority of councillors had declared publicly against reform. But, amazingly, the Rosner advocates won 10–6. That should have ended the matter. In March 1978, however, new elections were held and several of the Rosner partisans were voted out of office. When the council met again in May, they voted 11–5 to reverse the earlier decision. As one German observer commented, the decision to stand by the Daisenberger text was a testimony to "the stubbornness of the people of Oberammergau" and "a rigid and retrograde way of thinking."[13]

Tanenbaum attributes the abrupt reversal to the late intervention of the Anti-Defamation League. Charging that

Messrs. Perlmutter, Kameny, and Freedman failed to understand the intricacies of Oberammergau politics, Rabbi Tanenbaum claims that the ADL's insistence upon revisions within Daisenberger undercut support for a substitute Rosner play. Reactionaries like Anton Preisinger, who had spoken against foreign meddling, could not align themselves with more moderate traditionalists and muster votes necessary to repudiate the Rosner play. "There was a moment when Rosner seemed in, with any changes we desired," says Rabbi Tanenbaum. "Then came the reversal. It was terrible, one of the saddest days in my involvement in Jewish communal life."[14]

Of course, others see it differently. Professor Swidler and Ted Freedman both acknowledge the role played by people like Tanenbaum and Joachim Prinz in sensitizing villagers to Jewish feelings. But Swidler (who regards neither play as "any great advance over the other") contends that the American Jewish Committee and American Jewish Congress were involved with Oberammergau for more than a decade, with little impact. Rabbi Tanenbaum served the role of "beater," says Swidler. "By being so hypercritical, Tanenbaum forced Zwink and the others into the arms of the ADL people who they felt were more reasonable."[15] That impression was reinforced by Hans Maier who told me, "I am convinced that Mr. Tanenbaum wants to eliminate the Passion play. He would find fault in any Passion play."[16]

The instigator of the controversy, Hans Schwaighofer, still insists the Rosner text is better than Daisenberger, which, with all its modifications, is *schlecht* (wretched, inferior). "I am no scholar," he told me, "but I know that the *Umschreibungstext* is not in agreement with the *Evangelium*. It is not accurate in its historical foundation. Jews who come as spectators are offended by the version and then naturally there is damage between Jews and Christians." Asked why the villagers reverted to Daisenberger, if Rosner had been so well received, Schwaighofer added: "They want to make business. Sure business. Money. That is why they had to play one hundred days. It's business. But people would come if it was the *Rosnerspiel*. They would come even if it

were a *Mickeymousespiel.*"[17] For his dedication, Schwaighofer has earned the enmity of some who blame him for
creating a rift in the tightly knit community.

According to Bürgermeister Zwink, there is no more controversy. "There is no problem," Zwink informed me. "Daisenberger is a tradition for the people of Oberammergau—their Passion. The people of Oberammergau have
seen the Rosner play and have said, 'No, this is not the Passion play for Oberammergau.' They voted to see it. 'Please
Mr. Schwaighofer, we want to see the Rosner in 1977.' We
have seen the play and it was very good, but it was not for
Oberammergau. The allegory was not interesting for the
people of Oberammergau."[18]

Like Zwink, the people in Oberammergau try to present a
united front to outsiders. During my stay in town, I spoke
with a number of lumberyard workers who had participated
in the Passion. When asked which play they preferred,
the men immediately and firmly replied, "Daisenberger."
Which play would be performed in the future? "Daisenberger." What of Rosner? "I don't like it. It's not true to the
Gospels." "It's too poetic." "The Rosner play was removed
because of its *Frechheit* [offensiveness]." "With the Devil
and other characters, it's like Carnival in Rio." Did these
men agree with Zwink's suggestion that the play was *Voll-
kommen* (perfect): "No play is ever perfect. Even man is not
perfect." "Such a thing cannot be. It has to be adapted to the
time." All denied that there was any *Streitfrage* (controversy) in town. Yet as I walked away from the lumberyard,
four villagers were arguing forcefully among themselves
about the nature of Jews in Jerusalem at the time of Jesus, which gospel should be the basis of the Passion, and
whether Mary had been "graced" or "impregnated" by the
Holy Spirit.[19]

Denying the existence of a continuing dispute over
Rosner or Daisenberger does not wipe away the bitterness of
the past ten years. Opponents of the Rosner Passion are
quick to offer denunciations of a play they hope will not be
performed. Said Pater Rümmelein, "I am against Rosner because it is not fitting for Oberammergau. It is impractical.

Some people tried, but failed. Orff tried to write the music, but it was not quite right for the people. The people did not like it. Rosner is tasteless. Formerly, they showed many cruel details, like the death of Judas. Daisenberger is finer. Thank God, everything trivial has been eliminated."[20] Director Hans Maier concurs: "Daisenberger's version is easier to understand, fits better in our time. All who see it are inspired by it. With its rhyme form, Rosner needs an audience like Salzburg. I also feel Rosner has more anti-Semitism in it. If the purpose of a Passion play is to preach the Gospel, the basis of the Catholic faith, Daisenberger follows the Gospels faithfully. Not so Rosner."[21] Participating in a forum on the subject with Schwaighofer, Dr. Franz Rappmannsberger, culture editor for Bavarian radio, explained the continuing hostility in Oberammergau, saying, "The people have fear of this baroque, post-expressionistic composition of a play that appears somehow *unheimlich* [strange]." Rappmannsberger argued that the people of Oberammergau could not relate to characters onstage representing Jealousy, Avarice, Death, and Despair. The baroque period, with all its beauty, belonged in the past.[22]

It is ironic that the Rosner play, which is condemned for being a throwback, is also faulted for being too progressive. Of Schwaighofer's staging with bold sets, stylized costumes and props, new electronic and acoustic methods, Anton Preisinger, the ex-Nazi who played Christ in 1950 and 1960, said, "These are pop colours, but we want to enact our faith."[23] Preisinger took the lead in denouncing Stephan Schaller's attempted reforms in 1970, calling the changes "dramatic catastrophe." He also has been the most outspoken in denouncing those who suggest that Rosner is closer to contemporary theology. Unlike the Daisenberger text, which clearly pins guilt upon the Jews, the Rosner version supposedly emphasizes the individual's responsibility for his sins. In Rosner, for example, spectators are instructed, "Don't say the Jews there betray your man. We all have done that and often enough." Later, we hear, "Don't be frightened by the fall of Judas, for you have a God who is benevo-

lent and merciful to repentance." And again, "There is no
guilt so great that through true repentance cannot be redeemed."[24] Informed that such concepts conform to recent
Vatican changes, Preisinger has said, "The people come to
us. Do you believe they are coming for modern theology?
What we need today are no intellectuals, no theologians, and
no journalists. What we need today in the Church of God are
Poverellos [true believers from the time of the Holy Roman
Empire]."[25]

Substituting the Rosner play for Daisenberger, frankly,
solves few problems. The villagers fret about what will happen to Dedler's music which has acquired an almost sacred
aura.[26] Hans Schwaighofer himself confesses to a distaste for
Orff's proposed score, which bears closer relation to Gregorian chants than opera. The Oberammergauers worry about
tripping over the archaic iambic tetrameter in Rosner. As
one example, when Peter denies Jesus, he does so in the
following singsong:

> Fliesst nur, ach fliesst, ihr heissen Tränen,
> jetzt kann ich erst mein Schachheit kenne.
> Kaum dass mich Jesus angeblickt,
> hat er mir Weh ins Herz geschickt.
> Sein Blick—er war ein Blick der Liebe,
> doch nur damit ich mich betrübe
> und durch sein Gnad erkennen soll,
> wie schwach ich bin, wie sündenvoll.[27]

In reviewing the text, Monsignor Genewein of the archbishop's office in Munich laughed at Rosner's "poetische"
nature. But Genewein, too, was troubled by potential anti-
Jewish elements in the Rosner script. "No," he told me, "it's
not any better than Daisenberger. It couldn't be played like
that. Even the Rosner text would have to be revised."[28]

There is sufficient evidence to suggest that Rosner conforms more to medieval Jew-baiting than to post-Vatican II
ecumenism. Rosner relied upon a device common to mystery plays—the personification of human frailties. Thus we

have a *Schutzgeist* (guardian angel) as Prologue or Narrator, *Verzweiflung* (Despair) as a companion of Judas, *Neid* (Envy) playing a double role as a Jewish priest along with *Satan*, a host of his adherents (including *Acheroth*, the counterpart of Baal, *Beelzebub*, Milton's fallen angel from *Paradise Lost*), and executioners who derive their names (*Cacus*, a man-eating giant, *Momus*, god of censure and ridicule, and *Janus*, a two-faced deity of war and peace) from classical mythology.

It is difficult to imagine how Rosner could have woven a Passion about these characters alone, and in fact he did not. Just as Daisenberger, his play abounds with invented passages which are offensive not merely to Jews but to any thinking Christian. In a scene reminiscent of an ancient Egyptian legend,[29] Judas appears onstage with his alter ego, Despair. The disciple laments that thirty silver coins do not compensate for the risk he took, the harm he had done to his master. "Had I known it would come to this," he laments, "I would not have undertaken it." Judas decides to return the blood money to the Sanhedrin, over the objections of Despair who tells him he is confused.[30] Judas then appears before the high court in a desperate attempt to redeem Jesus. The exchange with the high priests and the ubiquitous "Rabbi" is as bad or worse than what is found in the Daisenberger text:

> CAIAPHAS: What was done was done properly. You will see no more of it.
>
> JUDAS: I tell you that I never gave him over to you for his death.
>
> RABBI: We know that he is guilty and that you are his betrayer.
>
> JUDAS: I repent what I began. I was seized by a delusion. The sin gives me no rest, no quiet . . .
>
> CAIAPHAS: That is no concern of ours. It's your business.

Judas continues to protest, but is taunted by the hard-hearted council members:

SARAS: You have money, go buy a rope and send your
    soul to the Devil.
JUDAS: Damned coin, cursed sort, through which I
    have become a traitor. There, you have the blood
    profit. (He throws the coins to the floor.) Take it. Give
    me my master.
ONE OF THE PRIESTS: Your master is already finished.
ALL: For yet today, yet today he must die!
RABBI: I will take the money back, but the guilt remains
    with you.
ANNAS: Go, you have nothing more to say here.[31]

Judas curses the priests and exits, accompanied once more
by Despair. As in Daisenberger, he offers a soliloquy where
he asks rhetorically: "Should the earth bear me? Should I
not be struck by lightning? I have sought out Hell myself and
am eternally cursed." Judas damns the hour of his birth and
wishes he had never seen the light. Despair offers him no
solace. Rather, it declares, "You can hope for nothing more
than Hell. Life is for you only torment. Therefore, it must be
ended soon." Hearing this, Judas tears his garments and
walks to the rear of the stage. He opens a curtain, revealing
Satan who is sitting in a tree, with a ladder nearby:

JUDAS: So, I will hang myself and send my soul to the
    fire.
DESPAIR: Yes. I wish you much luck and present you
    this rope.
JUDAS (takes the rope, kisses it, and speaks to it): Come,
    dear band, you will not break. (He pulls on it to see if
    it is strong enough.) You must avenge God because
    he has denied me his mercy and has given me no
    possibility.
DESPAIR: Don't think of mercy. Hang yourself to this
    tree. You need so much courage, so much strength for
    this task.

Judas climbs the ladder and throws the rope over the
branch. Satan eagerly helps as Judas speaks again: "I can

repent my sins no more now. Forever will I be estranged from God, and this is the compensation for avarice. Look, Devil, look. I am coming." He pushes the ladder away and hangs. Satan pulls him above by the neck, while Beelzebub and Acheroth pull from his feet. Another crowd of evil spirits make a circle around the tree, hold hands, and dance. The grisly scene continues:

> SATAN: Keep going! He ended his life with the rope.
> DESPAIR: Come on! Look on this man who finally ended Despair.
> ACHEROTH: Come on! Pull both of his feet. He must split in two.
> DESPAIR: Come on! Look what a good meal our ravens have here.
> BEELZEBUB: He belonged to us in his last hour.
> ALL: Come Judas, our dearest brother. You are the best of Hell's vultures. You'll have good tidbits for eternity.
> ACHEROTH: Let's see if there are any more silver coins in his sack. It is empty. Ah, poor man, who also cannot pay for his grave.
> BEELZEBUB: He needs nothing. Is the fire in our pit not dear enough? His life and soul are sufficient wages for us all.

In former times, the demons would batten on Judas's innards, donuts, which came spilling out of his costume. That, at least, was deleted from the modern revival. But the scene ends when a trapdoor opens onstage and the flames of Hell shoot out. Despair exclaims: "Here we are by the kingdom of flames. Come, let us disappear together!" Satan's minions joyfully grab hold of Judas's battered body, pitch it into the opening onstage, and leap in after.[32]

Rabbi Tanenbaum and director Schwaighofer contend that the Rosner script looks worse on paper than onstage, that the total effect of the play is to cast responsibility for men's sins upon the devil. Granted, the actual production may translate Judas's death scene into anything from horror to farce, it must be remembered that Judas traditionally personified the Jewish people. His betrayal of Christ stems from no hypnotic spell of Satan but, as Judas admits, from simple greed, a fault which anti-Semites still attribute to Jews. His suicide, too, comes after minimal encouragement, no real pressure, from Satan. I am not so certain that the concept—"the Devil made me do it"—a spiritual cop-out, has any relevance in twentieth-century theology. In a play which supposedly holds out salvation for all sinners, there apparently is no hope for Judas or his people. Just as in the Daisenberger text, their irredeemable villainy is etched not with a pen but with a sledgehammer.

As in Daisenberger, Pontius Pilate is an unwilling participant in the affair. When Jesus is returned from Herod, the high priests, including one referred to as "Rebi," demand his death. Pilate, however, considers Jesus no more than a fool and cannot sentence him to die when the Jewish "Osterfest" is so near. According to custom, he will set either Jesus or Barabbas free:

> PILATE: Tell me, who is dearer to you?
> ALL: Barabbas should be free from chains and Christ remain, him to death!
> ANNAS: Christ must die. This solution has been well considered by us.
> ALL: Christ dies. Barabbas lives!

Disgusted by their obstinacy, Pilate asks the priests to leave for a short time. As they go off, they continue to chant, "Christ dies! Barabbas lives!" Mindful that he can no longer rely upon his friend Sejanus to protect him from accusations of misgovernment, the Roman procurator reluctantly agrees to have Jesus beaten. "Perhaps this torment will suffice to raise some pity," he says.[33] When the short flogging scene ends, Pilate calls the high council and people together:

> ANNAS: It is once and forever decided not to annul the crucifixion.

RABBI: Scourging is insufficient punishment to be the judgment.

AMOS: The sun should lose its luster and no stars adorn the heavens if Christ should survive today.

SOLOMON: Our resolve is universal. He must be crucified today!

PEOPLE: Today he must be crucified!

ANNAS: We are bound to a law which finds enough guilt in him. He represented himself as the son of God and therefore the cross is his reward.

PEOPLE: He represented himself as the son of God and therefore the cross is his reward.

RABBI: If there were no other crime, this alone would suffice to command a punishment of death.

AMOS: So have the council and the people spoken.

ALL: So have the council and the people spoken.

PILATE: Is that the people that call to me?

AMOS: To the cross! All our voices cry.

PILATE: I find no guilt in him. Can't you agree with that?

SOLOMON: No!

ALL: No! He must be crucified!

AMOS: To the cross! All our voices cry!

ONE: To the cross!

ALL: To the cross! To the cross with him!

CAIAPHAS: If you let the villain get away, you hate Caesar.

ANNAS: Whoever speaks against us here is no friend of Caesar.[34]

Pilate continues to hedge, asking the mob if he should kill their king. Growing restless, they clamor, "We want no such king! We are subject to Caesar!" The last thing the Roman procurator needs on his hands is a riot, so he orders his soldiers to form a protective cordon. Pilate also mulls aloud, "Many hounds seek the rabbit's death." With the mob still shouting for Jesus' death, Barabbas and Christ are brought forward. As Barabbas is unfettered, Pilate declares, "From me you earn no pardon. I have done my duty and set you free upon your word. Let us promptly hang a bloody flag, as is customary, outside my house."[35]

Upon hearing that the symbol of condemnation will be given, the crowd erupts in jubilation. At one side of the stage, the character *Neid* (Envy) tells the audience: "I have so blinded the Jews that they themselves don't understand. I will not yet go from here. I will stand invisible at the judgment and what yet happens I will report exactly to Lucifer."[36] Once more, the intent in Rosner may be to shift responsibility away from people to the devil, but because the revelation from Envy is so fleeting, it fails. If anything, spectators will understand that *Neid,* who also doubles as "Rebi," identifies the Jewish people with perfidy.

When the condemnation scene resumes, the script directs Pilate to address the *Schreiber* (Scribes), *der Rat* (Sanhedrin), and not the *Volk* or *Masse,* as before, but "alle Juden."[37] That all are Jews and not a mob or crowd as mentioned in the Gospels of Matthew, Mark, or Luke is evident in Pilate's speech:

> PILATE: You Jews, listen. I openly acknowledge before the people and before the Council that Jesus has committed no crime for which I could condemn him to the cross. I therefore take no guilt upon me and I acknowledge this publicly. The end has been decided, so listen to what end it has been brought.
> (Scribe reads the judgment.)
> PILATE: The judgment is completed. I break my staff and wash my hands.
> CAIAPHAS: You have decided as you should and we want to thank you. You could do nothing else because the law finds him guilty. Let us carry to an end and without delay the slaughter of this sacrifice which our law demands.
> ALL: Out with him to Golgotha![38]

Rosner's Crucifixion scene is far more barbaric than anything conceived by Daisenberger. Jesus is abused as he makes his way slowly along the Via Dolorosa. He is jeered and taunted as he is murdered. The Rabbi sarcastically offers Christ a drink, saying, "Refresh yourself with this drink. You must have majestic strength." The executioners strip the cloak from "this great Jewish king" and prepare his "throne" that his "sovereignty might be well displayed":

> NATHAN: Now bind his hands and feet because we must stretch his limbs.
> (They lay a rope to him and pull, tying him to the cross.)
> COSMUS: It's okay. Give me the hammer.
> CACUS: We have no more pity.
> COSMUS: We have finished the matter.
> NATHAN: Now turn around his feet.
> CAPTAIN: Now the punishment must be fully executed.
> JANUS: Enough. Now give me the hammer.
> MOMUS: Strike until he finally turns white (from death).[39]

The scene continues for another fifteen or twenty minutes as Jesus, blood dripping from the wounds of nails, hangs in agony. Caiaphas, the Rabbi, Amos, and other Jews, easily identifiable by their names, stand before him and ridicule. The executioners toss dice for the cloak, laugh, and ask Jesus' blessing before each roll. One of them, Momus, offers a drink of gall, vinegar, and myrrh to the crucified prisoner and mocks, "What, has your great thirst disappeared?"

> JESUS: Eli! Eli! My god, why have you forsaken me?
> RABBI: Look. He despairs and calls for help from Elias because he can no longer help himself and is also without power in death.
> JESUS: It is fulfilled. It is done. Now father, into thine hands I give my spirit. My life is over.

At that point, "Christus neiget [sic] das Haupt." His head dips.[40]

Obviously, the Rosner version is not an improvement over Daisenberger. If anything, the high priests are more sadistic, Jewish identification with the forces of Satan more specific, and eternal damnation via Judas assured. When, upon entering Jerusalem, Jesus proclaims, "From the land of the Jews the heathen band sentences me to my death,"[41] it just may be that he is referring not to Romans or Gentiles but to his own people. With all its poetry and symbolism, the play reflects a brutal, medieval mentality. The lengthy scenes of gore combined with ridicule cannot fail to evoke emotional responses of anger and hate, even in the most sophisticated, modern audience. A reading of the Rosner text indicates that it, not the Jewish people, is irredeemable. As Dr. Nathan Levinson, one of the few remaining Jews in Germany, noted several years ago, the Rosner Passion "is not only terrible theology, but also terrible theater."[42]

Most regrettably, the Rosner controversy has bruised egos and generated resentment within the Jewish community in this country. Yet ultimately the American Jewish Committee, American Jewish Congress, and the Anti-Defamation League are striving for the same goal. Says Ted Freedman of the ADL: "The Rosner text is more allegorical in nature, uses the symbolism of the devil. But everybody knows what is inferred when you talk about the devil and the Jews. It doesn't solve the problem, just because people don't understand it. You might put it on in Swahili, then nobody would know what's being said. That's not the way to deal with the problem. The reality is there are people who are portraying the passion in a language they want to understand. It is an emotional experience. Our task is to make such changes so it can be a positive one for them, but certainly not a negative one for us."[43]

12

A Contemporary Passion?

Can a Passion, any Passion, be a positive experience for Christians without being a negative one for Jews? Or are we left with the gloomy proposition advanced by Hans Lamm that "every Passion play by necessity is anti-Jewish, as much as the Gospels are"? And "they are not going to rewrite the New Testament to please the Anti-Defamation League."[1]

The task of reconciling those disparate goals for 1980 was given to Pater Gregor Rümmelein, a modest, diminutive monk from Ettal. Because of his labors, visitors to Oberammergau that summer were greeted by a socially conscious Prologue who hailed "the brothers and sisters of the people who brought forth the Redeemer." The audience was further instructed not to seek blame in others but "let each of us recognize his own guilt in these events."[2] What they did not see or hear was almost as important. Gone from Rümmelein's revision were references to servants of Mammon, bloodhounds, Satan, and tableaux dealing with Joseph and Vashti. Lengthy scenes of merchants complaining to priests, priests conspiring, the Sanhedrin before Herod, and Jewish leaders at Golgotha were all halved. Despite the welcome changes, Rabbi Tanenbaum said of the 1980 Passion, "I came, I saw, and I was appalled."[3] The play was, he felt, "still structurally anti-Semitic."[4]

Tanenbaum's assessment may have been somewhat overdrawn. For his part, Pater Rümmelein insists: "We were interested in eliminating anything that could insult the Jews. We were very concerned to do everything to please the Jews. Cardinal Ratzinger declared there was nothing anti-Jewish in the play anymore. As the play is now presented, it totally corresponds with the Gospels, and that is what Oberammergau desires. None will say, 'The Jews are guilty of Christ's death.' It is expressly stated, 'Everybody should recognize his own guilt.' Catholics realize that just a few people wanted Jesus crucified. The gospel itself does not mention it, but we can assume that some of the people were against crucifixion. Something like in Hitler's time. The ones against Hitler were too quiet, and the ones for Hitler were tremendously noisy. Now all of Germany is blamed, to some extent rightfully, because Hitler's enemies should have been more vocal. Not enough people voted against Hitler in that first election, in 1933. In this respect, we have to accept the blame. Of course, the Jews nowadays have nothing to do with Christ's death. In like manner, the young Germans today have nothing to do with Hitler and do not want to accept blame." For Rümmelein, the current edition of the Oberammergau Passion is "friedlicher, rühiger, und frömmer" (more peaceful, quiet, and devout), and his only regret is that he was not able to revise the play earlier.[5]

Frankly, Oberammergau's Passion in 1980 was neither as good as Rümmelein and other villagers maintained nor as horrid as Tanenbaum suggested. If there were a continuum or scale of anti-Semitism, with Julius Streicher's *Der Stürmer* at 100 and Felix Salten's *Bambi* at 0, the 1970 play would probably be placed near 80. Thanks to Rümmelein's efforts, the 1980 play should be marked no worse than 40. Its retention of stereotypes, a broken covenant, an innocuous Pilate, crowds shrieking for Jesus' crucifixion, prevents the current text from satisfying the reforms outlined by the ADL or American Jewish Committee.

Let us assume for one moment that no further changes will be made in the Daisenberger text (and I do not believe this will happen), that Oberammergau's Passion continues to project anti-Semitic images. Is the only option, then, Rosner? Clearly, this is unacceptable. I asked Pater Rümmelein, Bürgermeister Zwink, Spielleiter Maier, Hans Schwaighofer, and Monsignor Genewein if a totally new text, one consistent with contemporary church dogma, might be presentable in Oberammergau? Would the villagers accept a Passion based not on the Gospels of Matthew and John, as are both Rosner and Daisenberger texts? Would a Passion based on the Book of Luke—one which emphasized the continuity or flow of Judaism and Christianity, which omitted the incident with the money changers and the charge of blasphemy, which condensed the plotting of the priests, saw Jesus condemned by a "mob" without any utterance of a blood curse, and which portrayed "a great crowd of the people and of women who were bewailing and lamenting" on the way to Golgotha, an equally great crowd returning from the Crucifixion "beating their breasts"—be possible?[6]

With the exception of Monsignor Genewein, all those associated with the play responded no to the above questions. The archbishop's representative affirmed that it is possible to do a Passion play without offending Jews. The starting place, he agreed, was the Book of Luke. "And if not Luke," he told me, "then something else." All the others flatly declared it could not be done. Some worried about what would happen to Dedler's semisacred music. Pater Rümmelein, obviously for personal reasons, opined that a new play was unnecessary. In a rare moment of agreement, Hans Maier and Hans Schwaighofer, advocates of rival versions of the Passion, declared that the people in Oberammergau "hardly" would accept a new version. Bürgermeister Zwink put it more diplomatically: "This man is not born. We have not seen this book. We must first see before we say if it is possible or not possible. But the man is not born."[7]

The man may not have lived who could write a twentieth-century Passion play that is relevant to the needs of Christians and merciful to all "who love and keep the commandments." But there is a woman who has done it. Catherine De Vinck, a renowned poetess,[8] published *A Passion Play* in 1975. Hers is an extraordinary work which truly can be called a hymn of reconciliation. The play, which consists of three acts, each with three scenes, takes us from Jesus in the house of Simon of Bethany to his reappearance before the apostles in the upper room of Acts. It thus parallels both the Daisenberger and Rosner versions but has the advantage of brevity, lasting no more than two hours in all.

Pilate is still the austere, reluctant Roman who inquires, "What is truth?" Deterred by Procula's dream, he turns Jesus over to Herod, after learning Jesus hails from troublemaking Galilee. Upon his return, the procurator has him flogged. De Vinck retains both brutal scenes of beating and crucifixion. With these few exceptions, however, De Vinck's Passion fulfills the requisites of sensitivity proposed by the Catholic Bishops' Conference, Vatican II, Professor Swidler, the ADL, and Rabbi Tanenbaum.

De Vinck's Passion has no need of an explosive scene with money changers, lengthy plotting of priests, or a blood curse. Her Judas is a weak, one-dimensional character. His motivation stems not from some intrinsic racial flaw, greed, or an external demon. Rather, Judas betrays Jesus because he followed what he believed to be a political revolutionary and was dismayed to find his leader actually believed himself to be the son of God. Judas's anguish and suicide are also omitted from De Vinck's play.

There is no need for a scene dealing with Judas's final remorse because the guilt for Christ's death is borne not by one symbolic person or the Jewish people but by all mankind. The high priests who orchestrate Jesus' murder are anonymous figures who wear "dark and brilliant masks" as in ancient Greek drama. Their repeated affirmations that "the Law is an iron woman, death spirited and blind" reflect upon every intransigent, hypocritical hierarchy in history.[9] The witnesses who denounce Jesus are patently false and not even the high priests who angrily order them out are fooled by their claims. The crowd that marches off to apprehend Jesus in Gethsemane is a "band of ill-assorted peo-

ple" who "carry chains, ropes, all kinds of daggers, sub-
machine guns, huge revolvers and over-sized clubs."[10] They
are the faceless, hate-filled mobs of history, and to emphasize the point, De Vinck has them wear animal masks,
some long-snouted or long-eared as pigs, donkeys, and apes,
others with plumes to suggest birds. The crowd that is hastily
assembled to denounce Jesus is exactly that—a crowd. They
shout "Kill him! Kill him!" and "Barabbas! Barabbas! Barabbas!" and "Nail him to the cross!" But they are not all Jews.
They do not shriek on endlessly. They do not accept eternal damnation for their actions. They do not taunt Jesus at
Golgotha.[11]

De Vinck's language is simple, understandable, relevant
to our own age, where nonconformists often are ridiculed.
Jesus' *Am-ha-Aretz* (poor followers) appear as "the sandaled
boys, the girls with flowing hair who puff the word 'peace' in
the air fine like dandelion seed."[12] Contemporary cynicism
is expressed by the Roman soldiers who pummel Jesus and
deride his efforts saying, "The world shall be unchanged;
the whore will open the same legs to the same stranger."[13]
Today's disenchantment with political opportunists is expressed by a member of the crowd who denies that Jesus is a
king, for "a true king would bring us armies, gunpowder and
gold; he would pass under our windows waving dollars and
flags; he would promise jobs, lower prices, better wages,
ivory, elephants, and slaves, a new sun, a fresh moon, our
stars forever flashing over the entire world."[14]

The one truly admirable character in De Vinck's Passion is
Jesus, clearly identifiable as a Jew. His greeting to his disciples is the traditional "Peace be to You" or *Shalom Aleichem*
of Hebrew.[15] He offers a blessing over the bread at the Last
Supper.[16] When he appears before the high priests, they ask:
"What is your name, your address? I see a number tattoed on
your wrist and David's star tacked to your coat: you will be
burned, gassed, hanged, pressed into soap and tallow."[17]

Jesus proclaims no new covenant. Rather, he says: "I did
not come to abolish the Law: let it tick, let it ring the change
of transgression and sin. I did not come to brand my people
with new ciphers, but to deliver them from the worm swol-

len with the rot of their fear."[18] His fate is linked with that
of Koheleth, as the narrator recites: "There is a season for
everything under the heavens: a time for being born, a time
for dying, a time for weeping, a time for healing."[19] His fate
is linked with that of Jews and other oppressed peoples
throughout history when he speaks to the women of Jerusalem along the Via Dolorosa:

> From age to age
> why is guilt pressed upon your souls?
> Crush the myrrh, prepare the linen
> store the ointment for your distant children.
> The desert, the rock-pile, the lime-pit
> this is where you keep house, my sisters!
> With you I mourn, with you I am sent
> by cattle-car to sealed rooms
> deep into a smoky darkness.
> My sisters, in my dying I sing Kaddish with you.
> I am not a God of nowhere, but Myriam's son;
> my roots stand firm in your soil, Israel!
> Who is killing me? A few Romans
> a handful of Jews? Here and now, yes;
> but my death grows elsewhere, hangs
> in a thousand evil trees. The hands
> that kill hold the club, aim the gun
> drop the bomb; the eyes that hunt me
> glow in dark forests of time; I die
> in all places of terror, at all hours
> —Rome, Constantinople, Auschwitz
> Hiroshima, Baby-Yar, Mylai—
> names are tattooed on my flesh
> numbers are carved in my wrists
> while the world writes its history
> with the iron alphabet of war.[20]

On the cross, Jesus utters the memorable lines from Luke
23:34 which are omitted from *all* Oberammergau Passions:
"Father, forgive them; they do not know what they are
doing." Significantly, De Vinck's Jesus continues:

Have mercy on my brothers
Have pity on my sisters:
with them I rise and grow
on the stem of time; with them
I ripen from seed to fruit.
Now and forever I am a man:
my city is of earth, of flesh
of these feeble lights we call
suns, stars and moons.
Rained over, snowed under, plowed
by the claws of the wind
I am Lord of this small estate.
Forgive my people:
would they kill me if they knew
I am the firebrand in their ashes
the bread in the dish of their hunger?
Father, this body stretched in pain
on the hard bed of this world
this is the house of your mercy
the hive where bees
will come and go from age to age.
Let them find their honey
Let them feed in their long winter![21]

Like Andre Schwarz-Bart's immortal Ernie Levy,[22] De Vinck's Jewish Jesus attempts to bolster the courage of his doomed companions. As the thieves are about to expire, Jesus tells them: "Have no fear: I pass with you through the smeared bloody gate. Sleep, my brother. We are going home."[23] When Christ himself dies, the people leave, slowly, some beating their breasts. According to stage directions, there is a long pause. Then, with the stage empty except for the bodies of Christ and the thieves, "a woman's voice rises singing Kaddish."[24]

Cardinal Ratzinger told the people of Oberammergau that they should seek the brightness of God's face in the story of the crucified and resurrected Jesus Christ. Here, at last, in the De Vinck Passion do we find a genuine hymn of reconciliation and love. Upon his return in the final act, Jesus tells his disciples, "Come to me all who thirst and hunger." He advises them not to keep ancient photographs of his face for "I am not in the past: I am the presence." The play ends, not with despair or martial vindication, but hope. "Fear not," Jesus says quietly. "I am with you always until the end of the world."[25]

De Vinck's play is faithful to the Gospels, responsive to Jewish sensitivities, literate, and artistically compelling. Yet it will never be performed in Oberammergau—because she is a woman, because she is not a resident of the village, because her play dares to evoke images of the Holocaust in a town anxious to forget its Nazi past, and because it employs some avant-garde staging techniques. If the hidebound villagers would not embrace one of their own (Rosner), it is highly unlikely they would break with tradition and use an American version translated into German.

Realistically, there is no alternative to Daisenberger. It is the basic text that will be employed in 1984, 1990, and 2000. That being so, additional changes, beyond a mere cosmetic touch-up, must be effected. Future Passions in Oberammergau should

1. be shortened by as much as two hours, through cuts in choral interludes and other redundancies;

2. improve upon the poor translations currently in use which contain numerous misspellings and references to Jews as a race;

3. introduce properly pronounced Hebrew words or greetings;

4. place Jesus clearly within a Jewish religious and historical milieu, including identification of the Last Supper as a seder of freedom, replete with matzos, *tallisim*, and *barochot*;

5. reduce invented dialogue among merchants, Judas, and high priests;

6. delete gratuitous insults against Jews, offered in choral passages;

7. play down the greedy aspects of Judas's nature and stress his disillusionment with the manner in which Jesus was moving ahead;

8. eliminate mythical symbols like the horned head-dresses, Latin decalogue, and black-garbed rabbis which reduce the Passion to a simplistic Manichaean struggle;

9. costume all participants, including temple guards and Romans, in outfits which at least have a semblance of historical validity;

10. demonstrate some passing acquaintance with the operation of talmudic law in the time of Christ;

11. emphasize a continuity of Old and New Covenants, through a closer adherence to the Book of Luke;

12. coordinate tableaux to emphasize not a break in God's blessing but an expansion thereof to all mankind;

13. portray Pilate as the amoral villain he truly was;

14. de-emphasize the blood and gore of Jesus' corporal and capital punishment through the abbreviation of such scenes which can appeal only to sadomasochistic audiences;

15. leave no doubt that a *mob* clamored for Jesus' execution, that within such mob there were more than a handful who spoke out against the unjust verdict;[26]

16. delete the insidious blood curse of Matthew and at least half of the screams for Jesus' death;

17. indicate in the text that condemnatory lines are spoken not by Jews or "the people" but by a mob;

18. include Christ's lines of forgiveness offered from the cross, lines which have notably been absent from the traditional Oberammergau Passion;

19. incorporate a Kaddish somewhere in the Crucifixion scene;

And lastly, somehow, more than is now evident, use the play as a vehicle for education, emphasizing the love and ethical teachings of Jesus. Nowhere in either the Rosner or the Daisenberger text do we get a glimmer of the Sermon on the Mount, Christ's parables, homilies, or the Golden Rule. Nowhere is there a glimmer of what Monsignor Genewein called the "Shalom Jahwe" (the peace of Jehovah) when he addressed the people of Oberammergau on Ash Wednesday in 1980. Instead, the play still retains too much of what Rosemary Ruether calls an anti-Jewish virus. The product of medieval anti-Judaism, the ancient death wish against

Jews was exploited by the Nazis and is still maintained in the East where "myths still live and glowing embers are easily fanned into new flames." Wrote Ms. Ruether, "If the Christian Church wants to purify its message and its life from the anti-Jewish virus, it will have to remove this left hand of Christology."[27]

Continued change is extremely important and necessary. Says the ADL's Ted Freedman, "The Oberammergau play in and of itself is nothing. What really is important is the symbolism of the play. I came away with the feeling that in spite of the pronouncements of Vatican II and the National Council of Churches, the Episcopalians and Lutherans with regard to deicide, and the related kinds of things, that that information has not generally filtered down to the masses. I have a sense that the distance between Rome and the Vatican and 823 UN Plaza [headquarters of the ADL] or New York City is closer than the distance from the Vatican to Palermo or Venice or the suburbs of Rome. When you look at the comments of the newly elected Southern Baptist president, who believes everything, every word of the Bible is divine, and that God does not hear the prayers of the Jews, I think what you have is the bedrock of the continuation of some of the problems which have plagued Jews. We're really saying that in spite of the progress, in spite of the pronouncements, that the Passion story and certain forms of religious education continues and perpetuates anti-Semitism into the twenty-first century."[28]

The villagers in Oberammergau have made a commitment to change.[29] The question is how far are they willing to go in compromising what they consider to be the essence of the Passion. According to Freedman, "My best estimate is that the text they're using now is the text they're going to use. The changes that may be forthcoming cannot be of sufficient nature that they disrupt the whole thing for them. They just won't do it. They'll close down on you." After his meetings with Bürgermeister Zwink and Pater Rümmelein, Freedman came away believing that the play will not stagnate, nor will it backslide to an earlier level of anti-Semitism.[30]

Freedman's point about knowing when and how to apply

moral suasion is extremely important. There are some traditionalists in Oberammergau who do not want to yield any
more ground. There are even those, I suspect, who long for
the kind of Passion performed in 1934 or 1950. Moderates,
too, may react with pique to adverse comments offered by
American Jews after they have made what appear to be major
concessions. Practically, then, can anybody dictate changes
suggested above?

The obvious answer would seem to be the archbishop of
Munich, Cardinal Ratzinger. Oberammergau lies within his
diocese and the bulk of its population is Roman Catholic.
Since Pope John XXIII, the church has been officially committed to bettering relations between Jews and Christians.
Subtle pressure from the archbishop's office would achieve
more than a dozen visits from American critics. There are
those, however, who deny that the church has any authority
over the villagers' pageant. Hans Lamm, for example, argues
that "The church's hands are bound because the play is not
done or approved by the church. The people could always
tell each cardinal to go to Hell and 'We don't care whether
you come and preach or whether you like the play.' He has
no jurisdiction over them. Informally, he talked with them,
and they took some of his advice. I don't say out of the kind-
ness of their hearts—because I'm not so sure their hearts are
very kind—but out of realization it's not desirable to have
world Jewry, which they overestimate very much in importance, or the church, or the cardinal against them. None of
the texts in 1980 or 1960 had the imprimatur of the church."[31]

Cardinal Ratzinger's representative in Munich, Monsignor Genewein, basically agreed with Lamm. "As a matter of
fact," he told me, "we have nothing to do with the text. It's
the people of Oberammergau, who are a little bit special. We
are not so happy with the Daisenberger text. The cardinal
would have preferred the Rosner text, but you know they
had elections. The cardinal worked personally on this text. It
is emended now, but in my opinion, the Passion play is a
little bit too long, a little bit too complicated. The Rosner text
would be much better from a point of view of theology."[32]

The Passion at Oberammergau may not bear the printed

seal of the Vatican, but throughout history, the church has taken more than fleeting interest in its performance. In the eighteenth century, villagers managed to circumvent the ban against religious dramas because of continuing turmoil in Germany and their remoteness in the Bavarian hills. Modern communication and transportation would rule out such behavior today. In fact, in this century numerous high-ranking Catholic officials have cloaked the Passion with unofficial sanction by their attendance. In 1900, Cardinal Ratti (later Pius XI) saw Anton Lang play Christus for the first time. In 1922, the pope dispatched his papal nuncio in Bavaria to witness the drama and carry his blessing to the Passion players.[33] Speaking to the people of Oberammergau in 1970, Cardinal Döpfner sidestepped any formal criticism, conceding that the statements of Vatican II were nearer to Catholic liturgy and the Gospels than "a Volksplay which comes from another root." Döpfner had much praise, however, for the play, which he regarded as "an expression of believing piety," "an historical event, full of symbolism and possibilities for us, for the guests, for the church and for the world."[34] Cardinal Ratzinger has been aware of the criticisms of the Oberammergau text and upon his return from New York where he met with Rabbi Tanenbaum in the winter of 1979–80, he recommended specific changes in the Daisenberger text. Accordingly, there were cuts and altera-tions in about three dozen places.[35] The church, then, has not been powerless in effecting changes. There is no need for a specific ban, withholding of sacraments, or threat of interdict. All that is required is for the Vatican Secretariat on Jewish Relations to take a more active role in supervising the script at Oberammergau. That is precisely what transpired during the winter of 1982–83. For some months, a confer-ence of German bishops under the direction of Franz Muss-ner labored over proposed changes for the 1984 text. As of this writing (April 1983), however, it was unknown what the bishops would recommend. At the very least, the church should insert a preface reflecting contemporary theology into all playbooks, to assist spectators in understanding the true purpose of the Passion.

All principals involved in the Oberammergau controversy avow their commitment to improved Christian-Jewish relations. Former Bürgermeister Zwink informed me, "Wir haben guten Beziehungen zu den Jüdischen Familien." (The Jewish man is the same friend for me as another man.)[36] The same message was stressed in Cardinal Ratzinger's opening sermon to the people of Oberammergau in May 1980. Monsignor Genewein sounded the identical theme in his Ash Wednesday address to the villagers. More eloquent than his superior, Genewein reminded the Oberammergauers that there was "too much war, too much hate, too much jealousy, too much want, too much misery on this earth." All men were "workers in a vineyard," struggling alongside their redeemer to create a rule of God, the previously mentioned "Shalom Jahwe" on earth. For that reason, the Passion should never create a trench of misunderstanding between peoples.[37]

Monsignor Genewein advocates, among other things, interfaith prayer sessions. More important, the Munich diocese mandates that all ordained priests make pilgrimage not to the Holy Land (a euphemism favored by some Christians over a term they deem "political") but to Israel. "For me," says Genewein, "the most important thing would be for more and more Germans to visit Israel. That's one of the best things. You see where it all happened. And you see the people, from Germany, from Yemen, a melting pot, making a garden out of a desert."[38]

Hopefully, Genewein and others like him represent the wave of the future. For twenty years, Jews and Christians have striven to reform what was a relic of the anti-Semitic past. Joachim Prinz and the American Jewish Congress paved the way back in 1960, and other Jewish groups built upon that foundation. None would have succeeded without the cooperation of righteous Gentiles like Monsignor Oesterreicher, Father Flannery, Sister Louis Gabriel, Annemarie Weiss, Rosemary Ruether, Leonard Swidler, or Sister Gloria Coleman. Nor would they have succeeded without the saintly intervention of Pope John XXIII who pressed for the declaration which said of Christ's death, "His passion cannot be attributed without distinction to all Jews then alive, nor can it be attributed to the Jews of today."[39] Finally, no progress could have been possible without the sensitivity of people like Ernst Zwink, Stephan Schaller, Hans Schwaighofer, Hans Maier, and Gregor Rümmelein, all of whom desired to make of the Oberammergau Passion a genuine hymn of reconciliation.

In 1900, a mournful rabbi from Philadelphia, Joseph Krauskopf, returned from Oberammergau and said: "When I considered the falsity I had listened to, the hatred and malice I had seen enacted, when I reflected upon the wrong that has been done to us, I could not but ask myself: How will it end? When will justice be done to the Jew?"[40] More than eighty years later, we still ask the same questions.

Postscript

On May 7, 1983, authorities in Oberammergau issued a press release which read, in part, "The Passion Play
Village Oberammergau has still not forgotten the charges of
anti-Semitism which in 1970 led to a temporary boycott with
the result that in August/September often whole sections of
the Passion Playhouse remained empty."[1] As evidence of
their sensitivity, village representatives met with Bishop
Karl Flügel, hoping to incorporate recommendations of the
German Bishops' Conference. On May 18, Oberammergau's
press service declared, "It was confirmed by a team of
theological experts that the text (of the 1984 Passion Play) is
in accord with the insights of the Council (Vatican II) and is
free of all possible anti-Judaism. . . . The Oberammergau
people can now with assurance begin the auditions for the
Jubilee Passion Play 1984 since the text has been unani-
mously approved by all experts."[2]

Were it only so. According to the Anti-Defamation
League's Ted Freedman, "No Jewish experts or representatives were consulted in this entire revision procedure for the
1984 production."[3] At the close of the 1980 performances,
Bürgermeister Zwink did request a detailed list of objections from the ADL and American Jewish Committee. Materials authored by Judith Banki and Professor Leonard Swid-

ler were sent. Their recommendations were appended to the formal report compiled by Professor Franz Mussner for the Bishops' Conference and the villagers this past spring. Of twenty-eight suggestions made by Swidler alone, only five were adopted, and these, in the view of both Swidler and Ted Freedman, were "insubstantial," "bare minimums," and "have no bearing on the matter of anti-Judaism."[4]

A combination of unfortunate circumstances, mistrust, and misunderstanding contributed to the present situation. The death of Mayor Zwink (through leukemia early in 1981) and the transfer of Cardinal Ratzinger from his post in Munich removed two sympathetic activists from the scene. Ratzinger's chair in Munich remained empty for a year before Archbishop Frederick Wetter was named as his replacement. Wetter delegated responsibility for an assessment of the Passion to Professor Mussner. The latter inadvertently attached the recommendations of Banki and Swidler to his own formal report, without translating the English into German. Professor Swidler believes the villagers and bishops may have assumed that Mussner's recommendations encompassed those of the Americans. To compound matters, the ADL which had offered to participate in discussions was notified May 3, 1983, that Archbishop Wetter was to meet with the villagers *two days later*, a time frame which made it virtually impossible to send any American or Jewish representative.

Professor Swidler believes that the Americans should have been afforded an opportunity to critique changes before they were announced. To date, appeals from Jewish organizations have proved fruitless. Bishop Flugel feebly maintains the church has fulfilled its original mandate (to meet with and seek a response from the Oberammergauers) and is unwilling to broach the subject again. Inquiries to Bürgermeister Frank Hofmann have elicited the response that further changes in the Passion text are "impossible." The reaction of Spielleiter Hans Maier has been equally disconcerting. Says Swidler, "I did reach Maier by telephone, but he became very, very, very huffy. He said they were not going to change another letter in the whole play."[5] Adds Ted Freedman, "The townspeople have the misguided notion that they made changes, why aren't we happy?"[6]

The answer to that last question is supplied by Professor Swidler, himself a Christian. If the Passion is to be a first-rate religious, dramatic, and musical production, writes Swidler, it must be "totally free from anti-Semitic and anti-Judaic elements," and must also "show forth the Jewishness of Yeshua and his followers, exhibit a sensitivity to and love for the Judaism that was the life-long religion of Yeshua and all his followers, and thereby foster love, not hate, between Jews and Christians."[7] As of this writing (December 1983), that has not been the case. Lamentably, the half-million tourists that already have guaranteed Oberammergau of sellout performances this coming summer will suffer more unhistorical kitsch.

Notes

Selected Bibliography

Index

Notes

New Testament Roots of Christian Anti-Semitism

1. Clark M. Williamson, "The 'Adversus Judaeos' Tradition in Christian Theology," *Encounter* 39 (1978): 273.

2. *Contra Celsum*, 4, 23; in Migne, *Patrologiae cursus completus*, series Graeca, 2:1060, cited in Léon Poliakov, *The History of Anti-Semitism*, vol. 1, trans. Richard Howard (New York: Vanguard Press, 1965), 23.

3. Migne, *Patrologiae* 46: 685, cited in Poliakov, *History*, 25.

4. Migne, *Patrologiae* 25: 830, in ibid.

5. John V. Chamberlain, "Anti-Semitism and the Gospel in the New Testament," *Saint Luke Journal of Theology* 23 (1980): 195.

6. See Gal. 4, Rom. 9–11.

7. Williamson, "The 'Adversus Judaeos' Tradition in Christian Theology."

8. Samuel Sandmel, *We Jews and You Christians: An Inquiry into Attitudes* (Philadelphia and New York: J. B. Lippincott, 1967), 20.

9. Williamson, "The 'Adversus Judaeos' Tradition in Christian Theology."

1. The Way to Oberammergau

1. Joseph Lutz, "A Leisurely Journey to Oberammergau," in *Oberammergau and Its Passion Play 1960*, official guide published by community of Oberammergau (London: Ernest Benn, 1960), 17.

2. Hermine Diemer, *Oberammergau and Its Passion Play*, rev. Dr. Franz Bogenrieder, trans. Walter Kloeck (Munich: Carl Aug. Seyfried, 1930), 3. Four generations of Ms. Diemer's family resided in Oberammergau and served as choirmasters through the 1930s. Her commentary was written for the playbook in 1900, twenty-four years before her death.

3. Rohtraut Moritz, "Gespräche mit evangelischen Passionsspielbesuchern," *Emuna Horizonte* 5 (August 1970): 222.

4. Annemarie Weiss, "Gespräche mit katholischen Passionsspielbesuchern," *Emuna Horizonte* 5 (August 1970): 223–24.

5. "Dokumentation der Schlussdiskussion des Forums," in Franz Mussner, *Passion in Oberammergau: Das Leiden und Sterben Jesu als geistliches Schauspiel*, Schriften der Katholischen Akademie in Bayern (Düsseldorf: Patmos Verlag, 1980), 106–7.

6. Concerning the press for tickets, see *New York Times*, 8 July 1979, sec. 20, and 10 August 1980, sec. 10; *Cleveland Plain Dealer*, 16 September 1979, sec. D; and *Youngstown Vindicator*, 13 January 1980, sec. B.

7. Practically everyone I interviewed offered the same estimate—that more than 60 percent of the audience at Oberammergau came from English-speaking countries. Professor Leonard Swidler of Temple University, perhaps the leading authority on the passion, contends that the 60 percent figure relates specifically to Americans. See *The Oberammergau Passionsspiel 1984*, ed. Leonard Swidler and Gerard Sloyan (New York: Anti-Defamation League, 1981), vi.

8. Interviews with American tourists, Munich and Oberammergau, 15–19 June 1980.

9. Diemer, *Oberammergau and Its Passion Play*, 3–4.

10. Gertrude Richardson Brigham likened the region to the Lake District of England "which is permeated with Wordsworth" (see "The Passion Play at Oberammergau 1922," *Art and Archaeology* 15 (January 1923): 36).

11. Ludwig II lived in a "befogged mental condition." He rode through the Bavarian mountains in a chariot, while attended by liveried servants. His Schloss Linderhof, fifteen kilometers away from Oberammergau, remains a major tourist attraction. Ludwig also presented the villagers with the *Marxersteig*, a Crucifixion group five hundred meters up the north slope of the Kofel (Janet M. Swift, *The Passion Play of Oberammergau* [New York and Chicago: Fleming H. Revell, 1930], 34–35).

12. The Kofel has actually claimed several lives—relatively un-trained mountain climbers who foolishly tried to scale the difficult frontal slope. On the many legends in the region, see *Larousse Encyclopedia of Mythology* (London: Paul Hamlyn, 1959), 260; John P. Jackson, *The Ober-Ammergau Passion Play* (London: Chiswick Press, 1880), 3.

13. Swift, *The Passion Play of Oberammergau*, 31.

14. Dr. Friedrich Springorum, "Ways to Oberammergau," in *The Passion Play at Oberammergau*, official 1950 text rev. Municipal-ity of Oberammergau (New York: Thomas Crowell, 1950), 27–29; Diemer, *Oberammergau and Its Passion Play*, 19–20.

15. Theodor Geus, "Das biblische Jerusalem in den bayerischen Bergen," *Frankfurter Allgemeine Zeitung*, 4 June 1980, sec. R.

16. Swift, *The Passion Play of Oberammergau*, 30–31. See also Jackson, *The Ober-Ammergau Passion Play*, 6–7; Diemer, *Ober-ammergau and Its Passion Play*, 5–9.

17. Diemer, *Oberammergau and Its Passion Play*, 19–20.

18. Ibid., 21.

19. Ibid., 21.

20. Mattie Johns Utting, *The Passion Play of Oberammergau* (Philadelphia: Dorrance, 1937), 25–27.

21. Diemer, *Oberammergau and Its Passion Play*, 76–79.

22. *The Passion Play at Oberammergau*, official 1950 text, 58–63.

23. *Oberammergau Passion 1980*, leaflet of Gemeinde Ober-ammergau, Geschaftsstelle der Passionsspiele, 1980, 22. Some have even remarked how there is a perceptible stoop among vil-lagers who spend so much time at the woodcarver's bench (Ashley Dukes, "Scene in Europe," *Theater Arts Monthly* 18 [September 1934]: 661).

24. Dr. Kurt Pfister, "Woodcarving and the Passion Play in Oberammergau," in *The Passion Play at Oberammergau*, official 1950 text, 79–86.

25. Vernon Heaton, *The Oberammergau Passion Play* (London: Robert Hale, 1970), 23.

26. R. L. Edsall, "Impressions of Oberammergau," *Common-weal* 13 (24 December 1930): 207.

27. Heaton, *The Oberammergau Passion Play*, 29.

28. Winold Reiss, "The Oberammergau Players," *Century* 104 (September 1922): 737.

29. J. J. Walsh, "Oberammergau," *Commonweal* 12 (20 August 1930): 403.

30. On the nature of typhus and pandemics, see Hans Zinsser, *Rats, Lice and History* (Boston: Little, Brown, 1935).

31. Carlton Hayes, Marshal Baldwin, and Charles Cole, *History of Europe* (New York: Macmillan, 1956), 549.

32. *Passion Oberammergau*, official illustrated guide, published by the community of Oberammergau, 1980, 6. The only previous attack against Ettal occurred in 1552 when followers of Prince Elector Moritz of Saxony killed two persons in the monastery and desecrated some of the sacred objects (Diemer, *Oberammergau and Its Passion Play*, 21).

33. Diemer, *Oberammergau and Its Passion Play*, 22.

34. Heaton, *The Oberammergau Passion Play*, 30–35. The Reverend Robert Coyle claims the eighty-four deaths occurred in a thirty-three-day span. *The Passion Play at Oberammergau* (Denver: Fisher, 1910), 8. It is also claimed that the pestilence claimed the lives of two priests who kept the "Death Book," namely the Reverends Primus Christeiner and Marcellus Ftiga (Werner Zwick, "Oberammergau to Mark 350th Anniversary of Passion Play in 1984," *Youngstown Vindicator*, 19 January 1983).

35. Diemer, *Oberammergau and Its Passion Play*, 22.

36. Montrose Moses, *The Passion Play of Oberammergau* (New York: Duffield, 1909), xxxvii.

37. Diemer, *Oberammergau and Its Passion Play*, 74. On the other plays in the region, see Heaton, *The Oberammergau Passion Play*, 29; Jackson, *The Ober-Ammergau Passion Play*, 5; and "Oberammergau's Tradition," *Living Age* 313 (27 May 1922): 553.

38. *John L. Stoddard's Lectures: India and the Passion Play*, vol. 4 (Chicago and Boston: Geo. Shuman, 1910), 229–30.

39. Walsh, "Oberammergau," 403.

40. M. Dillon, "Love, Peace, and Goodwill," *Scholastic* 55 (7 December 1949): 5T.

41. Swift, *The Passion Play of Oberammergau*, 38.

42. Coyle, *The Passion Play at Oberammergau*, 9.

43. Moses, *The Passion Play of Oberammergau*, xv.

44. Reinhold Niebuhr, "At Oberammergau," *Christian Century* 47 (13 August 1930): 983.

45. William Allen Butler, *Oberammergau 1890* (New York: Harper and Bros., 1891), 38. Similar paeans were sketched by Mildred Peterson who went on at length about the "air of friendliness," the "vigorous everyday piety" of the people, the sweet smell of "nature's perfume" which hung heavy over the Ammer Valley, the "immaculate streets," and absence of poverty in this "simple,

natural and quiet" village ("Inside the Homes of Oberammergau," *Better Homes and Gardens* 13 [April 1935]: 36–39, 78–79).

46. Stoddard joked that he counted one roof with 197 stones. If it were severely shaken, he added, the passerby below might play the role of the martyr Stephen (*Stoddard's Lectures*, 238).

47. E. A. Steiner, "Fashion Play of 1930," *Christian Century* 47 (13 August 1930): 985. Before the turn of the century, visitors to Oberammergau considered themselves fortunate if they secured lodging in any building in the village. Legend has it that the duke of Alencon and his brother, the prince of Brazil, were forced to spend one rainy night in a hansom coach. When they emerged, half-drowned the next morning, they still declared, "Even if we collapse entirely, we intend to see the Passion Play" (*New York Times*, 29 April 1934, sec. 4).

48. Regina Jais, *Legendary Germany: Oberammergau and Bayreuth* (New York: Dial Press, 1930), 118.

49. Moses, *The Passion Play of Oberammergau*, xv.

50. Geus, "Das biblische Jerusalem," *Frankfurter Allgemeine Zeitung*, 4 June 1980, sec. R.

51. Hannes Burger in the *Süddeutschen Zeitung*, quoted in Hans Lamm, "Atempause für Oberammergau," *Allgemeine Jüdische Wochenzeitung*, 6 June 1980.

52. Seventy years ago, Josephine Helena Short praised the villagers as "refined, cultivated people, sensitive to all that is beautiful and good about them" ("Oberammergau: A Village of Actors," *Current Literature* 49 [July 1910]: 84). Already, however, L. C. Morant had noted a change in attitude, scrambling and pushing, which he attributed to the unruly behavior of the audience, specifically American tourists ("The Vulgarising of Oberammergau," *Nineteenth Century* 48 [1900]: 821–22).

2. The Origins of the Passion

1. Theodor Gaster, *Thespis: Ritual, Myth, and Drama in the Ancient Near East* (reprint, New York: Harper Torchbook, 1966), 23.

2. Ibid., 23–25.

3. Gustave von Grunebaum, *Medieval Islam: A Study in Cultural Orientation* (reprint, University of Chicago: Phoenix Books, 1966), pp. 192–93.

4. On Mithra, see Robert Pfeiffer, *History of New Testament Times* (New York: Harper, 1949), 161 ff.

5. On the Egyptian Sed ceremony, see Alan Gardiner, *Egypt of*

the Pharaohs (New York: Oxford University Press, 1966), 85, 269, 331; and James Henry Breasted, *A History of Egypt* (1905; reprint, New York: Bantam, 1967), 32.

6. Dr. Josef Ziegler, "Dokumentation der Schlussdiskussion," in Mussner, *Passion in Oberammergau*, 106. Dr. Ziegler was professor of Theology at the University of Mainz.

7. Sandro Sticca, *The Latin Passion Play: Its Origins and Development* (Albany: SUNY Press, 1970), 125.

8. Karl Young, *The Drama of the Medieval Church* (Oxford University Press, 1933), 1: 492.

9. S. G. F. Brandon, *The Trial of Jesus* (New York: Stein and Day, 1968), 156–58. According to Professor Brandon, early Christian art avoided Crucifixion scenes in favor of Jesus' miracles, cures of paralytics, and the raising of Lazarus. Brandon attributes the change to Byzantine influence.

10. Sticca, *The Latin Passion Play*, 43–44.

11. V. A. Kolve contends there is no link between classical drama and religious plays of the medieval era, adding that the latter were "a fresh beginning, unrooted in any formal tradition of theater" (Kolve, *The Play Called Corpus Christi* [Stanford University Press, 1966], 8). Ashley Dukes disagrees, pointing to the "plain debt owed by the modern producer of the Passion Play to the conceptions of the Attic drama" (Dukes, "Scene in Europe," 661). A. W. Ward found "no essential difference between the functions of this Chorus and that of Greek tragedy, from which it is derived" (Ward, "The Oberammergau Passion Play in 1871," *Living Age* 261 [27 August 1910]: 525). In a letter to Goethe in 1820, Supiz Boisseree also rhapsodized about the connection between Oberammergau and Greek drama (Dr. Hans Bocherdt, "The Style of the Oberammergau Passion Play and Its Historical Background," in *The Passion Play at Oberammergau*, official 1950 text, 71).

12. John Gassner, *Medieval and Tudor Drama* (New York: Bantam Books, 1971), 3–11.

13. Joseph Reider, "Jews in Medieval Art," in *Essays on Antisemitism*, ed. Koppel Pinson (New York: Conference on Jewish Relations, 1946), 98.

14. On the development of medieval drama, see Edmund Chambers, *The Medieval Stage* (Oxford: Clarendon Press, 1903), 14 ff.

15. Kolve says, "In England during the Middle Ages, one would say we will play a game of the passion" (*The Play Called Corpus Christi*, 12–16).

16. Oscar Cargill, *Drama and Liturgy* (New York: Columbia University Press, 1930), 37–43, 132–35.

17. Moses, *The Passion Play of Oberammergau*, xxix–xxx.

18. Cargill, *Drama and Liturgy*, 28; Gassner, *Medieval and Tudor Drama*, 36–38; and Sticca, *The Latin Passion Play*, 41, 122–29.

19. Sticca, *The Latin Passion Play*, 18. Monte Cassino also has yielded the *Codex Purpureus Rossanensis*, purportedly a sixth-century manuscript from the Rossano Cathedral in Calabria, Italy. The 188 extant pages, roughly half the original, tell of the trial of Jesus before Pilate and contain some of the earliest illuminations of gospel scenes. More remarkable, the scenes constitute stage directions for location of figures. To this day, Pilate is enthroned on a tribunal, while Jesus stands to his right and bystanders to the left (Sticca, *The Latin Passion Play*, 93).

20. See Cargill, *Drama and Liturgy*, 42; Moses, *The Passion Play of Oberammergau*, xx; Gassner, *Medieval and Tudor Drama*, 33; Sticca, *The Latin Passion Play*, 19; and Rolf Kulli, *Die Ständesatire in deutschen geistlichen Schauspielen des ausgehenden Mittelalters* (Bern: Francke Verlag, 1966), 7–9.

21. Karl Young, Eduard Nechssler, and George Coffin Taylor see the roots of the Passion in the *Planctus Mariae*, but the similarities with the *Visitatio* seem too compelling to ignore (Sticca, *The Latin Passion Play*, 9; Gassner, *Medieval and Tudor Drama*, 35; and Cargill, *Drama and Liturgy*, 28).

22. Moses, *The Passion Play of Oberammergau*, xx–xxii.

23. *The Oberammergau Passion Play 1980*. English text (parish of Oberammergau, 1980), 11–12.

24. Gassner, *Medieval and Tudor Drama*, 34.

25. Sticca, *The Latin Passion Play*, 52.

26. Kolve, *The Play Called Corpus Christi*, 177.

27. Ibid., 36.

28. Sticca, *The Latin Passion Play*, 169.

29. Moses, *The Passion Play at Oberammergau*, xxxii–xxxv.

30. Leon Poliakov, *The History of Anti-Semitism from the Time of Christ to the Court Jews*, trans. Richard Howard (New York: Schocken Books, 1974), 130–31.

31. Kolve, *The Play Called Corpus Christi*, 50–72.

32. Moses, *The Passion Play of Oberammergau*, xxxvii, lxi.

33. A. W. Ward counted no fewer than 503 such plays, including the celebrated Sterzing plays discovered in 1860 ("The Oberam-

mergau Passion Play in 1871," 522). On the origins of the medieval theater in Germany, see Hans Knudsen, *Deutsche Theater Geschichte* (Stuttgart: Alfred Kröner Verlag, 1959); Rudolf Vey, *Christliches Theater in Mittelalter und Neuzeit* (Zurich: Christiana-Verlag, 1960); Heinz Kindermann, *Theater Geschichte Europas I, Antike und Mittelalter* (Salzburg: Otto Müller Verlag, 1957). See also Mattie Johns Utting, *The Passion Play of Oberammergau* (Philadelphia: Dorrance, 1937), 13.

34. Cargill claims the novitiate Balbulus Notker was supplying words for melodies at Saint Gall by 887 (*Drama and Liturgy*, 13–14).

35. *John Stoddard's Lectures*, 230; and Moses, *The Passion Play of Oberammergau*, xlvi.

36. Jackson, *The Ober-Ammergau Passion Play*, 1.

37. Dr. Holland, quoted in Diemer, *Oberammergau and Its Passion Play*, 32.

38. Ibid., 32. See also *Passion Oberammergau*, official illustrated guide (1980), 7. Hartmann's work is available in the U.S. from a dozen libraries (August Hartmann, *Das Oberammergauer passionsspiel in seiner ältesten gestalt* [Leipzig: Breitkopf und Härtel, 1880]).

39. Diemer, *Oberammergau and Its Passion Play*, 32.

40. Ibid., 31.

41. Bogenrieder, "The Passion Play and Its History," *The Passion Play at Oberammergau*, official 1950 text, 35.

3. The Daisenberger Passion

1. Dr. Alois Fink, "Notes on the Question of a New Version of the Text," *Oberammergau and Its Passion Play 1960*, official guide published by the community of Oberammergau (London: Ernest Benn, 1960), 33.

2. *Passion Oberammergau*, official illustrated guide (1980), 7.

3. Arthur Maximilian Miller, "Experiments on the Text of the Passion Play," *Oberammergau and Its Passion Play 1960*, 39. Oscar Cargill suggests that the inspiration for this baroque revision may have been "Les Vierges Sages et Les Vierges Folles," a French mystery play telling of the damnation of foolish virgins and employing the characters of Christus, Fatuae, Prudentes, and Mercatores (*Drama and Liturgy*, 45). Cargill also points out that Marius Sepet discovered a medieval *lectio* (lesson) in 1867 in which various Old Testament characters appear as prophets of Christ. The

apocryphal lectio, found in the diocese of Artes, is attributed to Augustine. See also reference to Old Testament plays appended to the Christmas liturgy (ibid., 65 ff).

4. Bogenrieder, "The Passion Play and Its History," *The Passion Play at Oberammergau 1950*, 35. In 1770, Elector Maximilian Joseph declared, "Be it known to the supplicants of the community of Oberammergau that their petition has been rejected once and forever." Despite the absolute ban, the people continued to perform the Passion (Diemer, *Oberammergau and Its Passion Play*, 23). See also D. M. Young, "Reader's Choice," *Travel* 113 (April 1960): 40.

5. Diemer, *Oberammergau and Its Passion Play*, 23-24; Moses, *The Passion Play of Oberammergau*, xlv-xlvix; Heaton, *The Oberammergau Passion Play*, 40-44.

6. Swift, *The Passion Play of Oberammergau*, 77.

7. Tradition has it that the bells in Oberammergau's church steeple were cast from cannon captured from the French in the Franco-Prussian War. William T. Stead, *The Story That Transformed the World: The Passion Play at Ober Ammergau in 1890* (London and New York: office *Review of Reviews*, 1890), 18.

8. Diemer, *Oberammergau and Its Passion Play*, 41.

9. *Passion Oberammergau* (1980), 7.

10. Pabst, "The Oberammergau Passion Music," *The Passion Play at Oberammergau, 1950* text, 46-50. See also Dr. Erica Jaeger, "Rochus Dedler, Creator of the Passion Play Music," *Oberammergau and Its Passion Play 1960*, 49-56; and H. L. Gideon, "Music of the Passion Play at Oberammergau," *Forum* 44 (December 1910): 733-37.

11. Diemer insists that "the one thing that must not be said of him is that he was a remodeller of the passion-text" (*Oberammergau and Its Passion Play*, 51). Yet Walter Rauschenbusch of the Rochester Theological Seminary long ago blamed Daisenberger for "flatten(ing) everything out like a prosaical pedagog" (Rauschenbusch, "The Religion of the Passion Play," *Independent* 69 [29 September 1910]: 692). Even the 1980 guidebook refers to Daisenberger's "careful working-over of the Othmar Weis text" (*Passion Oberammergau 1980*, 7). The text employed in the village bears Daisenberger's name.

12. Jackson, *The Ober-Ammergau Passion Play*, 13.

13. Swift, *The Passion Play of Oberammergau*, 75-76.

14. *The Oberammergau Passion Play*, 1980 English text, 112.

15. Interview with Bürgermeister Ernst Zwink, 18 June 1980.

Between pageants, villagers kept themselves in a state of readiness by presenting other Daisenberger scripts which dealt with the lives of Otto von Wittelsbach, Ludwig the Bavarian, Joseph in Egypt, Judith, and Naboth. Such plays were enacted in a smaller theater and included such titles as "Die Pestnot Anno 1633," "Das Judasspiel," and "Whitsuntide Orgen" (Therese Bauer-Preissenberg, "Other Plays Performed at Oberammergau," *Oberammergau and Its Passion Play 1960*, 95–98).

16. In 1979–80, Monika Lang took the issue of whether an older, married woman might play Mary to the German courts. A Munich tribunal ruled that the issue was not a matter of constitutional rights. The villagers yielded anyway, granting permission to forty-one-year-old Irmi Dengg to serve as one of two Marys ("Passionate Issues behind the Passion Play," *Volker Buhbe*, 19 March 1980, in *German Tribune*, 6 April 1980).

17. Jackson, *The Ober-Ammergau Passion Play*, 10.

18. Niebuhr, "At Oberammergau," 983.

19. Dr. Hans Borcherdt, "The Style of the Oberammergau Passion Play and Its Historical Background," *The Passion Play at Oberammergau*, 1950 text, 71–72.

20. Baroness Jemima Tautphoeus, *Quits* (New York: G. P. Putnam's, 1863). This two-volume work is, quite frankly, abysmally dull.

21. Hans Christian Andersen, *Pictures of Travel* (New York: Hurd and Houghton; Cambridge: Riverside Press, 1871), 260–67.

22. George Shuster, "Oberammergau: After Ten Years, the Passion Play in Bavaria," *Saturday Review* 43 (12 March 1960): 44.

23. "Oberammergau Awakes," *Literary Digest* 105 (14 June 1930): 19.

24. Ibid., 19.

25. Benjamin Henrichs, "Jesus und die Biedermänner: Das Spiel von Oberammergau: Passion der Kompromisse," *Die Zeit*, 30 May 1980.

26. Niebuhr, "At Oberammergau," 984. The *Guardian*'s Michael Billington attended the 1980 Passion and found it inoffensive, adding, "It is pious pageant rather than a powerful drama" (see "Passion for Pageant," *Manchester Guardian*, 15 June 1980).

27. "Piety with Profit," *Time* 76 (11 July 1960): 56.

28. Hannes Burger of the *Suddeutsche Zeitung* cited in Hans Lamm's "Atempause für Oberammergau," 6.

29. T. F. Driver, "Play That Carries a Plague," *Christian Century* 77 (7 September 1960): 1016–17.

30. W. A. Darlington, *Literature in the Theatre* (New York: Holt, 1968), 59.

31. J. B. Priestley, *Self-Selected Essays* (New York: Harper, 1937), 216–18.

32. Ibid., 219.

33. "The Passion Play Judged as Secular Drama," *Literary Digest* 74 (9 September 1922): 30–31.

34. "Germany Shocked at Oberammergau," *Literary Digest* 106 (16 August 1930): 15.

35. "Aus den Interviews der Ökumenischen Studiengruppe," 221.

36. "Piety with Profit," 56.

37. Driver, "Play That Carries a Plague," 1016.

38. Ibid., 1016. *Time*'s critic was a bit more generous, saying of the living pictures that they contribute little "but an impression of so many Bavarian countryfolk assembling for a photograph in Biblical costume" ("Piety with Profit," 56).

39. Interview with Theodore Freedman, 13 June 1980, New York City. The complaint dates back more than a century. A. W. Ward had advocated the deletion of several tableaux and the shortening of choral interludes ("The Oberammergau Passion Play in 1871," 526).

40. Driver, "Play That Carries a Plague," 1016. Seventy years ago, A. W. Ward noted the doughty, slow, and heavy nature of the chorus: "the men are fine fellows, generally better-looking than the women" ("The Oberammergau Passion Play in 1871," 521, 524). The *Guardian*'s Billington recently conceded, "I couldn't help thinking that the Passion Play itself could be improved if it were allowed to smile occasionally" (*Manchester Guardian*, 15 June 1980).

41. Dr. Hans Mallau, "Beobachtungen eines Alttestamentlers zu den lebenden Bildern des Oberammergauer Passionsspieles," in *Emuna Horizonte* 5 (August 1970): 235–41.

42. R. I. Edsall, "Impressions of Oberammergau," 207.

43. *The Oberammergau Passion Play 1980*, English text, 28. Little has changed since A. W. Ward, generally an advocate of the play, wrote in 1910 that "very few individual performers rose above respectable mediocrity" ("The Oberammergau Passion Play in 1871," 527).

44. Correspondence between the author and editors of Pennsylvania, Kent State, and Wayne State University presses, respectively.

45. *Random House Dictionary of the English Language,* 1967.

46. A colleague, Professor Charles Darling, who teaches the history of folk music and has published a volume on the subject, suggests that if Woody Guthrie rates a 10 on the scale of folk importance, then Dorrance Weir is a 3. "The man's a racist," says Darling (interview, 13 January 1983).

47. Even Glassie concedes "prejudice is its foundation," *Folksongs and Their Makers* (Bowling Green University Press, n.d.), 52.

48. Harold N. Lee, *Perception and Aesthetic Value* (New York: Prentice-Hall, 1938), 124–25. Lee warns, however, that "bad taste," which he defines as crude, undeveloped, or vulgar, is unacceptable at any time, 142.

49. Mikel Dufrenne, *The Phenomenology of Aesthetic Experience,* trans. Edward Casey, et al. (Evanston: Northwestern University, 1973), 504. Art is true, says Dufrenne, "When it helps us to know the real," 543.

50. Monroe Beardsley, *Aesthetics: Problems in the Philosophy of Criticism* (New York: Harcourt, Brace, 1958), 574. This brilliant book poses other crucial questions. Is the work "uplifting or inspiring"? Is it effective social criticism? Does it promote desirable social or political ends? Does it give insight into a universal human problem? Is it self-contradictory? Is it replete with "obviously false passages"? Is it new and original or trite? Does it show skillful or poor workmanship? Is it well organized? Is it dull and monotonous? Is it full of vitality or is it insipid? Is it "tender, ironic, tragic, graceful, delicate and richly comic"? When judged by these standards, Oberammergau's Passion is a disaster (see Beardsley, 142, 286, 456–62).

51. Gillo Dorfles, *Kitsch: The World of Bad Taste* (New York: Universe Books, 1970), 11, 63–64, 293. Dorfles condemns artists who intentionally and consciously use kitsch for ends diametrically opposed to the ends of art.

52. Beardsley, *Aesthetics,* 456–62.

4. Guidelines Rejected: A New Covenant

1. Heaton, *The Oberammergau Passion Play,* 115.

2. Moritz, "Gespräche mit evangelischen Passionsspielbesuchern," *Emuna Horizonte,* 222.

3. Interviews with Pater Gregor Rümmelein, Ettal, 19 June 1980, and Bürgermeister Franz Zwink, 18 June 1980.

4. Leonard Swidler and Gerard Sloyan, "Recommendations for the Oberammergau Passionsspiel 1984" in *The Oberammergau Passionsspiel 1984*, ed. Swidler and Sloyan (New York: Anti-Defamation League, 1981), 33. Paul Winter also faults the Gospels as representations of communal preaching and tradition rather than actual history. *On the Trial of Jesus* (Berlin: Walter de Gruyter, 1961), 3–6.

5. S. G. F. Brandon, *The Trial of Jesus of Nazareth* (New York: Stein and Day, 1968), 14. A good example of one such apocryphal document that church authorities had the sense to reject early on was the so-called Gospel of Peter which fixes blame for the denunciation, beating, and Crucifixion directly upon the Jews. In this terse document, the Jews also perform the hand-washing ritual normally ascribed to Pilate (see *Lost Books of the Bible* [New York: Alpha House, 1926], 282–86).

6. Hans Conrad Zander, "Rommes Theater oder die Passionsspiele von Oberammergau," *Emuna Horizonte* 5 (August 1970): 229.

7. Sister Louis Gabriel, "The Gospels and the Oberammergau Passion Play," *Catholic World* 211 (April 1970): 13–17.

8. "Stellungnahme zu den Passionsspielen in Oberammergau," *Emuna Horizonte* 5 (August 1970): 246.

9. *Guidelines for the Oberammergau Passionsspiel and Other Passion Plays*, prepared by Leonard Swidler, ADL flyer, 1980.

10. Judith Banki, *What Viewers Should Know about the Oberammergau Passion Play*, 1980 (New York: American Jewish Committee, 1980), 11.

11. Swidler and Sloyan, *The Oberammergau Passionsspiel 1984*, 35.

12. Interviews with four village craftsmen, Oberammergau, 19 June 1980, and Gregor Breitsamter, 19 June 1980. Breitsamter insisted, "All people know that Christ was a Jew." Hans Lamm of the Munich Jewish community also defended the villagers, saying that if Americans don't understand Jesus was a Jew, it is a result of lack of education and sophistication on the part of people in "Scranton or Kansas City."

13. Charles Glock and Rodney Stark, *Christian Beliefs and Anti-Semitism* (New York: Harper and Row, 1966), 48–49.

14. Weiss, "Gespräche mit katholischen Passionsspielbesuchern," 225.

15. Frederick Schlegel and Friedrich Schleiermacher de-

nounced any links between Judaism and Christianity about the time Othmar Weis was penning his Passion. By 1878, Wagner wrote in his *Bayreuther Blätter* that identifying Jesus with Jews was "one of the most terrible derangements of world history." Twenty years later, Wagner's son-in-law, Houston S. Chamberlain, "scientifically" established that Galilee was really the *Gelil Haggoyim* (district of Gentiles). All of which suited Hitler, who constantly fulminated that Jesus most certainly was an Aryan (see *Hitler's Secret Conversations* [New York: Octagon Books, 1972], 63, 117, 586). See also Peter Viereck, *Meta-politics: The Roots of the Nazi Mind* (reprint, New York: Capricorn, 1965); George Mosse, *Toward the Final Solution* (New York: Harper, 1978); Waldemar Gurian, "Anti-Semitism in Modern Germany," in Pinson, *Essays on Antisemitism*, 236 ff; Chamberlain, *Foundations of the Nineteenth Century* (New York: John Lane, 1912).

16. Winter, *On The Trial of Jesus*, 16–19.

17. Roland De Vaux, *Ancient Israel: Religious Institutions* (New York: McGraw-Hill, 1965) 2: 398–99; see also Exod. 28:36 ff, Lev. 8:9.

18. Joshua Trachtenberg's *The Devil and the Jews: The Medieval Conception of the Jews and Its Relation to Modern Antisemitism* (Yale University Press, 1943) is the best work on this subject. See also Marvin Lowenthal, *The Jews of Germany* (Philadelphia: Jewish Publication Society of America, 1936), 65–66, 97; Poliakov, *The History of Anti-Semitism*, 123–72; Salo Baron, *A Social and Religious History of the Jews* (Columbia University Press, 1967), 11: 122–91; and B. Blumenkranz, "On Roman Church and the Jews to the Twelfth Century," in *The World History of the Jewish People*, ed. Cecil Roth, 11: 69–97.

19. Rosemary Ruether, *Faith and Fratricide: The Theological Roots of Anti-Semitism* (New York: Seabury Press, 1974), 213.

20. See statements of Nat Kameny, chairman of ADL's Program Committee and Rabbi Marc Tanenbaum of the American Jewish Committee, *Buffalo Jewish Review*, 6 June 1980.

21. Professors Swidler and Sloyan have urged the deletion of this nefarious character for more than three years (*The Oberammergau Passionsspiel 1984*, 35).

22. Again, Professors Swidler and Sloyan note that the names "automatically set up in the minds of the audience an opposition between the 'Old' and the 'New' Testaments" (ibid., 34).

23. Winter, *On The Trial of Jesus*, 33. According to Winter, the

Gospels actually give a "shadowy" or "undetermined" role to Caiaphas. Acts 4:6 refers to Annas only, and Winter questions the validity of this reference, concluding that the confusion stems from errors in interpretation and copying. In 1900, Rabbi Joseph Krauskopf argued that it was impossible to have more than one man reigning in Israel. Moreover, the Reform rabbi from Philadelphia charged Jewish literature knew of no high priest by either name (Krauskopf, *A Rabbi's Impressions of the Oberammergau Passion Play* [Philadelphia, E. Stern, 1901], 98). According to Krauskopf, there simply were no references to Caiaphas or Annas in the Talmud or the writings of Flavius Josephus, the two principal commentaries for this era. Twenty-five years after Krauskopf voiced his objections, Professor Joseph Klausner of Hebrew University attempted to resolve some of the problems. For Klausner, Annas was Ananus ben Seth, who served as high priest for nearly a decade (6–15 A.D.) before being deposed by Valerius Gratus. Five of his sons subsequently became high priests, as did his son-in-law Joseph ben ha-Khayyaf (Caiaphas), who served in this prestigious office during the procuratorship of Pontius Pilate (26–36 A.D.). That Annas and Caiaphas simultaneously bore the title of high priest was not remarkable, as it was legitimate for any man who had served even one day to carry the title the rest of his life, much the same as former U.S. presidents. Klausner based his identifications upon talmudic references to priestly families known as the Bet Hanin (Pes. 57a) and House of Kophai (Yeb. 15b). The Mishnah also tells of a high priest called Elionaeus ha-Kayyaf and the Tosefta (Yeb. i:10) mentions a priestly family named Kaiapha. As for Josephus, Klausner found a disparaging reference to the abortive rule in the year 62 of the willful, conceited Sadducee, "Anan, son of Anan, son of Seth." See Klausner, *Jesus of Nazareth* (New York: Macmillan, 1929), 162, 339–40; and articles by Leo Roth in *Encyclopedia Judaica* (Jerusalem: Keter Pubs., 1971), namely "Caiaphas, Joseph," 5:19; "Elionaeus," 6:663; "Anan ben Seth," 2:922; and "Anan, Son of Anan," 2:919.

24. *The Passion Play at Oberammergau*, official 1934 text (Munich: J. C. Huber, 1934), 73–74.

25. Interview with Hans Lamm, Munich, 22 June 1980.

26. Bo Reicke, "Die historischen Umstände bei der Passion Jesu," in Mussner, *Passion in Oberammergau*, 18. Reicke also properly refers to the holiday as *Passatag* or *Passafest*.

27. Ruether, *Faith and Fratricide*, 10.

28. Interview with Hare, 2 March 1981. See also Hare's *The Theme of Jewish Persecution of Christians in the Gospel According to St. Matthew* (Cambridge University Press, 1967); and Alan Davies, *Anti-Semitism and the Foundations of Christianity* (New York: Paulist Press, n.d.).

29. Luke 2:21–41 and Sandmel, *Anti-Semitism in the New Testament?* (Philadelphia: Fortress Press, 1978), 71–75.

30. Krauskopf, *A Rabbi's Impressions of the Oberammergau Passion Play*, 73.

31. Graetz, *History of the Jews* (reprint, Philadelphia: Jewish Publication Society of America, 1956), 2:155–56.

32. Winter, *On the Trial of Jesus*, 132–35.

33. Arthur Gilbert, *The Vatican Council and the Jews* (Cleveland and New York: World, 1968), 275–76.

34. Ibid., 275, 277.

35. Leonard Swidler and Gerard Sloyan, *A Commentary on the Oberammergau Passionsspiel in Regard to Its Image of Jews and Judaism* (New York: Anti-Defamation League, 1978), 57–58.

36. *The Passion Play at Oberammergau*, 1934 text, 38–39. Professors Swidler and Sloyan have duly noted slight changes in the 1960 and 1970 versions, but the chorus still concluded with the words "Ein bess'res Volk wird er sich wählen" (Swidler and Sloyan, *A Commentary on the Oberammergau Passionsspiel*, 13).

37. Reider, "Jews in Medieval Art," in Pinson, *Essays on Antisemitism*, 99.

38. Ibid., 93.

39. Swidler and Sloyan, *The Oberammergau Passionsspiel 1984*, 19.

40. Malcolm Hay, *Thy Brother's Blood: The Roots of Christian Anti-Semitism* (reprint, New York: Hart, 1975), 3–67.

41. *Das Oberammergauer Passionsspiel 1980*, textbuch, 36–37.

42. *The Oberammergau Passion Play 1980*, English text, 36–40, 88, 111–12.

43. Interview with Pater Rümmelein, 19 June 1980.

44. Ruether, *Faith and Fratricide*, 5.

45. Ibid., 8. Ruether calls such tendencies "symbolic imperialism."

46. Interview with Stanley Milgram, 20 April 1983.

47. Interview with Msgr. Dr. C. M. Genewein, Munich, 16 June 1980.

5. History Ignored: The Sanhedrin and Pilate

1. Krauskopf, *A Rabbi's Impressions of the Oberammergau Passion Play*, 19.

2. Henry Bamford Parkes, *Gods and Men: The Origins of Western Culture* (reprint, New York: Vintage, 1965), 388.

3. Haim Cohn, *The Trial and Death of Jesus* (New York: Harper and Row, 1971), 54. Cohn suggests it was "not improbable" that Jesus came upon a huckster who was cheating or profiteering, 57.

4. Graetz, *History of the Jews*, 2: 161.

5. Josephus, *Jewish Wars*, bk. 2, chap. 9.

6. Louis Finkelstein, *Akiba: Scholar, Saint, and Martyr* (reprint, New York: Meridian, 1962), 51.

7. Hugh Schonfield, *The Passover Plot* (New York: Bantam Books, 1965), 116.

8. S. G. F. Brandon, *The Trial of Jesus of Nazareth*, 83.

9. Gen. 22:9; Exod. 29 ff; Lev. 16:26–27; Num. 5:7, 19; Deut. 21:3. See also De Vaux, *Ancient Israel*, 415–16; "Sacrifices," *The Encyclopedia of the Jewish Religion*, ed. R. J. Zwi Werblowsky and Geoffrey Wigoder (New York: Holt, Rinehart and Winston, 1965), 338.

10. *The Oberammergau Passion Play 1980*, English text, 111–12.

11. Krauskopf, *A Rabbi's Impressions of the Oberammergau Passion Play*, 63.

12. Brandon, *The Trial of Jesus of Nazareth*, 84, and T. S. Kepler, "Oberammergau , the Jews, and Pilate," *Christian Century* 78 (26 July 1961): 898.

13. *The Passion Play at Oberammergau*, 1934, 17.

14. Sanh. 4:36a.

15. Matt. 3:4; Mark 14:1 ff; Luke 22:1; John 5:29.

16. Krauskopf says flatly that no such armed force existed at the time. *A Rabbi's Impressions of the Oberammergau Passion Play*, 82. Cohn concedes that while Jewish "constables" were sent after Jesus, they were accompanied by "ruffians and brigands." *The Trial and Death of Jesus*, 73–74, 82. For Winter's reference to the *Cohors Secunda Italica* and Greek auxiliaries from Sebaste and Caesarea, see *On the Trial of Jesus*, 29, 35, 45–48.

17. Reicke, "Die historischen Umstände bei der Passion Jesu," in Mussner, *Passion in Oberammergau*, 18; and Cohn, *The Trial and Death of Jesus*, 112.

18. Klausner, *Jesus of Nazareth*, 341.

19. Ibid., 29.

20. Brandon, *The Trial of Jesus of Nazareth*, 88; William Wilson, *The Execution of Jesus* (New York: Charles Scribner's Sons, 1970), 9; George Foot Moore, *Judaism* (reprint, New York: Schocken Books, 1971), vol. 2.

21. Winter, *On the Trial of Jesus*, 67–70. See also Solomon Zeitlin, *Who Crucified Jesus?* (New York: Bloch, 1964).

22. Robert Seltzer, *Jewish People, Jewish Thought* (New York and London: Macmillan, 1980), 218–19.

23. Jacobs argues that "there is no question . . . of a uniform *halakhah*, even at this early period, handed down from generation to generation in the form the *halakhah* assumes in the tannaitic period." "Halakhah," *Encyclopedia Judaica*, 7: 1162.

24. "Sanhedrin," *Encyclopedia Judaica*, 14: 840. See also "Talmud Babylonian," *Encyclopedia Judaica*, 15: 761–66.

25. De Vaux, *Ancient Israel*, 1: 155.

26. Ibid., 155–56.

27. Reicke, "Die historischen Umstände bei der Passion Jesu," 15. Winter, who is normally critical of those who apply talmudic standards to the proceedings, maintains the Supreme Court would hardly have convened en masse to review a prima facie case against Jesus (*On The Trial of Jesus*, 26). Brandon also argues that the hearing at Caiaphas's house could not have constituted a formal trial (*The Trial of Jesus of Nazareth*, 92). Cohn grants the possibility that all of the councillors were in attendance at what he terms a preliminary hearing. But the Israeli judge contends the Sanhedrin actually tried to save Jesus (*The Trial and Death of Jesus*, 26, 331).

28. Winter, *On the Trial of Jesus*, 73–74.

29. Mark 26:67, 14:65. Luke 23:70–71 spares us this physical abuse. John says nothing of any of these beatings or taunts.

30. Cohn, *The Trial and Death of Jesus*, 61. Cohn adds, "By asserting he would be privileged in heaven to sit at God's right hand did not in any way infringe the oneness of God," 127–30. Douglas Hare agrees that Jesus' statements could not be termed blasphemy as defined in his age. *The Theme of Jewish Persecution of Christians*, 27–29.

31. Krauskopf, *A Rabbi's Impressions of the Oberammergau Passion Play*, 100. Neither Winter, 25, nor Brandon, 90, considers the charge of blasphemy to have any merit.

32. Sanh. 7:66a provides for death to those who "desecrate" the Sabbath. Saving lives has never been interpreted to mean desecration.

33. Krauskopf, *A Rabbi's Impressions of the Oberammergau Passion Play,* 73–74.

34. Ibid., 99.

35. Cohn, *The Trial and Death of Jesus,* 60.

36. Winter, *On the Trial of Jesus,* 50.

37. Swidler and Sloyan, *The Oberammergau Passionsspiel 1984,* 44.

38. Klausner, *Jesus of Nazareth,* 348.

39. Ibid., 348.

40. Josephus, *Jewish Wars,* bk. 2, chap. 9, sec. 2.

41. Philo, *De Legatione ad Gaium,* 10.299–305.

42. Kolve dislikes the presentation, calling it artistic oversimplification (*The Play Called Corpus Christi,* 232–33). For a more positive interpretation see Arnold Williams, *The Characterization of Pilate in the Towneley Plays* (East Lansing: Michigan State University Press, 1950).

43. *The Passion Play at Oberammergau,* 1934, 97.

44. *The Oberammergau Passion Play 1980,* English text, 79.

45. Ibid., 82.

46. *The Passion Play at Oberammergau,* 1934, 109.

47. It is unclear in the 1980 text, 79 and 109, whether he is relying upon a Roman or Jewish practice. If the latter, the concept is patently false, for Professor Winter has noted, "The Jews, usually meticulous about recording the details of national observances, have failed to preserve any trace of, or reference to, this 'custom' " (*On the Trial of Jesus,* 93).

48. *The Passion Play at Oberammergau,* 1934, 118.

49. Ibid., 118.

50. Brandon, *The Trial of Jesus of Nazareth,* 98.

51. Cohn, *The Trial and Death of Jesus,* 145.

52. Ibid., 171–73.

53. Ibid., 181.

54. Klausner, *Jesus of Nazareth,* 346.

55. Cohn, *The Trial and Death of Jesus,* 166–67.

56. Ibid., 158.

57. Ibid., 267–69.

58. Wrote Winter, "The more Christians are persecuted by the Roman state, the more generous becomes the depiction of Pontius Pilate as a witness to Jesus' innocence." The purpose was to remind the emperor "how different the attitude of his forbears toward Judaism was from his own" (*On the Trial of Jesus,* 59–60).

59. Niebuhr, "At Oberammergau," 984.

60. Interview with Zwink, 18 June 1980.

61. Interview with Pater Rümmelein, 19 June 1980.

62. Driver, "Play That Carries a Plague," 1018.

63. Krauskopf, *A Rabbi's Impression of the Oberammergau Passion Play*, 42. Rabbi Krauskopf argued that the grossest violence had been done to Jewish history and laws, and it is difficult to disagree with him.

64. Cohn, *The Trial and Death of Jesus*, 319.

6. Hymn of Reconciliation or An Anti-Semitic Play?

1. "Oberammergau: Telling It Straight," *Christianity Today* 14 (19 June 1970): 22.

2. "Forgetting the Hymn of Hate," *Literary Digest* 72 (25 March 1922): 30–31.

3. Dr. Karl Ipser, "1970 The Passion: A Dramatic Play Illustrating the Life of God Among Men," *Das Passionsspiel Oberammergau*, official illustrated catalogue (Verlag Gemeinde Oberammergau, 1970), 1.

4. Mimeographed copy, Cardinal Ratzinger's Sermon at Oberammergau, 18 May 1980, issued by Anti-Defamation League, 4–6.

5. Interview with Rümmelein, 19 June 1980.

6. Interview with Zwink, 18 June 1980.

7. Stead, *The Story That Transformed the World*, 159.

8. "Is the Passion Play Anti-Semitic?" *Literary Digest* 106 (13 September 1930): 21.

9. Niebuhr, "At Oberammergau," 984.

10. H. B. Kuhn, "Concerning Oberammergau: 1980," *Christianity Today* 22 (19 May 1978): 70.

11. "Discussion," *Christian Century* 77 (14 December 1960): 1476.

12. Brown was theological secretary for the International Fellowship of Evangelical Students, based in Lausanne, Switzerland. See his articles "Oberammergau: Is It Anti-Semitic?" *Christianity Today* 14 (19 June 1970): 24; "The Current Passions," *National Review* 22 (25 August 1970): 890.

13. Krauskopf, *A Rabbi's Impressions of the Oberammergau Passion*, 60.

14. "Is the Passion Play Anti-Semitic?" *Literary Digest*, 21.

15. Ibid., 21.

16. Statements on the Oberammergau Passion Play released by American Jewish Congress, 16 November 1966, 1, and 30 January 1968, 3.

17. Phil Baum, "Background of Oberammergau Passion Play," issued by American Jewish Congress, 7 November 1966, 4.

18. Driver, "Play That Carries a Plague," 1017.

19. Ibid., 1018.

20. "Time for a New Vow at Oberammergau," *Christian Century* 83 (2 November 1966): 1329. See also Cynthia Bourgeault, "Passion Drama: History and Perspective," in *Face to Face: An Interreligious Bulletin* (published by Anti-Defamation League) 7 (Summer 1980): 21–23. Dr. Bourgeault, a priest of the Episcopal church, is currently dramatic director for the University of Pennsylvania Collegium Musicum.

21. Judith Banki, *What Viewers Should Know about the Oberammergau Passion Play*, 5.

22. Release of American Jewish Congress, 6 March 1968.

23. Release of American Jewish Congress, 13 August 1975.

24. Poliakov, *History of Anti-Semitism*, 124.

25. Baron, *A Social and Religious History of the Jews*, 11: 133.

26. Ibid., 159.

27. Zander, "Frommes Theater oder die Passionsspiele von Oberammergau," 230.

28. *The Passion Play at Oberammergau*, 1934, 13.

29. Poliakov, *History of Anti-Semitism*, 126.

30. Gassner, *Medieval and Tudor Drama*, 38–39. A like theme is expressed by Maistre Arnoul Gréban who has the Virgin say, "These accursed Pharisees from whom nothing comes but treason." For a view of French Passion plays, see Grace Frank, *The Medieval French Drama* (Oxford: Clarendon Press, 1954).

31. Kolve, *The Play Called Corpus Christi*, 115.

32. *The Passion Play at Oberammergau*, 1934, 50.

33. Trachtenberg, *The Devil and the Jews*, 23, and Poliakov, *History of Anti-Semitism*, 126.

34. Trachtenberg, *The Devil and the Jews*, 22. Other Passions which attempted to represent the Jews at prayer merely lampooned the chants of the synagogue (see M. Blakemore Evans, *The Passion Play of Lucerne* [London: Oxford University Press, 1966]). Evans claims that the play represents the one medieval Passion which could be reproduced today without the slightest danger of serious error from its original. Apart from the use of horns (196), the

chorus sings a strange mixture of nonsense which is a composite of eighteen different languages (68). A similar magical incantation was uttered at Frankfurt where Jews allegedly sang:

> Chodus chados adonay
> sebados sissim sossim
> cochun yochun or nor
> yochun or nor gun
> ymbrabel et ysmabel
> ly ly lancze lare
> vezerando ate lahn dilando
> sicut vir melior yesse
> ceuc ceuca ceu
> capiasse, amel!

See Kulli, *Die Ständesatire in deutschen geistlichen Schauspielen*, 17.

35. *The Passion at Oberammergau*, 1934, 21, 22, 78, 85, 102, 125.

36. Wilm Sanders, "Was man auch sehen muss beim Passionsspiel von Oberammergau," *Emuna Horizonte* 5 (August 1970): 243.

37. Zander, "Frommes Theater oder die Passionsspiele von Oberammergau," 229. Dr. Georg Schroubek maintains that Daisenberger did not want the high priests to carry the burden of guilt alone, so he introduced the intrigue of the expelled Jewish merchants outside the temple (Schroubek, "Erbauliches Spiel oder Ärgernis?" *Emuna Horizonte* 5 [August 1970]: 234).

38. *The Passion at Oberammergau*, 1934, 34.

39. Ibid., 41–42. The lines are substantially the same in the 1980 version (*The Oberammergau Passion Play 1980*, 28, 33).

40. Swidler and Sloyan argue that speeches in the current text suggest that the Torah values human life less than is actually the case. They recommend significant changes in references to the thirty pieces of silver (*The Oberammergau Passionsspiel 1984*, 44).

41. *The Passion at Oberammergau*, 1934, 80, 94. Both lines have been deleted from 1980, but the action proceeds along the same way.

42. Moses, *The Passion Play of Oberammergau*, xv–xviii; Diemer, *Oberammergau and Its Passion Play*, 39.

43. Trachtenberg, *The Devil and the Jews*, 22.

44. Krauskopf, *A Rabbi's Impressions of the Oberammergau Passion*, 77.

45. Ibid., 77.

46. Baron, *A Social and Religious History of the Jews*, 131. Virtually the same point was made by Vamberto Morais, *A Short History of Anti-Semitism* (New York: W. W. Norton, 1976), 88. S. G. F. Brandon suggests the name Iscariot may have been derived from the futile revolt of the Sicarii (dagger men) (Brandon, *The Trial of Jesus*, 149).

47. *The Passion at Oberammergau*, 1934, 126.

48. The character was in the play until 1970 (see Joseph Gaer, *The Legend of the Wandering Jew* [New York: Mentor, 1961]).

49. *The Passion at Oberammergau*, 1934, 27. There has always been confusion as to which of the priests directed the plot against Jesus. Neither the book of Luke (chap. 23) nor Mark (chap. 14) refers to the two priests by name in the scene where Jesus is interrogated by the Sanhedrin. In Matthew (26:57) Jesus is led directly to Caiaphas's palace following his arrest. In John (18:12 ff) Annas is the principal malefactor and Caiaphas only enters the plot tangentially.

50. *The Passion at Oberammergau*, 1934, 24–25. The specific lines have been cut, but the scene with its conspiracy remains intact.

51. Ibid., 59–60. Once more, the tone of the scene is intact, with some lines muted, in the 1980 version.

52. Ibid., 19. Nathaniel may well have served as the inspiration for the nefarious Zerah in Zefferelli's NBC production of the Passion. Like Nathaniel, Zerah was an advocate of collaboration with Rome, promoted the conspiracy, and delighted in the torment of Jesus, and was an invention of the director.

53. Ibid., 57.

54. Ibid., 59–60.

55. Matt. 26:3–4, Mark 14:1–2, and Luke 22:1–6 hardly justify the present two hundred lines in the Rümmelein redaction.

56. *The Passion at Oberammergau*, 1934, 83–84. The 1980 version is practically identical (*The Oberammergau Passion Play 1980*, 67–69).

57. *The Passion at Oberammergau*, 1934, 86.

58. Ibid., 95. Cf. *The Oberammergau Passion Play 1980*, 78.

59. 1934 text, 98–101.

60. 1980 text, 83.

61. 1934 text, 104–7. Cf. 1980 text, 83–85.

62. 1934 text, 109–10.

63. 1934 text, 111–12. Cf. 1980 text, 87.

64. Edsall, "Impressions of Oberammergau," 207.

65. 1934 text, 114–15.

66. Pater Rümmelein notes: "The gospel itself does not mention it, but we can assume that some of the people were against Crucifixion. Something like in Hitler's time. The ones against Hitler were too quiet and the ones for Hitler were tremendously noisy" (interview 19 June 1980). Though Ted Freedman and others consider the scene effective, I think it only exaggerates the disparity of support.

67. 1980 text, 90–91.

68. Ibid., 92.

69. Ibid., 93.

70. 1934 text, 120. The whole scene could have been taken verbatim from act 9 of the twelfth-century Montecassino play (Sticca, *The Latin Passion Play*, 75).

71. 1980 text, 95.

72. Ibid., 100.

73. Again, the scene is remarkably similar to those performed at Wakefield and Bodley (Gassner, *Medieval and Tudor Drama*, 156–68; Kolve, *The Play Called Corpus Christi*, 188).

74. John Schonfield, *The Passover Plot* (New York: Bantam, 1966) disputes the use of nails in the Crucifixion and argues that Jesus planned to be revived after being "executed" on the eve of the Sabbath.

75. *John Stoddard's Lectures*, 328. Before the twentieth century, actors who portrayed Christ wore flesh-colored underwear, which made concealment of a wired corset and blood pouch a little easier than today.

76. 1934 text, 135.

77. Ibid., 134.

78. Ibid., 136; cf. 1980 text, 105–6.

79. Moritz, "Gespräche mit evangelischen Passionsspielbesuchern," 222; Sanders, "Was man auch sehen muss beim Passionsspiel von Oberammergau," 242.

80. Ward, "The Oberammergau Passion Play in 1871," 530.

81. Rauschenbusch, "The Religion of the Passion Play," 691.

82. W. T. Stead, "Oberammergau: A Third Visit," *Review of Reviews* 42 (August 1910): 180.

83. Baum, "Background of Oberammergau Passion Play," American Jewish Congress release, 2.

84. "Dokumentation der Schlussdiskussion des Forums," in Mussner, *Passion in Oberammergau*, 101.

85. Letter to author from Bettelheim, 24 April 1983.

86. Driver, "Play That Carries a Plague," 1017. Wrote the editors of *Christian Century:* "It is hard to imagine a more unfortunate scene than the staging of the life and death of Jesus Christ in a manner that increases Jewish-Christian tensions" (see "Bad Scene at Oberammergau," *Christian Century* 87 [27 May 1970], 651). Despite his general defense of the play, Michael Billington also grants the scene before Pilate's house is "as chilling as any representation of mob-rule" (*Manchester Guardian*, 15 June 1980).

7. The Impact of Anti-Semitism

1. Erich Fromm, *The Anatomy of Human Destructiveness* (New York: Holt, Rinehart and Winston, 1973), 266.

2. See S. Garattini and E. B. Sigg, *Aggressive Behavior* (New York: John Wiley and Sons, 1969), and Bail Eleftheriou and John Paul Scott, *The Physiology of Aggression and Defeat* (New York and London: Plenum Press, 1971). The former was a compendium of papers delivered before an international symposium at Milan's Institut di Ricerche Farmacologiche, while the latter dealt with findings of the American Association for the Advancement of Science held in Dallas in 1968.

3. Konrad Lorenz, *On Aggression,* trans. Marjorie Wilson (New York: Harcourt, Brace and World, 1963), 49, 51, 56.

4. Alfred Kinsey, et al., *Sexual Behavior in the Human Female* (Philadelphia: Saunders, 1953).

5. Lorenz, *On Aggression,* 272. See also Gordon W. Allport, *The Nature of Prejudice* (New York: Doubleday Anchor, 1958), 385–93.

6. *Rage, Hate, Assault, and Other Forms of Violence,* ed. Denis Madden and John Lion (New York: Spectrum Publications, Hasted Press, 1976), 35–47. Note that 70 percent of the government researchers who contributed to the surgeon general's report felt that they had established some link between visual stimuli and violence and that their recommendations had been ignored or hedged upon.

7. Goldaber terms this potentially dangerous phenomenon "violence for vicarious power" (Bil Gilbert and Lisa Twyman, "Violence: Out of Hand in the Stands," *Sports Illustrated* 58 [31 January 1983]: 70). Dr. Bill Beausey, executive director of the Academy for the Psychology of Sports, concurs, noting that there are some sports (e.g., auto racing, football, hockey, and boxing) which have a greater potential for violence than others (golf, ten-

nis, billiards) ("Psychologist Develops Sports Violence Ratings," *Youngstown Vindicator*, 19 December 1982, sec. D). Ashley Montagu takes a different point of view, suggesting that such vicarious outlets are healthy (Montagu, *The Nature of Human Aggression* [New York: Oxford University Press, 1976], 281).

8. *Rage, Hate, Assault*, 33–34.

9. Andersen, *Pictures of Travel*, 264.

10. Stead, "Oberammergau: A Third Visit," 183. Mayr, who had played Christ in 1870, 1880, and 1890, had received a letter from the pope which pardoned all his own sins—past, present, and future—as well as the sins of his children (Morant, "The Vulgarising of Oberammergau," 824). Apparently, he could not cope with the advance of age. John Stoddard, for one, was dismayed by Mayr's capacity to absorb beer (*Stoddard's Lectures*, 267). For other glimpses of the Passion players, see Reiss, "The Oberammergau Players," 742; L. P. Richards, "Life Stories of the Oberammergau Players," *McClure's* 35 (August 1910): 388–401; Moses, *The Passion Play of Oberammergau*, lviii; Swift, *The Passion Play of Oberammergau*, 76.

11. Coyle, *The Passion Play at Oberammergau*, 10.

12. Darlington, *Literature in the Theatre*, 61.

13. *New York Times*, 29 April 1934, sec. 4.

14. Interview with Dr. Charles Waltner, Youngstown, 3 February 1981.

15. Krauskopf, *A Rabbi's Impressions of the Oberammergau Passion*, 33.

16. Ibid., 26.

17. Diemer, *Oberammergau and Its Passion Play*, 84. About the same time, Carl Link was telling how a woman refused to stay in the home of Anton Lang (Christus) because of her own "unworthiness." Another female visitor left the village "distracted" when told she had stayed in Judas's house. Link, "Painting the Passion Players in Their Homes," *Ladies Home Journal* 34 (September 1922): 84.

18. Weiss, "Gespräche mit katholischen Passionsspielbesuchern," 224.

19. Moritz, "Gespräche mit evangelischen Passionsspielbesuchern," 220–21.

20. J. J. Walsh, "Oberammergau," *Commonweal* 12 (20 August 1930): 404.

21. Weiss, "Gespräche mit katholischen Passionsspielbesuchern," 224.

22. Sanders, "Was man auch sehen muss beim Passionsspiel von Oberammergau," 242–43.

23. Interviews with English-speaking tourists, Oberammergau, 18–19 June 1980.

24. Mussner, "Wer trägt die Schuld am gewaltsamen Tod Jesu?" in Mussner, *Passion in Oberammergau*, 32.

25. Anthony Storr, *Human Destructiveness* (New York: Basic Books, 1972), 13; Rollo May, *Power and Innocence: A Search for the Sources of Violence* (New York: W. W. Norton, 1972), 165–79; Allport, *The Nature of Prejudice*, 337.

26. Fromm, *Anatomy of Human Destructiveness*, 272–73. As evidence of man's propensity to violence, the Research Institute of America reports that in the twenty-two years following World War II, more than seven million people were killed throughout the world in "tribal acts of violence" *Rage, Hate, Assault*, 71.

27. Storr, *Human Destructiveness*, 86.

28. Irenäus Eibl-Eibesfeldt, *Love and Hate: The Natural History of Behavior Patterns*, trans. Geoffrey Strachan (New York: Holt, Rinehart and Winston, 1971), 99–102.

29. Stanley Milgram, *Obedience to Authority* (New York: Harper and Row, 1969).

30. Eibl-Eibesfeldt, *Love and Hate*, 81.

31. Lorenz, *On Aggression*, 268–72.

32. Interview with Dr. Sol Levin, NEOUCOM, 27 February 1981.

33. Interview with Dr. Irving Goldaber, 14 February 1983. Goldaber thinks it not unlikely that one day there will be an actual assassination carried out at Oberammergau as a result of the emotions generated by the play.

34. Hans Toch, *Violent Men: An Inquiry into the Psychology of Violence* (Chicago: Aldine, 1969), 211–12.

35. See especially Allport, *The Nature of Prejudice*, 14–15, 57–58, 175–79, 195, 283–89, 457–58. Allport claims that linguistic tags are the first step in learning prejudice. To have enemies, one must have labels. A long period of verbal complaint facilitates movement to the next stage of prejudice, which may be violence. "It was Hitler's anti-locution that led Germans to avoid their Jewish neighbors," said Allport. The final step in the "macabre progression was the ovens at Auschwitz."

36. Morse Peckham, *Man's Rage for Chaos: Biology, Behavior, and the Arts* (New York: Schocken, 1967), 314.

37. Interview with Levin, 27 February 1981. To gain insight into

people's responses to visual stimuli alone, a survey was conducted among history classes at Youngstown State University in the fall of 1980. Two groups (one numbering twenty-two students, the other thirty-three) were chosen at random and shown a set of thirty-six slides. The students, mostly products of lower middle-class, Catholic, urban families, were to identify and/or offer reactions to what they saw. Slides included pictures of Franklin Roosevelt (whom most could not identify), Sigmund Freud (for irony), African blacks, Anne Frank, several Holocaust scenes, and at least eight photos taken from the Oberammergau playbook. Practically all of the students identified the scenes of the Passion and offered empathetic comments. A slide of Jesus with thorns prompted remarks like "pain," "sorrow," "love," "confusion," "savior," "sorrow and joy," "sacrificial lamb," "humanity," "gentle," "merciful," "crying for his people." That of the Crucifixion elicited "fear," "sadness," "died for no reason," "sad moment and then not sad because he took his life for us," "the man is in pain, why don't people help him?" "died for no reason," "remorse," "pain, love, guidance, support." Nearly identical comments accompanied the photos of Anne Frank—"sympathy," "innocence," "admiration," "sorrow," "inspiration"—and those of the concentration camps—"pity cum outrage," "sorrow and pity," "sadness," "despair," "intolerable," "unmerciful," "how could they?" The slides also roused what we have termed negative passions. One of the late Shah of Iran prompted statements like "US puppett [sic]," "dislike," "selfish tyrant," "disgust," "regret," "slyness." More telling were the violent reactions to Ayatollah Khomeini: "rat, crazy, nuts," "anger," "dislike," "fanatic," "fanaticism," "mean," "hatred, revenge," "dictator," "senile old man," "tyrant," "ignorant," "thinking up another catastrophe," "jerk, should be shot," "should be taught a lesson," "asshole," "mentally sick," "expletive deleted," "anger, kill him," "hatred, death, war," "hatred, confusion, dislike," "bomb Iran," "disgust," "I hope he doesn't start World War III." If photos alone could prompt such strong emotions among Americans who were not immediately threatened by the Iranian ruler, even with fifty-two of their countrymen in captivity, imagine the rage and anger which must have been stored up in Europe's Christian population against Jews whom they had been taught to revile for centuries.

38. Dolf Zillmann, *Hostility and Aggression* (Hillsdale, N.J.: Lawrence Erlbaum, 1979), 321.

39. Ibid., 321.

40. "Is the Passion Play Anti-Semitic?" *Christian Century* 47 (20 April 1930): 1007.

41. Baron, *Social and Religious History of the Jews*, 189. See also Morais, *Short History of Anti-Semitism*, 99.

42. Poliakov, *History of Anti-Semitism*, 129.

43. Interview, Dr. Goldaber, 14 February 1983.

44. Poliakov, *History of Anti-Semitism*, 135.

45. Ibid., 130.

46. Interview with Hans Lamm, Munich, 22 June 1980. Dr. Lamm was one of the few fortunate Jews in Bavaria who immigrated to the U.S. before the outbreak of World War II. He worked for several Jewish communities in this country before returning to his homeland as an intelligence officer with the American army. Subsequently, he decided to remain in Germany and is today the spokesman of the Munich Jewish community.

47. "Is the Passion Play Anti-Semitic?" 1006–7.

48. Ibid., 1006.

49. See report of *Stern*, cited in *Cleveland Plain Dealer*, 17 March 1981, sec. A.

50. Zander, "Frommes Theater oder die Passionsspiele von Oberammergau," 229.

51. "Documentation der Schlussdiskussion des Forums," *Passion in Oberammergau*, ed. Franz Mussner, 108.

52. Weiss, "Gespräche mit katholischen Passionsspielbesuchern," 226.

53. Interview, Dr. C. M. Genewein, Munich, 16 June 1980.

54. Krauskopf, *A Rabbi's Impressions of the Oberammergau Passion*, 19.

55. Interview with Douglas Hare, 2 March 1981.

56. Interview with Professor Leonard Swidler, 25 February 1981.

57. Interview with Dr. Levin, 27 February 1981. Nearly identical conclusions were reached by Jules Isaac and Jean-Paul Sartre in their respective works, *The Teaching of Contempt* and *Jew and Anti-Semite*.

58. Interview with Dr. Waltner, 3 February 1981.

59. Interview with Dr. Goldaber, 14 February 1983.

60. Letter from Dr. Robert Jay Lifton, 10 May 1983.

8. The Tercentenary: The Passion Play as Nazi Propaganda

1. *The Passion Play at Oberammergau*, 1950 text, 9–10.

2. *New York Times*, 16 May 1934.

3. *New York Times*, 2 July 1933, sec. 8.

4. Gordon Zahn defines this *Gehorsam* mentality as one which stressed *Pflicht* (duty), *Ehre* (honor), *Treue* (loyalty), *Volk* (people), *Vaterland* or *Heimat* (homeland), *Obrigkeit* (obedience), and *Opferbereitschaft* (sacrifice for the community), precisely the virtues emphasized by the Nazis (Zahn, *German Catholics and Hitler's Wars: A Study in Social Control* [New York: Sheed and Ward, 1962], 19–39, 189). Guenther Lewy of the University of Massachusetts also argues that the *Kulturkampf* left many German Catholics suffering from an inferiority complex which they could only resolve with "superheated patriotism" Lewy, *The Catholic Church and Nazi Germany* [New York: McGraw-Hill, 1964], 15–16). The signing of the Concordat created a temporary state of euphoria among German Catholics (ibid., 103–8, and Ernst Helmreich, *The German Churches under Hitler: Background, Struggle, and Epilogue* [Detroit: Wayne State University Press, 1979], 101–6, 262–73).

5. Max Gallo, *The Night of Long Knives*, trans. Lily Emmet (New York: Harper & Row, 1972). It should also be noted that Hitler was plotting the death of Engelbert Dollfuss and the overthrow of the Austrian republic at the same time.

6. *New York Times*, 6 August 1934.

7. *Völkischer Beobachter*, 1 June 1934.

8. George Mosse, *Nazi Culture: Intellectual, Cultural, and Social Life in the Third Reich* (New York: Grosset and Dunlap, 1966), 153–58.

9. *The Speeches of Adolf Hitler*, ed. Norman Baynes (New York: Howard Fertig, 1969), 1: 568.

10. Ibid., 569–84.

11. *New York Times*, 2 July 1933, sec. 8.

12. *Allgemeine Jüdische Wochenzeitung*, 6 June 1980.

13. *Hitler's Secret Conversations, 1941–1944* (New York: Octagon Books, 1972), 457.

14. Wagner toyed with the idea of an opera dealing with Jesus as early as 1849. Lacking the support of even his friend Franz Liszt, he shelved the project. His later works owe much of their inspiration to the Gospels (see Richard Wagner, *My Life* [New York: Tudor, 1936], 469, 472, 500; *Richard Wagner's Prose Works*, trans.

William Ellis (London: Kegan, Paul, Trench, Trübner, 1895), 4: 74–75, 112. Hitler shared Wagner's enthusiasm for the Passion tale, offered that "mystery" lay at the heart of Bayreuth, and indicated in January 1942, "I already rejoice at the idea that one day I shall be able to resume the pilgrimage" (*Hitler's Secret Conversations*, 198).

15. On Hitler's Oedipal relationship with his mother, see Richard Koenigsberg, *Hitler's Ideology: A Study in Psychoanalytic Sociology* (New York: Library of Social Science, 1975), 55–59; Robert Waite, *The Psychopathic God: Adolf Hitler* (New York: Basic Books, 1977); Walter Langer, *The Mind of Adolf Hitler* (New York: Basic Books, 1972).

16. *The Speeches of Adolf Hitler*, 1: 19.

17. Ibid., 333–41.

18. Ferdinand Friedensburg, "On Nazism and the Church Struggle," in *The German Church Struggle and the Holocaust*, ed. Franklin Littell (Detroit: Wayne State University Press, 1974), 242.

19. Maurice Samuel, *The Great Hatred* (New York: Knopf, 1941), 105–28. Dr. Waltner makes the same point: "Why were they after the Jews? Children rebel against the father. God is the universal father. We cannot rebel against him. Only Lucifer did. So you rebel against his people, the Jews. They are different anyway. It is displaced rebellion against the children of God" (interview, 3 February 1981). On Hitler's commitment to "tear up Christianity root and branch" in Germany, see also Josef Tenenbaum, *Race and Reich* (New York: Twayne, 1956), 49–50.

20. Michael Ryan, "Hitler's Challenge to the Churches: A Theological Political Analysis of *Mein Kampf*," in Littell, *The German Church Struggle and the Holocaust*, 163, 267.

21. See Lewy, *The German Catholic Church and Nazi Germany*, 25 ff; Tenebaum, *Race and Reich*, 52–56; Littell, *The German Church Struggle*, 134–35; Karl Barth, *The German Church Conflict* (Richmond: John Knox Press, 1965).

22. Littell, *The German Church Struggle*, 14.

23. Frederick Schweitzer, *A History of the Jews since the First Century A.D.* (New York: Macmillan and Anti-Defamation League, 1971), 222.

24. Ruether, *Faith and Fratricide*, 7. Father John Pawlikowski adds: "Whatever position one takes on the New Testament basis for the legacy of anti-Semitic teachings in the Church, it cannot be denied that interpretations of New Testament teachings by Christian teachers and preachers throughout the centuries created an

atmosphere which contributed directly to the acceptance of Nazi attitudes towards the Jewish people" (Pawlikowski, *The Challenge of the Holocaust for Christian Theology* [New York: Anti-Defamation League, 1978], 27).

25. Richard Mandell points out these very aspects of Nazi society impressed tourists during the 1936 Olympic Games. See his excellent work, *The Nazi Olympics* (New York: Macmillan, 1971).

26. *New York Times*, 16 May 1934.

27. *Travel* 62 (April 1934): 32–33. I suspect that some favorable reviews were planted in journals (see "Oberammergau's Jubilee Year," *Review of Reviews* 89 [April 1934]: 54–55; A. Dukes, "Scene in Europe," *Theatre Arts Monthly* 18 [September 1934]: 660–62).

28. *Times* (London), 16 May 1934.

29. E. H. Browne, "This Year's Passion Play," *Commonweal* 20 (21 September 1934): 481–82.

30. *Times* (London), 18 May 1934.

31. *New York Times*, 15 January 1933, sec. 6.

32. Ibid., 2 July 1933, sec. 8.

33. Ibid., 16 May 1934.

34. *Times* (London), 23 August 1934.

35. Ibid., 19 July 1934.

36. Ibid., 1 June 1934.

37. *New York Times*, 25 April 1933.

38. *Völkischer Beobachter*, 24 May 1934.

39. Robert Gorham Davis, "Observer at Oberammergau," *Commentary* 29 (March 1960): 198.

40. H. Sutton, "Longest Run on Record," *Saturday Review* 33 (22 April 1950): 36.

41. W. A. Heaps, "Oberammergau Today," *Christian Century* 63 (4 December 1946): 1469. See also Report of Erich Adler to chief of Intelligence, Munich Detachment, Information Control Division, Office of Military Government for Bavaria, 25 February 1947, in Melchior Breitsamter Folder, Records of the U.S. Occupation Headquarters, World War II, Office of Military Government for Germany, Bavaria, Information Control, 10–48–2. All references hereafter to these documents located in the General Archives Division of the National Archives Records Center in Suitland, Maryland, are to OMGUSB Records.

42. See eleven-page "Eidesstattliche Erklärung des Bürgermeisters Josef Raab," 14 April 1946, OMGUSB.

43. Two Jews came forward to testify on behalf of Lang. Thus

the panel, which included Hans Huber, a survivor of the concentration camps, dealt leniently with Lang (*New York Times*, 28 May 1947).

44. Letter of Bürgermeister Raab to Theater and Music Control Section, Information Control Division, Breitsamter Folder, OMGUSB, 1–48–2, 1 May 1946.

45. Interview with Hans Maier, Oberammergau, 19 June 1980.

46. Letter of Bürgermeister Raab, 1 May 1946, OMGUSB, 1–48–2.

47. Ferdinand Reyner, "Christ in Oberammergau," *Atlantic Monthly* 130 (November 1922): 599, 602.

48. Driver, "Play That Carries a Plague," 1018.

49. *New York Times*, 2 July 1933, sec. 8.

50. *New York Times*, 11 August 1949.

51. Phil Baum, "Background of Oberammergau Passion Play," release of American Jewish Congress, 7 November 1966, 3.

52. *The Passion Play at Oberammergau*, 1934, 10.

53. Ibid., 9.

54. *The Speeches of Adolf Hitler*, I: 386–87. In *Mein Kampf*, Hitler also raged against the spiritual pestilence that was worse than the Black Death and that had splashed filth over German art and literature.

55. Mosse, *Nazi Culture*, 259.

56. Ibid., 257–58. Faulhaber's reluctance to speak out should not surprise. The cardinal did not protest Nazi hooliganism directed against the Friedensbund deutscher Katholiken in 1933 (Zahn, *German Catholics and Hitler's Wars*, 110–15). Nor did he speak out in November 1933, when Dr. Muhler, former head of Catholic Action in Munich, was arrested for reporting atrocities in Dachau (Lewy, *German Catholic Church and Nazi Germany*, 111). When he did protest treatment of Catholic youth groups to Bavarian Minister of Interior Wagner, he uttered no outcry against the demeaning treatment of Jews (*Times* [London], 28 April 1934). Actually, Faulhaber's silence was no worse than his colleagues who, said William Allen, "consistently showered gratuitous and unsolicited declarations of loyalty upon Hitler" (Allen, "Objective and Subjective Inhibitants in the German Resistance to Hitler," in Littell, *The German Church Struggle*, 121). Waldemar Gurian also makes note of this quiescent attitude (Lewy, *German Catholic Church and Nazi Germany*, 171).

57. *New York Times*, 18 May 1934. Ashley Dukes concedes there

were suggestions of contemporary influence, but "to say that it (the Passion) has already been Nordicized is going too far" (see "The Scene in Europe," 662).

58. *Times* (London), 18 May 1934.

59. *Völkischer Beobachter,* 14 August 1934.

60. Ibid., 10.

61. Ibid., 10. See also *New York Times,* 14 August 1934, where it is claimed that Hitler arrived sans fanfare and used a ticket in a block anonymously reserved for "a Nordic travelling group."

62. Interview with Bürgermeister Zwink, 18 June 1980.

63. Heaps, "Oberammergau Today," 1468.

64. Annex of Personnel in Passion play who were prisoners of war in Russian, American, English, or French camps (Breitsamter Folder, Information Control Division, OMGUSB, 1–48).

65. Heaton, *The Oberammergau Passion Play,* 50.

66. One of the first American units to enter Oberammergau was a Naval Technical Mission dressed in army uniforms. The team was seeking Herbert Wagner, chief design engineer for the Henschel HS-293 Aircraft, and others who had worked on German missile projects. With its Messerschmidt and BMW factories operating at full tilt toward the end of the war, Oberammergau was not the innocent little provincial village it pretended (see Clarence Lasby, *Project Paperclip: German Scientists and the Cold War* [New York: Atheneum, 1971]).

67. Heaps, "Oberammergau Today," 1468. I am especially indebted to Dr. Jim Elder of Youngstown, a Jewish survivor of the Oberammergau labor camp, for glimpses of the village in wartime (interview, 29 October 1980). Michael Elkins claims that one Nazi who sought refuge in Oberammergau after the war was tracked down by members of the Jewish revenge group known as DIN. In 1958 SS Lt. Georg Kurt Mussfeld, responsible for killing Jews in Lublin during the war, was hanged in the kitchen "of the pilgrims inn" which he operated in Oberammergau (Elkins, *Forged in Fury* [New York: Ballantine Books, 1971], 186).

9. The 1950 Revival

1. *New York Times,* 30 April 1950.

2. "Passion in 1946?" *Time* 46 (16 July 1945): 62.

3. Lucius D. Clay, *Decision in Germany* (Garden City: Doubleday and Co., 1950), p. 231. Clay served as deputy military governor

under Eisenhower and McNarney, then as military governor in the American Zone from 1947 to 1949.

4. Heaps, "Oberammergau Today," 1468–69.

5. Clay, *Decision in Germany*, 256.

6. Interview with Jim Elder, 29 October 1980. Another Jewish survivor, George Jacobs, tells substantially the same story. Jacobs, whose odyssey began in Polish Silesia before the war, spent more than a year in this region and recalls the frigid welcome extended to refugees (interview, 14 January 1981).

7. Norbert Muhlen, *The Return of Germany* (London: Bodley Head, 1953), 167.

8. *The Papers of General Lucius D. Clay, Germany, 1945–1949*, ed. Jean Edward Smith (Bloomington: Indiana University Press, 1974), 1: 47.

9. Ibid., 273.

10. Victor Bernstein of *PM*, Carl Levin of the *New York Herald-Tribune*, Ed Morgan of the *Chicago Daily News*, and Ray Danniell of the *New York Times* all criticized the policies of Third Army Commander George Patton (*Clay Papers*, 89).

11. Ibid., 61.

12. Elkins, *Forged in Fury*, 253.

13. *Clay Papers*, 142.

14. Ibid., 131.

15. Some officials estimated a need for 500 denazification tribunals manned by 22,000 persons. As a result, before the end of 1946, many cases were turned over to local tribunals staffed by non-Nazi Germans (Whitney Harris, *Tyranny on Trial: The Evidence at Nuremberg* [Dallas: Southern Methodist University Press, 1954], 541).

16. *Clay Papers*, 228.

17. Ibid., 260.

18. Ibid., 285.

19. Ibid., 576–77, 659.

20. Clay, *Decision in Germany*, 262.

21. Ibid., 281.

22. Ibid., 283. See also John Gimbel, *The American Occupation of Germany: Politics and the Military, 1945–1949* (Stanford University Press, 1968), 245–52. As recently as April 1983, Simon Wiesenthal estimated that more than four million former members of the Nazi party were still living in West Germany (speech at Youngstown State University, 14 April 1983). On the failure of

American denazification, see Constantine FitzGibbon, *Denazification* (New York: W. W. Norton, 1969).

23. See reports of Col. John Taylor, Dr. Thomas Alexander, and Dr. Herman Wells, in Clay, *Decision in Germany*, 299.

24. *New York Times*, 5 June 1947.

25. *Clay Papers*, 963–67.

26. Ibid., 161–62.

27. Heyl to Commanding General USFET, APO 757, 14 September 1945, Breitsamter Folder, Information Control Division, OMGUSB, 10–48–2. See accompanying letter of Father Bogenrieder, 1 May 1946.

28. Breitsamter *Fragebogen*, Information Control Business Questionnaire, 25 March 1946, Breitsamter Folder. See accompanying letter relating to the religious and biblical nature of the play from Raab to Gerald Van Loon, theater chief in Munich, 2 April 1946. Subsequently, Breitsamter would claim to having directed lesser productions like "Der Meister des Lebens" and "Der Verlorene Sohn." *Tätigkeitsbericht* for 1946 and 1947.

29. Young Gregor, who played Christ in 1980, had been a member of the Hitler youth at age fourteen.

30. Report of Adler to Team Chief, Munich Detachment, Information Control Division, 25 February 1947, Breitsamter Folder, OMGUSB, 10–48–2.

31. Report of Hart to Commanding Officer, Counter Intelligence Corps APO 170, 26 April 1946; and Martindale to same, Breitsamter Folder, Information Control Division, OMGUSB, 10–48–2.

32. A similar view was expressed by the *New York Times*, which noted that Oberammergau "for all its piety, was well-known in prewar days as a Nazi stronghold" (*New York Times*, 9 October 1946).

33. Report of Adler to Team Chief, Munich Detachment, Information Control Division, 25 February 1947, Breitsamter Folder, OMGUSB, 10–48.

34. Ibid.

35. Memo from Cramer to Walter Behr, Information Control Division, March 20, 1947, Breitsamter Folder, OMGUSB, 10–48–2.

36. Ibid.

37. Ibid.

38. Behr to Chief, Information Control Division, 15 April 1947, Breitsamter Folder, OMGUSB, 10–48–2.

39. Martindale to Chief, Information Control Division, 29 April 1947, Breitsamter Folder, OMGUSB, 10–48–2.

40. Memo of Kleitz for distribution, 2 May 1947, and memo of Halpin to Chief, Film, Theater, and Music Branch, Information Control Division, 6 May 1947, Breitsamter Folder, OMGUSB, 10–48–2.

41. Letter from Behr to Breitsamter, 9 May 1947, Breitsamter Folder, OMGUSB, 10–48–2.

42. Memo from Martin Mayes, Branch Chief, Film, Theater, and Music Branch, Information Control Division, to Director, Internal Affairs Division, 6 January 1948, Breitsamter Folder, OMGUSB, 10–48–2.

43. *New York Times*, 18 November 1949. Earlier, Wilhelm Link had told a denazification court that more than 1,000 Oberammergauers might be chargeable as "followers" (*New York Times*, 17 May 1947).

44. Georg Lang claimed he joined the party to prevent the Nazis from abolishing the Passion play (*New York Times*, 5 June 1947). Later, he rejected charges of anti-Semitism and refused to be drawn into a debate over his background or the political implications of the play. "We cannot possibly be expected to distort facts of religious history," he declared (*New York Times*, 9 March 1960).

45. "New Christus," *Time* 54 (21 November 1949): 49.

46. *New York Times*, 18 November 1949. Ironically, Walter Behr, one of those privy to the decision-making process in 1947, was furious about the cast selections in 1949 (see *New York Times*, 11 August 1949).

47. *Stars and Stripes*, 4 January 1949.

48. Lang to Military Government, Garmisch-Partenkirchen, 15 January 1949, Passionsspiel Folder, Intelligence Division, OMGUSB, 10–107.

49. Lang to William J. Garloch, Intelligence Division Commanding Officer, 2 February 1949, Passionsspiel Folder, OMGUSB, 10–107. Actually, the figure DM 2 million, or $600,000, was being publicly discussed by January 1949, and the Oberammergau Passion Committee was very open about the need to secure a "patron town in the United States to help subsidize the project" (*New York Times*, 16 January 1949, sec. 2).

50. Report of Joseph Bartos, Acting Finance Adviser, Office Finance Adviser, to Education, Cultural Relations Division, Cultural Affairs Branch, 24 August 1949, OMGUSB, 10–164.

51. See memo of William J. Moran, Deputy Director, Field Operations Division, 13 August 1949, Loan Folder, 1949, OMGUSB, 10–164.

52. Memo of Resch, Ministerialdirigent, Bavarian State Interior Ministry, to OMGUSB Finance Division, Munich, 1 October 1948, Loan Folder, 1948–49, Public Finance Branch, OMGUSB, 260.

53. *New York Times*, 30 April 1950.

54. Memo of Joseph Bartos, Finance Adviser Office, to Deputy Military Government, 25 August 1949, Loan Folder, 1949, OMGUSB, 10–164.

55. Application of Munich to Finance Adviser Officer, 10 November 1948, Loan Folder, 1949, OMGUSB, 10–164.

56. Letter of Hays to Murray Van Wagoner, Director, Office of Military Government for Bavaria, 19 May 1949, Public Finance Branch, Loan Folder, 1949, OMGUSB, 260, Box 132.

57. Letter from Van Wagoner to Hays, 27 April 1949, Finance Division Branch, Loan Folder, 1949, OMGUSB, 10–164.

58. Davis to Huebner, 29 August 1949, Finance Division Branch, Loan Folder, 1949, OMGUSB, 10–164. The one thing that did upset Davis was the handling charge of 3 percent being charged by the Bayrische Gemeinde Bank in Munich. The total interest of 9½ percent, which no American bank would have charged, left him "completely outraged."

59. Interview with John D. McCloy, 2 February 1980.

60. TWX from OMGUS HQ to OMG Bavaria, Office of the Finance Adviser, 13 August 1949, Finance Division Branch, Loans, 1949, OMGUSB, 10–164.

61. *New York Times*, 21 May 1950.

62. *New York Times*, 19 May 1950. The people of Oberammergau accorded an extraordinary honor to one little boy whose serviceman father hailed from Boise, Idaho. They permitted the youth to participate in the tableaux (*New York Times*, 22 May 1950).

63. Interview with John D. McCloy, 2 February 1980.

64. Joseph Maria Lutz, "The 1950 Play and Its Performers," *The Passion Play at Oberammergau*, 1950 text, 52–53. Mayor Zwink told me, "The people of Oberammergau did this. We said in 1949 or 1950, 'We want to play the Passion Play.' The American generals did not say no" (interview with Zwink, 18 June 1980).

65. Lutz, "The 1950 Play and Its Performers," 52.

66. Johnson believed his memo "was probably lost in the labyrinth of changing personnel and red tape" (see letter of Willard Johnson, *Christian Century*, 12 October 1960, p. 1184).

67. It was claimed that a shortage of printed materials compelled the use of the 1934 text (*New York Times*, 16 January 1949, sec. 2).

10. Profit from the Passion

1. Release of American Jewish Congress, 18 November 1966. See also "Amerikaner Idisher Kongres Ruft Velt-Boykot Kegen Antisemitishen Pasion-Spiel in Merv-Deytschland," *Tog*, 19 November 1966.

2. Release of American Jewish Congress, 13 August 1975.

3. Release of American Jewish Congress, 23 November 1966.

4. Zander, "Frommes Theater oder die Passionsspiele von Oberammergau," 227. Schaller had earlier indicated his commitment to revision, telling the Munich Society for Christian-Jewish Cooperation, "There are passages in the old play which could no longer be tolerated" "Oberammergau: A Felicitous Follow-Up," *Christian Century* 85 (19 June 1968): 809.

5. "Bad Scene at Oberammergau," *Christian Century* 87 (27 May 1970): 651.

6. *Buffalo Jewish Review*, 6 June 1980.

7. Release of American Jewish Congress, 13 August 1975.

8. Interviews with Zwink and Maier, 19–20 June 1980.

9. Originally the Passion was presented in Oberammergau's church. By 1674, however, lack of space prompted the townspeople to move it out of doors, to the yard overlooking the cemetery. A temporary stage was constructed on the north wall of the church between 1815 and 1820. In 1830, the presentation was moved several hundred meters to what came to be known as the Passion Meadow. A primitive theater was surrounded by high fences of wood. Spectators suffered through the all-day performances on benches, exposed to the elements. In 1880, the first true hall was constructed, to be followed by a permanent theater in 1890. Not until the turn of the century, however, was a roof raised over the audience section of the Greek-style amphitheater. Seats are still uncomfortable, but the audience is sheltered and the number of entry-exits constitute a miracle of efficiency. Five thousand people can get to and from their seats in a matter of minutes.

10. Though William Butler claims the income in 1890 was only $61,000 (*Oberammergau 1890*, 46), the *New York World* reported the higher figure for that year (see Moses, *The Passion Play at Oberammergau*, lxiii). The latter figure of $15 million was an estimate offered by Ted Freedman of the Anti-Defamation League, Bürgermeister Zwink, and Monsignor Genewein. A subsequent report placed the gross from 1980 at the equivalent of $11.3 million (*Youngstown Vindicator*, 19 January 1983).

11. Swift, *The Passion Play of Oberammergau*, 93.

12. *Stoddard's Lectures*, 246.

13. Swift, *The Passion Play of Oberammergau*, 95.

14. Diemer, *Oberammergau and Its Passion Play*, 68. One such example of health problems was Anton Mayr, Thomas in 1922. Weakened by the loss of one leg in World War I, Mayr contracted pneumonia and died after participating in the postwar extravaganza (Gertrude Brigham, "The Passion Play at Oberammergau, 1922," *Art and Archaeology* 15 (January 1923): 33).

15. Eugen Roth, "For God or Gain?" *The Passion Play at Oberammergau*, 1950 text, 94–100. See also Roth, "The Vow," *Oberammergau and Its Passion Play* 1960, 80–81.

16. Swift, *The Passion Play of Oberammergau*, 90.

17. Ibid., 91.

18. Ibid., 92. About the same time, Lang also received the offer of a free automobile from Henry Ford. Apparently he was forced to decline this honor as well.

19. "Oberammergau's Blow at Mammon," *Literary Digest* 75 (25 November 1922): 34.

20. Ibid.

21. Lang allowed that he was interested in such films as *Quo Vadis, Theodora,* and the works of Shakespeare. But he blasted "greedy," "get rich quick" managers who were pandering to the whims of the public (see "Christus in Oberammergau," *Living Age* 314 (26 August 1922): 550–51).

22. Swift, *The Passion Play of Oberammergau*, p. 94.

23. Karlheinz Simon to Information Control Division, Film Branch, OMGUSB, 16 December 1947, 10–164.

24. Interview with Bürgermeister Zwink, 19 June 1980. The reporter for the *Volker Buhbe* quoted the people of Oberammergau as saying, "We play first and foremost for ourselves and not for the others" (*German Tribune*, 6 April 1980).

25. "Oberammergau's Tradition," *Living Age* 313 (27 May 1922): 553.

26. Diemer, *Oberammergau and Its Passion Play*, 23.

27. Ibid., 23.

28. Ibid., 26–27.

29. The nonsectarian committee in America included such luminaries as Governor Al Smith, W. A. Harriman, Evangeline Booth, Burton Holmes, Frank Waterman, Mrs. Gutzon Borglum, Ida Tarbell, Archbishop Mundelein, Jane Addams, Bishop W. A. Leonard,

Newton D. Baker, Rabbi Abba Hillel Silver, and Minnie Maddern Fiske (Swift, *The Passion Play of Oberammergau*, 144).

30. Ibid., 145.

31. "Oberammergau's Rebuke to America," *Literary Digest* 80 (5 January 1924): 34. Lang was also quoted as saying, "We have but one object in our visit—the most adventurous ever taken by people of our little mountain village—and that is to secure work. This work is for our families so they may be saved to carry on the crafts of Oberammergau and again present the passion play" (Swift, *The Passion Play of Oberammergau*, 145).

32. Ibid., 150–51. Though the tour generated much publicity, orders fell off by the fall of 1925 (see "Oberammergau in Distress," *Living Age* 329[1 May 1926]: 287).

33. "Passion Play Profits," *Literary Digest* 109 (9 May 1931): 20.

34. Phil Baum, "Background of Oberammergau Passion Play," special report for American Jewish Congress, 7 November 1966, 4.

35. Roth, "For God or Gain?" *Passion Play at Oberammergau*, 1950 text, 99.

36. Interview with Monsignor Genewein, 16 June 1980. The villagers themselves spoke of a possible DM 100 million income, from which, of course, costs would have to be deducted (*German Tribune*, 6 April 1980). Current Bürgermeister Frank Hofmann recently told the press of the need for *Rathaus* and health-spa renovation (*Youngstown Vindicator*, 19 January 1983).

37. Statement of Cardinal Ratzinger, Oberammergau, 18 May 1980.

38. Baum, "Background of Oberammergau Passion Play," 2.

39. "Oberammergau: Living with a Vow," *Newsweek*, 21 April 1980, p. 27.

40. Interview with Bürgermeister Zwink, 18 June 1980. Pater Rümmelein offered the same explanation. "It is because so many come from the USA and Great Britain," he told me. "Seventy percent of all visitors come from these two countries. Many Germans cannot see it because the Americans take all the seats" (interview, 19 June 1980).

41. Interview with Schwaighofer, 18 June 1980.

42. Heaton, *The Oberammergau Passion Play*, 74.

43. K. M. Roof, "Moral Effect of the Tourist upon the Native," *Craftsman* 11 (March 1907): 675.

44. Coyle, *The Passion Play at Oberammergau*, 11.

45. Priestley, *Self-Selected Essays*, 219.

46. Darlington, *Literature in the Theatre and Other Essays*, 63.

47. Driver, "Play That Carries a Plague," 1017. A current projection by Werner Zwick holds that scalpers may receive as much as $200 per ticket in 1984. *Youngstown Vindicator*, 19 January 1983.

48. "Piety with Profit," *Time* 76 (11 July 1960): 56.

49. "Debate at Oberammergau," *Newsweek* 54 (23 November 1959): 114.

50. Sutton, "Longest Run on Record," 38.

51. Schroubek, "Erbauliches Spiel oder Argernis?" 232. See also Henry Becker, "The Oberammergau Passion Play," *Mentor* 10 (August 1922): 34–35. Becker raved about the countryside, but noted that the villagers "wax fat on the great influx of eager and generous tourists."

52. Edsall, "Impressions of Oberammergau," 207.

53. *New York Times*, 15 January 1933, sec. 6.

54. Heaton, *The Oberammergau Passion Play*, 60, 66, 74.

55. *German Tribune*, 6 April 1980.

56. *Frankfurter Allgemeine Zeitung*, 4 June 1980, sec. R.

57. Interview with Dr. Lamm, Munich, 22 June 1980.

58. "Heavenly Hosts; A Beginner's Guide to Television Evangelists," *Playboy* 27 (October 1980): 157–61.

59. Harvey Watts, "Pilgrimage Play at Hollywood, California," *Art and Archaeology* 15 (January 1923): 15–21. The Passion was in its third season in the El Camino Real Canyon, with Henry Herbert as Christ.

60. It was clear from statements issued by the Brazilian government that the Passion in Nova Jerusalem was intended to generate sufficient profits to pay for theater, props, actors, and access roads (*New York Times*, 9 December 1972). Profit has also enabled Val Balfour's Virginia-based troupe to remain in business for more than a quarter century. Based loosely upon the Oberammergau epic (the Strasbourg play lasts only two hours, has no music, and has some priests who oppose the denunciation of Jesus), Balfour's version is regarded as innocuous by the Anti-Defamation League (interview with Ted Freedman, 15 October 1981). The Lake Wales Passion is also an annual affair which draws from visitors to north-central Florida and Orlando. Its directors denied any connection with the spirit or tone of the traditional Oberammergau Passion in a letter to me, 16 February 1983.

61. Said Ted Freedman, "The issue is, of course, larger than Oberammergau; it is a matter of concern wherever the passion story

is reenacted." And further: "Our concern is with the negative concepts attributed to Jews and Judaism communicated through its drama and pageantry" ("Oberammergau: A Personal Account," *Face to Face* 7 [Summer 1980]: 18).

62. Some critics have likened the Union City pageant to the works of *Der Stürmer* (see *Union City Dispatch*, 22 March 1967; *New York Times*, 31 January 1968; *New York Times*, 24 March 1974). More recently, the revival of a musical version of a thirteenth-century Carmina Burana Passion has aroused protests from New York City to Bloomington. *ADL Update* (Winter 1983), p. 3.

63. *Arkansas 1978 Tour Guide*, 105–11. See also pamphlet of Gerald L. K. Smith, *An Inspired Cause, a Miraculous Outgrowth, a Prophetic Challenge*, published by Elna M. Smith Foundation (1973), 11–14.

64. Smith, *The Miracles on the Mountains*, pamphlet published by Elna Smith Foundation, Eureka Springs (1975 edition).

65. Smith, *An Inspired Cause*, 16.

66. Arnold Forster and Benjamin Epstein, *The New Anti-Semitism* (New York: McGraw-Hill, 1974), 20.

67. Ibid., 24–25.

68. Ibid., 25. Robert Hyde claims that "the Spirit of the Lord" is actually in the play. "The Great Passion Play," *Pentecostal Messenger* 53 (April 1979): 30.

69. Some members of the local Chamber of Commerce resigned in protest when Robertson was inducted (*New York Times*, 28 November 1969).

70. Despite protests from the ADL's Dore Schary, President Nixon (who earlier had called Smith a hatemonger) declined to override the Commerce Department's approval of assistance for roads to Eureka Springs (*New York Times*, 25 January 1970). For support given Smith by government officials, see Forster and Epstein, *The New Anti-Semitism*, 25–48 passim.

11. The Rosner Option

1. "Dokumentation der Schlussdiskussion des Forums," in Mussner, *Passion in Oberammergau*, 104–5.

2. Father Schaller informed Hans Lamm, "There are passages in the old play which could no longer be tolerated" ("Oberammergau: A Felicitous Follow-Up," *Christian Century* 85 (19 June 1968), 809.

3. Letter from Pater Schaller, 24 March 1980.

4. Zander, "Frommes Theater oder die Passionsspiele von Oberammergau," 227.

5. Ibid., 228. For a historical critique of the Rosner Passion see Pater Schaller's *Passio Nova: Das Oberammergau Passionsspiel von 1750* (Bern and Frankfurt: Verlag Peter Lang, 1974).

6. "Dokumentation der Schlussdiskussion des Forums," *Passion in Oberammergau*, 110.

7. Release of American Jewish Committee, 13 August 1975.

8. Telephone interview with Rabbi Tanenbaum, 23 April 1981.

9. *New York Times*, 8 June 1977, sec. 3; 16 August 1977.

10. "Dokumentation der Schlussdiskussion des Forums," *Passion in Oberammergau*, 106.

11. Interview with Rabbi Tanenbaum, 23 April 1981.

12. Interview with Lamm, 22 June 1980.

13. Claus Kolberg in *Kieler Nachrichten*, 21 April 1978, reprinted in *German Tribune*, 7 May 1978.

14. Interview with Rabbi Tanenbaum, 23 April 1981.

15. Interview with Swidler, 25 February 1981. Swidler allows that other organizations paved the way for the ADL reforms but insists that the past several years have also seen a change in the atmosphere in Germany. The "dramatic turnaround" in Christian-Jewish relations stems in part, he believes, from the teachings of Vatican II. More important was the impact of the television docudrama "Holocaust: Story of the Family Weiss." That production not only caused the West German government to reconsider its policy of amnesty on war crimes but also stirred the people to extensive thinking about their attitudes toward Jews and Judaism.

16. Interview with Maier, 19 June 1980.

17. Interview with Schwaighofer, 18 June 1980. Rabbi Tanenbaum says substantially the same thing. "The Arbeitsgemeinschaft said why get rid of a good thing? Why alienate peasants and visitors. Daisenberger was a far more pietist folk play" (interview with Tanenbaum, 23 April 1981).

18. Interview with former Bürgermeister Zwink, 18 June 1980.

19. The tape of this interview, done as I was strolling along the Ammer River, truly is humorous. From start to finish, the men insisted there was no problem in town. Yet none of them could get out a sentence without another interrupting (interview, 19 June 1980).

20. Interview with Pater Rümmelein, 19 June 1980.

21. Interview with Hans Maier, 19 June 1980.

22. "Dokumentation der Schlussdiskussion des Forums," *Passion in Oberammergau*, 103–4.

23. *German Tribune*, 27 January 1980. Earlier, Preisinger had played the aesthete, telling visitors, "The play has logic, is plainly constructed, and does not allow for too much of a change in its over-all concept" (see "Oberammergau: A Felicitous Follow-Up," 809). His concerns were shared by others who worried about the nature of the costumes, props, introduction of professional actors, all of which "will radically alter the deeper meaning of the play" (see H. B. Kuhn, "Concerning Oberammergau 1980," *Christianity Today* 22[19 May 1978]: 69–70).

24. "Synopse aus den drei Textfassungen Daisenberger 1970, Daisenberger 1980, Rosner-Probespiel 1977," in Mussner, *Passion in Oberammergau*, 113. Hereafter cited as Rosner Synopsis.

25. Zander, "Frommes Theater oder die Passionsspiele von Oberammergau," 230. Professor Bodo Richter of New York State University at Buffalo defines "Poverellos" as a term of endearment for poor men, beggars, the equivalent of Saint Francis.

26. Among the negative expressions on Rosner, see *New York Times*, 19 August 1977. Gregor Breitsamter, Pater Rümmelein, Maier, Zwink, and the other townsfolk expressed concern about the fate of Dedler's music. For his part, Schwaighofer claims he only had preliminary discussions with Orff about a new composition before the latter's death.

27. Rosner Synopsis, 126.

28. Interview with Monsignor Genewein, 16 June 1980.

29. The Berlin Papyrus from the Middle Kingdom expresses "The Dialogue of a Man Weary with His Soul." The frustration and anguish in that ancient document might well have served as a model for Judas's despair (see Jacob Erman, *The Ancient Egyptians: A Sourcebook of Their Writings* [1927; reprint, New York: Harper Torch, 1966], 86 ff).

30. Rosner Synopsis, 129–31.

31. Ibid., 132.

32. Ibid., 132–34.

33. Ibid., 135–36.

34. Ibid., 137–40.

35. In medieval times, it was customary for some kind of red ensign to be flown from the roof of a government house to notify people of an impending execution. Like the subsequent reference to breaking Pilate's staff, the citation reflects Rosner's eighteenth-century environment.

36. Rosner Synopsis, 142.
37. Ibid., 143.
38. Ibid., 143.
39. Ibid., 144–45.
40. Ibid., 146–51.
41. Ibid., 116.
42. "Dokumentation der Schlussdiskussion des Forums," *Passion in Oberammergau*, 109.
43. Interview with Ted Freedman, 13 June 1980.

12. A Contemporary Passion?

1. Interview with Hans Lamm, Munich, 22 June 1980.
2. *The Oberammergau Passion Play 1980*, 16.
3. *Buffalo Jewish Review*, 6 June 1980.
4. Interview with Rabbi Tanenbaum, 23 April 1981.
5. Interview with Pater Rümmelein, 19 June 1980.
6. Sandmel, *Anti-Semitism in the New Testament?* has an excellent discussion of the advantages of Luke, 71–85.
7. Interview with Zwink, 18 June 1980. Said Hans Schwaighofer, "It must be a special person. Maybe people would accept it. I don't believe it" (interview, 18 June 1980).
8. Born in Brussels in 1922, Ms. De Vinck immigrated to the U.S. in 1948. Since then, she has published seven books. In 1975 she was awarded the Keats Society (London) Prize for poetry. Writing the author to grant permission for citations from her passion play, Ms. De Vinck commented: "Christians should have feelings of love, of tenderness towards the Jews, should look upon them as their spiritual brothers and sisters. Alas, history spoke another language, a language of mistrust, persecution, hatred. As a Christian I have always been profoundly disturbed by this tragic flaw in the Church's understanding of Jesus. The Inquisition, the pogroms, the Holocaust are bloody stains on the fabric of Christianity" (25 April 1983).
9. Catherine De Vinck, *A Passion Play* (Allendale, N.J.: Alleluia Press, 1975), 13, 33.
10. Ibid., 27.
11. Ibid., 44–45.
12. Ibid., 39.
13. Ibid., 46.
14. Ibid., 49.
15. Ibid., 65.

16. Ibid., 17.

17. Ibid., 33.

18. Ibid., 34.

19. Ibid., 53.

20. Ibid., 52.

21. Ibid., 55–56.

22. From Schwarz-Bart's epic novel, *The Last of the Just* (New York: Atheneum, 1960).

23. De Vinck, *A Passion Play*, 57.

24. Ibid., 59.

25. Ibid., 66–68.

26. Some of my students have suggested that there be some jostling onstage between the various partisans.

27. Ruether, *Faith and Fratricide*, 12–13. Uriel Tal regards modern anti-Semitism as a continuation "mutatis mutandis" of Christian hatred of Jews as deicides and argues that this hatred was cultivated "for centuries by the church" (see Tal, *Christians and Jews in Germany: Religion, Politics and Ideology in the Second Reich, 1870–1914*, (trans. Noah Jacobs [Ithaca, N.Y.: Cornell University Press, 1975], 224–25). For an exposition of the teachings of some of the most sympathetic Christian theologians (Karl Barth, Wolfhart Pannenberg, Piet Schoonenberg, and others), see Eugene Borowitz's *Contemporary Christologies: A Jewish Response* (New York: Paulist Press, 1980).

28. Interview with Ted Freedman, 13 June 1980.

29. Already in 1960, Dr. Alois Fink had written of the villagers' sensitivity to change: "The people of Oberammergau deserve credit for their own constantly active critical discernment in recognizing the controversial passages in the present text and in seriously devoting themselves to the question of a revised version" (Fink, "Some Notes on the Question of a New Version of the Text," *Oberammergau and Its Passion Play 1960*, 36).

30. Interview with Ted Freedman, 13 June 1980.

31. Interview with Lamm, 22 June 1980.

32. Interview with Monsignor Genewein, 16 June 1980.

33. "Oberammergau's Blow at Mammon," *Literary Digest* 75 (25 November 1922): 34.

34. Zander, "Frommes Theater oder die Passionsspiele von Oberammergau," 229, and Sanders, "Was man auch sehen muss beim Passionsspiel von Oberammergau," 244.

35. Said Georg Krieger in the *Rheinischer Merkur/Christ und Welt:* "The Roman Catholic Church has given its implicit blessing

to the Oberammergau revision 1980 version, so the Church can hardly be accused of objecting to a new and deeper look at the theological message conveyed" (*German Tribune*, 8 June 1980).

36. Interview with Zwink, 18 June 1980.

37. Ash Wednesday, 1980 address of Dr. Curt M. Genewein in Pfarrkirche of Oberammergau (German transcription).

38. Interview with Genewein, 16 June 1980.

39. The celebrated encyclical *Nostra Aetate* is still flawed in several areas. What started out as a brief statement of the Catholic church's attitude "especially toward Jews" ultimately emerged as a sanitized declaration of the church's relationship "toward non-Christian religions." The Vatican found it necessary to offer "explanations" to Palestinian and other Arab representatives that the statement by no means altered its position vis-à-vis Israel. The Jewish problem was addressed in *Nostra Aetate* after reference had been made first to the Church's relationship with Hinduism, Buddhism, and Islam. And allegedly out of concern for Jewish sensitivities, the word *deicide* was never formally used (see Arthur Gilbert, *The Vatican Council and the Jews* [New York: World Publishing, 1968], 262 ff).

40. Krauskopf, *A Rabbi's Impressions of the Oberammergau Passion*, 85.

Postscript

1. Letter from ADL's Theodore Freedman to Bishop Flugel, Regensburg, 28 June 1983.

2. Ibid.

3. Ibid.

4. Interviews with Ted Freedman, 3 August 1983, and Leonard Swidler, 5 August 1983. Swidler's recommendations which were ignored included deletion of "Old Testament" names and the character known as "Rabbi," "a reluctant Pilate," "the handwashing Pilate," "a self-righteous Pilate," screams of "kill the Messiah," "we are all guilty," "Heil Israel," the emphasis on a new covenant and the destruction of Judaism.

5. Interview with Swidler, 5 August 1983.

6. Interview with Freedman, 3 August 1983.

7. Swidler and Sloyan, *The Oberammergau Passionsspiel 1984*, p. 45.

Selected Bibliography

Books

Allport, Gordon W. *The Nature of Prejudice.* New York: Double-day Anchor, 1958.

Andersen, Hans Christian. *Pictures of Travel.* New York and Cambridge: Riverside Press, 1871.

Banki, Judith. *What Viewers Should Know about the Oberammer-gau Passion Play, 1980.* New York: American Jewish Committee, 1980.

Barth, Karl. *The German Church Conflict.* Richmond: John Knox Press, 1965.

Beardsley, Monroe. *Aesthetics: Problems in the Philosophy of Criticism.* New York: Harcourt, Brace, 1958.

Brandon, S. G. F. *The Trial of Jesus.* New York: Stein and Day, 1968.

Brooke, C. F. Tucker. *The Tudor Drama.* Boston: Houghton Mifflin, 1911.

Burdett, O. "Passion Play." In *Critical Essays,* pp. 44–65. Faber, 1925.

Butler, William. *Oberammergau 1890.* New York: Harper and Bros., 1891.

Cargill, Oscar. *Drama and Liturgy.* New York: Columbia University, 1930.

Chambers, Edmund. *The Medieval Stage*. Oxford: Clarendon Press, 1903.

Childe, Francis. *The Passion of the Saviour*. N.p. 1871.

Clay, Lucius D. *Decision in Germany*. Garden City, N.Y.: Doubleday, 1950.

————. *The Papers of General Lucius D. Clay*. Edited by Jean E. Smith, Bloomington: Indiana University Press, 1974.

Cohn, Haim. *The Trial and Death of Jesus*. New York: Harper and Row, 1971.

Coyle, Robert. *The Passion Play at Oberammergau*. Denver: Fisher Books, 1910.

Darlington, W. A. *Literature in the Theatre and Other Essays*. New York: Books for Libraries Press, 1925.

DeVaux, Roland. *Ancient Israel*. New York and Toronto: McGraw-Hill, 1965.

De Vinck, Catherine. *A Passion Play*. Allendale, N.J.: Alleluia Press, 1975.

Dickie, J. F. *Passion Play of Oberammergau*. Berlin: Steinitz, 1900.

Diemer, Hermine. *Oberammergau and Its Passion Play*. Translated by Walter Kloeck. Munich: Carl Aug. Seyfried, 1930.

Dorfles, Gillo. *Kitsch: The World of Bad Taste*. New York: Universe Books, 1970.

Drew, Mary F. *The Passion Play of Oberammergau*. London: Burns and Oates, 1881.

Dufrenne, Mikel. *The Phenomenology of Aesthetic Experience*. Translated by Edward Casey. Evanston: Northwestern University, 1973.

Eibl-Eibesfeldt Irenäus. *Love and Hate: The Natural History of Behavior Patterns*. Translated by Geoffrey Strachan. New York: Holt, Rinehart and Winston, 1971.

Elkins, Michael. *Forged in Fury*. New York: Ballantine Books, 1971.

Evans, M. Blakemore. *The Passion Play of Lucerne*. Oxford University Press. Reprint. Millwood, N.Y.: Kraus, 1975.

FitzGibbon, Constantine. *Denazification*. New York: W. W. Norton, 1969.

Flannery, Edward. *The Anguish of the Jews*. New York: Macmillan, 1965.

Forster, Arnold, and Benjamin Epstein. *The New Anti-Semitism*. New York: McGraw-Hill, 1974.

Fromm, Erich. *The Anatomy of Human Destructiveness*. New York: Holt, Rinehart and Winston, 1973.

Gaer, Joseph. *The Legend of the Wandering Jew*. New York: Mentor, 1961.

Gassner, John. *Medieval and Tudor Drama*. New York: Bantam Books, 1971.

Gaster, Theodor. *Thespis: Ritual, Myth, and Drama in the Ancient Near East*. Reprint. New York: Harper Torchbook, 1966.

Gilbert, Arthur. *The Vatican Council and the Jews*. Cleveland and New York: World, 1968.

Gimbel, John. *The American Occupation of Germany: Politics and the Military, 1945–1949*. Stanford University Press, 1968.

Glassie, Henry. *Folksongs and Their Makers*. Bowling Green University Press, n.d.

Glock, Charles, and Rodney Stark. *Christian Beliefs and Anti-Semitism*. New York: Harper and Row, 1966.

Graetz, Heinrich. *History of the Jews*. Reprint. Philadelphia: Jewish Publication Society of America, 1956.

Grunebaum, Gustave von. *Medieval Islam: A Study in Cultural Orientation*. Reprint. University of Chicago Phoenix Books, 1966.

Hare, Douglas A. *The Theme of Jewish Persecution of Christians from the Gospel According to St. Matthew*. Cambridge University Press, 1967.

Hartmann, August. *Das Oberammergauer Passionsspiel in seiner ältesten gestalt*. Leipzig: Breitkopf und Härtel, 1880.

Hay, Malcolm. *Thy Brother's Blood*. New York: Reprint. Hart, 1975.

Heaton, Vernon. *The Oberammergau Passion Play*. London: Robert Hale, 1970.

Helmreich, Ernst. *The German Churches under Hitler: Background, Struggle, and Epilogue*. Detroit: Wayne State University Press, 1979.

Hitler, Adolf. *Hitler's Secret Conversations, 1941–1944.* New York: Octagon Books, 1942.

———. *The Speeches of Adolf Hitler, April, 1922–August, 1939.* Edited by Norman Baynes. New York: Howard Fertig, 1969.

Howe, Sarah W. *Oberammergau in 1900: The Village, the People, the Passion Play.* New York: Abbey Press, 1902.

Jackson, John. *The Ober-Ammergau Passion Play.* London: Chiswick Press, 1880.

Jais, Regina. *Legendary Germany: Oberammergau and Bayreuth.* New York: Dial Press, 1930.

Klausner, Joseph. *Jesus of Nazareth.* New York: Macmillan, 1929.

Koenigsberg, Richard. *Hitler's Ideology: A Study in Psychoanalytic Sociology.* New York: Library of Social Science, 1975.

Kolve, V. A. *The Play Called Corpus Christi.* Stanford University Press, 1966.

Krauskopf, Rabbi Joseph. *A Rabbi's Impressions of the Oberammergau Passion Play.* Philadelphia: E. Stern, 1901.

Kulli, Rolf Max. *Die Ständesatire in deutschen geistlichen Schauspielen des ausgehenden Mittelalters.* Bern: Francke Verlag, 1966.

Langer, Walter. *The Mind of Adolf Hitler.* New York: Basic Books, 1972.

Lee, Harold. *Perception and Aesthetic Value.* New York: Prentice-Hall, 1938.

Lewy, Guenther. *The Catholic Church and Nazi Germany.* New York: McGraw-Hill, 1964.

Littell, Franklin, ed. *The German Church Struggle and the Holocaust.* Detroit: Wayne State University Press, 1974.

Lorenz, Konrad. *On Aggression.* Translated by Marjorie Wilson. New York: Harcourt, Brace and World, 1963.

Madden, Denis, and John Lion, eds. *Rage, Hate, Assault, and Other Forms of Violence.* New York: Spectrum Publications, Halsted Press, 1976.

Mandell, Richard. *The Nazi Olympics.* New York: Macmillan, 1971.

Milgram, Stanley. *Obedience to Authority.* New York: Harper and Row, 1969.

Montagu, Ashley. *The Nature of Human Aggression*. New York: Oxford University Press, 1976.

Morais, Vamberto. *A Short History of Anti-Semitism*. New York: W. W. Norton, 1976.

Moses, Montrose. *The Passion Play of Oberammergau*. New York: Duffield, 1909.

Mosse, George. *Nazi Culture: Intellectual, Cultural, and Social Life in the Third Reich*. New York: Grosset and Dunlap, 1966.

Muhlen, Norbert. *The Return of Germany*. London: Bodley Head, 1953.

Mussner, Franz, ed. *Passion in Oberammergau: Das Leiden und Sterben Jesu als geistliches Schauspiel*. Düsseldorf: Patmos Verlag, 1980.

Oberammergau and Its Passion Play 1960. Official guide published by the community of Oberammergau. London: Ernest Benn, 1960.

The Oberammergau Passion Play of 1930. Pictures of the play and players. Official edition. Munich: F. Bruckmann, 1930.

The Oberammergau Passion Play 1980. English and German texts. Druckhaus Oberammergau, 1980.

Parkes, Henry Bamford. *Gods and Men: The Origins of Western Culture*. Reprint. New York: Vintage, 1965.

Passion Oberammergau. Official illustrated guide. Gemeinde Oberammergau, 1980.

The Passion Play at Oberammergau. 1934 text. Munich: J. C. Huber, 1934.

The Passion Play at Oberammergau. Official 1950 text. London: Ernest Benn; New York: Thomas Crowell, 1950.

Das Passions Spiel Oberammergau. Official illustrated catalogue. Verlag Gemeinde Oberammergau, 1970.

Pawlikowski, John. *The Challenge of the Holocaust for Christian Theology*. New York: Anti-Defamation League, 1978.

Peck, Abraham, ed. *Jews and Christians after the Holocaust*. Philadelphia: Fortress Press, 1982.

Pfeiffer, Robert. *History of New Testament Times*. New York: Harper, 1949.

Pinson, Koppel, ed. *Essays on Antisemitism*. New York: Conference on Jewish Relations, 1946.

Poliakov, Leon. *The History of Anti-Semitism from the Time of Christ to the Court Jews*. Translated by Richard Howard. New York: Schocken Books, 1974.

Priestley, J. B. *Self-Selected Essays*. London: Wm. Heinemann Ltd., 1937.

Ruether, Rosemary. *Faith and Fratricide: The Theological Roots of Anti-Semitism*. New York: Seabury Press, 1974.

Sandmel, Samuel. *Anti-Semitism in the New Testament?* Philadelphia: Fortress Press, 1978.

Schonfield, John. *The Passover Plot*. New York: Bantam, 1966.

Stead, William T., ed. *The Story That Transformed the World; or, The Passion Play at Oberammergau in 1890*. London: Office *Review of Reviews*, 1890.

Sticca, Sandro. *The Latin Passion Play: Its Origins and Development*. Albany: SUNY Press, 1970.

Stoddard, John. *John L. Stoddard's Lectures: India and the Passion Play*. Chicago: Geo. Shuman, 1910.

Swidler, Leonard, and Gerard Sloyan. *A Commentary on the Oberammergau Passionsspiel in Regard to Its Image of Jews and Judaism*. New York: Anti-Defamation League, 1978.

————, eds. *The Oberammergau Passionsspiel 1984*. New York: Anti-Defamation League, 1981.

Swift, Janet M. *The Passion Play of Oberammergau*. New York and Chicago: Fleming Revell, 1930.

Tal, Uriel. *Christians and Jews in Germany: Religion, Politics, and Ideology in the Second Reich, 1870–1914*. Translated by Noah Jacobs. Ithaca: Cornell University Press, 1975.

Tautphoeus, Baroness Jemima. *Quits*. New York: G. P. Putnam's, n.d.

Tenenbaum, Josef. *Race and Reich*. New York: Twayne, 1956.

Toch, Hans. *Violent Men: An Inquiry into the Psychology of Violence*. Chicago: Aldine, 1969.

Trachtenberg, Joshua. *The Devil and the Jews: The Medieval Conception of the Jew and Its Relation to Modern Anti-Semitism*. Reprint. Meridian, 1961.

Trench, Maria. *The Passion Play at Ober-Ammergau*. London: Kegan, Paul, Trench, Trübner, 1900.

Utting, Mattie Johns. *The Passion Play of Oberammergau*. Philadelphia: Dorrance, 1937.

Wagner, Richard. *Richard Wagner's Prose Works*. Translated by Wm. Ellis. London: Kegan, Paul, Trench, Trübner, 1895.

———. *My Life*. New York: Tudor, 1936.

Waite, Robert. *The Psychopathic God: Adolf Hitler*. New York: Basic Books, 1977.

Williams, Arnold. *The Characterization of Pilate in the Towneley Plays*. East Lansing: Michigan State University Press, 1950.

Winter, Paul. *On the Trial of Jesus*. Berlin: Walter de Gruyter, 1961.

Young, Karl. *The Drama of the Medieval Church*. Oxford University Press, 1933.

Zahn, Gordon. *German Catholics and Hitler's Wars: A Study in Social Control*. New York: Sheed and Ward, 1962.

Zeitlin, Solomon. *Who Crucified Jesus?* New York: Bloch, 1964.

Zillmann, Dolf. *Hostility and Aggression*. Hillsdale, N.J.: Lawrence Erlbaum, 1979.

Articles

"Bad Scene at Oberammergau." *Christian Century* 87 (27 May 1970): 651.

Baum, Phil. "Background of Oberammergau Passion Play." American Jewish Congress, 7 November 1966.

Bourgeault, Cynthia. "Passion Drama: History and Perspective." *Face to Face: An Interreligious Bulletin* 7 (Summer 1980): 21–23.

Bramston, M. "Oberammergau: Behind the Scenes." *Spectator* 65 (1890): 277.

Brigham, G. R. "Passion Play at Oberammergau." *Art and Archaeology* 15 (January 1923): 31–37.

Brisland, E. "Oberammergau in 1890." *Cosmopolitan* 10 (1890): 131 ff.

———. "Current Passions." *National Review* 23 (25 August 1970): 890.

Brown, H. O. "Oberammergau: Is It Anti-Semitic?" *Christianity Today* 14 (19 June 1970): 22–24.

Browne, E. H. "This Year's Passion Play." *Commonweal* 20 (21 September 1934): 481–82.

Burton, I. "Oberammergau in 1890." *New Republic* 2 (1890): 546 ff.

Cecil, A. "Ober-Ammergau—An Appreciation." *Blackwoods* 188 (November 1910): 616–22.

Cutler, M. "Passion Play." *Harpers Bazaar* 44 (August 1910): 490–91.

Davis, R. G. "Observer at Oberammergau." *Commentary* 29 (March 1960): 198–204.

"Debate at Oberammergau." *Newsweek* 54 (23 November 1959): 114.

Devrient, H. "Passion Play." *Forum* 29 (1900): 545 ff.

"Disposition of Receipts." *Nation* 52 (1890): 91.

Driver, T. F. "Play That Carries a Plague." *Christian Century* 77 (7 September 1960): 1016–18.

Dukes, Ashley. "Scene in Europe." *Theatre Arts Monthly* 18 (September 1934): 660–62.

Dutton, M. B. "At the House of David." *Critic* 47 (December 1905): 481–95.

Edsall, R. L. "Impressions of Oberammergau." *Commonweal* 13 (24 December 1930): 207–8.

Fisher, B. E. S. "300th Anniversary." *North American Review* 237 (March 1934): 11–12.

"Forgetting the Hymn of Hate." *Literary Digest* 7 (25 March 1922): 30–31.

Fuller, R. "World's Stage 1930." *Travel* 54 (April 1930): 24–27.

Gabriel, Louis, Sr. "Gospels and the Oberammergau Passion Play." *Catholic World* 111 (April 1970): 13–17.

"Germany Shocked at Oberammergau." *Literary Digest* 106 (16 August 1930): 15.

Gideon, H. L. "Music of the Passion Play at Oberammergau." *Forum* 44 (December 1910): 733–37.

Graham, J. "Oberammergau: The Village That Kept Its Vow." *Readers' Digest* 97 (July 1970): 193–94.

Hare, A. D. "Passion Play 1900." *Argosy* 71 (1900): 316 ff.

Harris, M. "Passion Play at Oberammergau." *Catholic World* 131 (April 1930): 22–28.

Heaps, W. A. "Oberammergau Today." *Christian Century* 63 (4 December 1946): 1468–69.

"Is the Passion Play Anti-Semitic?" *Christian Century* 47 (20 August 1930): 1005–7.

"Is the Passion Play Anti-Semitic?" *Literary Digest* 106 (13 September 1930): 21.

Kepler, T. S. "Oberammergau, the Jews, and Pilate." *Christian Century* 78 (26 July 1961): 897–900.

Kuhn, H. B. "Concerning Oberammergau: 1980." *Christianity Today* 22 (19 May 1978): 69–70.

Lang, A. "Christus in Oberammergau." *Living Age* 314 (26 August 1922): 550–51.

Lang, F. "Oberammergau Today." *Christian Century* 63 (25 December 1946): 1569.

Link, C. "Painting the Passion Players in Their Homes." *Ladies Home Journal* 39 (September 1922): 17 ff.

Mallau, Hans. "Beobachtungen eines Altestamentlers zu den lebenden Bildern des Oberammergauer Passionsspieles." *Emuna Horizonte* 5 (August 1970): 235–41.

Maxwell, G. "Oberammergau and Its Passion Play." *Fortnightly* 117 (June 1922): 1018–29.

Morant, L. C. "The Vulgarising of Oberammergau." *Nineteenth Century* 48 (November 1900): 820–24.

Moritz, Rohtraut. "Gespräche mit evangelischen Passionsspielbesuchern." *Emuna Horizonte* 5 (August 1970): 221–22.

Niebuhr, Reinhold. "At Oberammergau." *Christian Century* 47 (13 August 1930): 983–84.

"Oberammergau." *Christian Century* 47 (3 September 1930): 1065.

"Oberammergau: A Felicitous Follow-Up, Revision of Anti-Semitic Passages." *Christian Century* 85 (19 June 1968): 809.

"Oberammergau: A Village of Actors." *Current Literature* 49 (July 1910): 81–84.

"Oberammergau Awakes." *Literary Digest* 105 (14 June 1930): 18–19.

"Oberammergau in Distress." *Living Age* 329 (1 May 1926): 287–88.

"Oberammergau Passion Play." *Mentor* 10 (August 1922): 34–35.

"Oberammergau Ready for 300th Anniversary." *Newsweek* 3 (May 1934): 28.

"Oberammergau: The World's Greatest Drama." *Spectator* 152 (23 March 1934): 484.

"Oberammergau's Blow at Mammon." *Literary Digest* 75 (25 November 1922): 34.

"Oberammergau's Jubilee Year." *Review of Reviews* 89 (April 1934): 54–55.

"Oberammergau's Rebuke to America." *Literary Digest* 80 (5 January 1934): 34.

"Oberammergau's Tradition." *Living Age* 313 (27 May 1922): 550–53.

"Passion in 1946?" *Time* 46 (16 July 1945): 62.

"Passion Play." *Commonweal* 20 (25 May 1934): 102.

"Passion Play." *Travel* 62 (April 1934): 31.

"Passion Play Beards." *Newsweek* 33 (23 May 1949): 72.

"Passion Play Judged as Secular Drama." *Literary Digest* 74 (9 September 1922): 30–31.

"Passion Play Profits." *Literary Digest* 109 (9 May 1931): 20.

"Passion Revised." *Time* 75 (21 March 1960): 64.

"Passion's the Thing." *Newsweek* 75 (1 June 1970): 82.

Peterson, M. O. "Inside the Homes of Oberammergau." *Better Homes and Gardens* 13 (April 1935): 36 ff.

"Piety with Profit." *Time* 71 (11 July 1960): 56.

"Play Passions." *Time* 111 (22 May 1978): 64.

Rauschenbusch, W. "The Religion of the Passion Play." *Independent* 69 (29 September 1910): 689–93.

Reiss, W. "Oberammergau Players." *Century* 104 (September 1922): 727–42.

Reyher, F. "Christ in Oberammergau." *Atlantic* 130 (November 1922): 599–607.

Richards, L. P. "Life Stories of the Oberammergau Players." *McClure's* 35 (August 1910): 388–401.

Roof, K. M. "The Moral Effect of the Tourist upon the Native." *Craftsman* 11 (March 1907): 674–75.

Sanders, Wilm. "Was man auch sehen muss beim Passionsspiel von Oberammergau." *Emuna Horizonte* 5 (August 1970): 242–45.

Schroubek, Georg. "Erbauluches Spiel oder Argernis?" *Emuna Horizonte* 5 (August 1970): 231–34.

Shillito, E. "In the Uplands of Oberammergau." *Christian Century* 47 (1 October 1930): 1190.

Shuster, G. "Oberammergau: After Ten Years, the Passion Play in Bavaria." *Saturday Review* 43 (12 March 1960): 43–44.

"Spectacle at Oberammergau." *Life* 49 (25 July 1960): 58–59.

Stead, W. T. "Oberammergau: A Third Visit." *Review of Reviews* 42 (August 1910): 180–86.

Steiner, E. A. "Fashion Play of 1930." *Christian Century* 47 (13 August 1930): 983–84.

Sutton, H. "Longest Run on Record." *Saturday Review* 32 (22 April 1950): 36 ff.

"Time for a New Vow at Oberammergau: Anti-Semitism of Play." *Christian Century* 83 (2 November 1966): 1328–29.

Walsh, J. J. "Oberammergau." *Commonweal* 12 (20 August 1930): 403–4.

Ward, A. W. "The Oberammergau Passion Play in 1871." *Living Age* 266 (27 August 1910): 521–31.

Watts, Harvey. "Pilgrimage Play at Hollywood, California." *Art and Archaeology* 15 (January 1923): 15–21.

Weiss, Annemarie. "Gespräche mit katholischen Passionsspiel-besuchern." *Emuna Horizonte* 5 (August 1970): 223–24.

Woolcott, A. "Oberammergau This Way." *Colliers* 86 (26 July 1930): 116 ff.

"World's Most Popular Play." *Review of Reviews* 81 (May 1930): 133.

Young, D. M. "Reader's Choice." *Travel* 113 (April 1960): 40.

Zander, Hans. "Frommes Theater oder die Passionsspiele von Oberammergau." *Emuna Horizonte* 5 (August 1970): 227–30.

Index